KNOWING GOD
AND OURSELVES

The Holy Spirit 'enflames our hearts with the love of God and with zealous devotion' (*Institutes* III.1.3).

KNOWING GOD AND OURSELVES

Reading Calvin's Institutes Devotionally

David B. Calhoun

THE BANNER OF TRUTH TRUST

THE BANNER OF TRUTH TRUST

Head Office
3 Murrayfield Road
Edinburgh, EH12
6EL
UK

North America Office
PO Box 621
Carlisle, PA
17013
USA

banneroftruth.org

First published 2016
© David B. Calhoun 2016
Reprinted 2021

*

ISBN
Print: 978 1 84871 718 3
Epub: 978 1 84871 719 0
Kindle: 978 1 84871 720 6

*

Typeset in 10.5/13.5 Adobe Garamond Pro
at The Banner of Truth Trust, Edinburgh

Printed in the USA by
Versa Press Inc.,
East Peoria, IL

May the Lord grant that we may be engaged in the mysteries of his heavenly wisdom with a true increase of piety, for his glory and our edification. Amen.

Calvin's opening prayer from his daily lectures on the Bible

Contents

Preface

The goal of this book is to help students, especially beginning students, of Calvin's *Institutes* to better understand what you are reading and to encourage you to persist in working through this important but challenging book.

I have focused on what Calvin writes in the *Institutes*, not on what scholars have written about Calvin's theology. Rather than another book about Calvin's theology, this one is an invitation to read the *Institutes* for yourself. There are some surprises in store for you if you are reading the *Institutes* for the first time. B. B. Warfield judges that 'Calvin has suffered more than most men from … gratuitous attributions to him of doctrines which he emphatically disclaims' (*Calvin and Augustine*, 155).

I have generally avoided criticism of Calvin's teaching. I do not think that Calvin was always right. Neither did Calvin. He carefully makes the case for his own interpretation of any difficult passage of Scripture, and often explains on what grounds a reader might choose to interpret it differently. He ended his extensive treatment of the Lord's supper in the *Institutes* with the comment, 'I urge my readers not to confine their mental interest within these too narrow limits, but to strive to rise much higher than I can lead them' (IV.17.7). My goal in this book is to help you understand Calvin. Others may be able to help you 'rise much higher'.

To fully understand Calvin's thought it would be necessary to study his commentaries, treatises, and letters, as well as the *Institutes*— a daunting undertaking to be sure. We can get a good and accurate knowledge of Calvin's theology, however, by studying this, his most famous book. The final edition of the *Institutes*, completed just five years before his death, is the best source for his mature thinking, although Calvin's theology changed remarkably little during his lifetime. With the 1559 *Institutes* Calvin believed that he had finally 'embraced the sum of religion in all its parts' and 'arranged it in such an order' that his readers would be enabled to understand the Bible better (*Institutes* 1.3).

Books on specific topics of Calvin's theology are helpful but necessarily isolate a particular subject. Jane Dempsey Douglass writes, for example, that to talk about 'Christian freedom' in Calvin 'by discussing chapters of the *Institutes* devoted to it is a bit like walking into a theatre during the second act of a play and leaving before the final act' (*Women, Freedom, and Calvin*, 17). The same is true of any doctrine or topic in the *Institutes*. It is important to study the *Institutes* from beginning to end to understand the flow of Calvin's thought with its many connections and to come to appreciate the full range and force of his theology. There are hundreds of books about Calvin's life, influence, and theology, but not many treat the *Institutes of the Christian Religion* in its entirety.

Calvin intended the *Institutes* to be a guide in reading Scripture and a theological companion to his commentaries. Above all, he wanted his readers to respond to biblical truth with love for God and obedient lives. The subtitle of this book is *Reading Calvin's Institutes Devotionally*. Reading the *Institutes* devotionally is not merely one way of reading Calvin's book. It is the *only* way to read it.

The titles of the chapters in this book are Calvin's own words. I have looked especially for figurative expressions. 'Figures', Calvin says, 'are called the eyes of speech, not that they explain the matter more easily than simple ordinary language, but because they win attention by their propriety, and arouse the mind by their lustre, and by their lively similitude so represent what is said that it enters more effectively into the heart' (*Calvin: Theological Treatises*, 319). Following each title is a sentence from Calvin that contains the words of the title.

The quotation that follows, set apart in a box, states something important about that section of the *Institutes*.

The chapters in the *Institutes* to be read with each chapter of this book are indicated. The reading assignments are from the McNeill-Battles edition of the 1559 *Institutes*. The introductory material is given in page numbers of volume 1 (e.g. 1:33). The readings from the *Institutes*, and all references to the *Institutes* in the text, are given as Book, chapter, section: 'I.1.1', for example (Book I, chapter 1, section 1). Quotations from Calvin's commentaries are noted as Comm. plus the biblical text, for example 'Comm. John 3:16.'

You may prefer to read the briefer but ample 1541 French edition of the *Institutes*, translated by Robert White, and also published by the Trust. You will find in the appendix of this edition a 'Comparative Table of the 1541 and 1560 *Institutes* (823-36). Relevant chapter and page numbers for the 1541 edition have been added in square brackets to the 'Read' section at the head of each chapter in this guide.

The Scripture text for each chapter is a key passage for Calvin's thought on the topic of the chapter. These quotations are from the English Standard Version.

Each notable quote, from the *Institutes* or from Calvin's commentaries and sermons, illustrates the theme of the chapter in a striking and memorable way.

The prayer for each chapter has been selected from the wealth of Calvin's prayers—from his liturgies, sermons, and lectures, and his individual and family prayers.

'A look back and a look ahead' (beginning in chapter 2) reviews briefly what Calvin has already covered and prepares us for what is coming next. It is especially important for readers of the *Institutes* to be aware of its beautiful, and at times intricate and creative, connections.

Each chapter ends with 'Knowing God and ourselves', a short application and meditation on Calvin's content. This reminds us that we should be reading the *Institutes* devotionally.

Occasional quotations from various sources (in boxes) summarize, illustrate, or emphasize some aspect of Calvin's teaching.

I have avoided footnotes, but indicate sources of quotations in the text. With modern bibliographical aids, these sources can be located with little effort. The text of this book is thus freed from academic overload. The goal is for you to read Calvin, not footnotes!

'By nature I love brevity', Calvin wrote. Those words are found on page 685 of the first volume of the Battles translation of the *Institutes*! The length of the *Institutes* may not seem to justify Calvin's claim, but compared with many theologies, past and present, Calvin's book is remarkable for its lucid brevity. I have sought to follow Calvin's advice in this book. It is a short, and I hope lucid, guide to Calvin's *Institutes*, which is a guide to the Bible.

I did not read Calvin's *Institutes* until I was in my doctoral studies at Princeton Theological Seminary. I have been reading this book ever since, along with other writings by Calvin and books about Calvin. For twenty-five years, I taught a course in the *Institutes* at Covenant Theological Seminary. I do not idolize Calvin, but my respect for him as a teacher and pastor has grown through the years. Facing the daily task of living, with its many demands and pressures, struggling with incurable cancer, and trying to find a way to understand the chaos and grimness of world events unfolding around me, I have found Calvin a source of solidity and strength. Enjoying the gift of life, the blessing of love of family and friends, the joy of food and drink, the beauty of nature, and the wonder of it all, I have discovered in Calvin a fellow pilgrim whose words often reflected and focused my feelings and helped me to fix my eyes on heaven and to give thanks. Calvin also challenges me, rebukes me, and leads me on, gently but firmly, toward greater love for God and obedience to his word. I pray that your study of Calvin's *Institutes* will bring you great blessing also.

When he was a young pastor, Eugene Peterson heard a lecture by the Quaker philosopher Douglas Steere on John Calvin's *Institutes of the Christian Religion*. Peterson had little interest in theology and none at all in Calvin. But, 'after the hour's lecture', Peterson writes, 'most (maybe all) of my stereotyped preconceptions of both Calvin and theology had been dispersed'. Steere 'talked at length of the graceful literary style of the writing, the soaring architectural splendour of this spiritual classic, the clarity and breadth of the thinking, the penetrating insights and comprehensive imagination. The lecture did its work in me—if Calvin was this good after four hundred years, I wanted to read his book for myself. The next day I went to a bookstore and bought the two volumes and began reading them. I read them through in a year, and when I finished I read them again. I've been reading them ever since' (*Books & Culture*, September/October 2011, 17, 19).

Introduction to the Institutes

Calvin was the greatest exegete of the Reformation age: he was the Reformation's greatest theologian. And he was the practical genius of the Reformation. We do not say he was the practical genius of the Reformation in spite of his learned commentaries and his profound and profoundly reasoned theology. We would better say it was in large part because of them. Calvin probably never did a more practical thing than expound the Scriptures day by day with the penetrating insight and the clear, searching honesty of comment in which he is unsurpassed. And he certainly never did a more practical thing than write the *Institutes of the Christian Religion* (*Selected Shorter Writings of Benjamin B. Warfield*, 1:403).

Read: 'Introduction' by John T. McNeill (1:xix-lxxi), 'John Calvin to the Reader', 'Subject Matter of the Present Work', and 'Prefatory Address to King Francis I of France' (1:3-31). [*1541* 'Translator's Introduction' (vii-xiii), 'Outline of the Present Book' (xv-xvi), 'Prefatory Letter to Francis I' (xvii-xxxvi)].

Scripture Text: 'Do your best to present yourself to God as one approved, a worker who has no need to be ashamed, rightly handling the word of truth' (2 Tim. 2:15).

Notable Quote: 'When we read the word of God … we do it not to any other end and purpose, but to be instructed in good doctrine, that is to say in doctrine as is profitable to our salvation' (Sermon on Titus 1:1-4).

Prayer

O Lord, you who are the fountain of all wisdom and learning ... illumine my understanding, which of itself is blind, so that it may grasp the teaching that will be given to me; please strengthen my memory to be able to remember well, dispose my heart to receive what is taught willingly and with due eagerness, so that the opportunity you present to me may not be lost because of my ingratitude.

To do this, please pour out your Holy Spirit on me, the Spirit of all intelligence, truth, judgment, prudence, and teaching.

Grant that I may direct my study to the true purpose, which is to know you in our Lord Jesus Christ, to have full confidence of salvation and life in your grace alone, and to serve you rightly and purely, according to your pleasure.

Hear me, merciful Father, by our Lord Jesus Christ. Amen.

(John Calvin: Writings on Pastoral Piety, 212-13.)

> 'Calvin was a sickly, diligent pastor, scholar, diplomat, and polemicist, who wrote theology of breathtaking beauty and tough-mindedness as well as line-by-line commentary on most books of the Bible' (Robinson, *The Death of Adam*, 175).

John Calvin's *Institutes of the Christian Religion*, according to John T. McNeill, 'holds a place in the short list of books that have notably affected the course of history' (1:xxix). Calvin's book has been called 'one of the masterpieces of world literature' (Nichols, *Primer for Protestants*, 61). It is the Reformation's 'most eloquent theological statement' (Ozment, *The Age of Reform 1250-1550*, 372) and 'contains the outline and breathes the genius of the Reformed faith' (Mackay, *Christianity on the Frontier*, 86).

The first edition of this remarkable book was published in 1536, when its author was in his mid-twenties and had been a Protestant for only two or three years. The *Institutes* came fifteen years after Philip Melanchthon's *Loci Communes*, and about ten years after summaries of theology by the Swiss Reformed pastor Ulrich Zwingli and by Calvin's countryman and friend William Farel. When Calvin's *Institutes* appeared Farel advised people to put aside his own book and read Calvin's instead.

Title

In the sixteenth century the common word for a book of theology was *summa*, meaning 'summary' or 'substance', as the *Summa Theologiae* of Thomas Aquinas. Calvin, educated in law, chose the word *institutio* for his book, a word often used for manuals in subjects such as law. *The Institutes of the Christian Religion* is a manual, a book of basic instruction in the Christian religion. The word 'religion' in the title probably bears the common sixteenth-century meaning of Christian life or practice.

More than a *summa theologiae*, Calvin's *Institutes* is a *summa pietatis*. It is a book about Christian piety, about Christian discipleship, about loving and serving God.

Purpose

'One thing that has marked all great theologians, from the apostle Paul onward, is that their finest theology has been called forth by specific requests for help' (Battles, *The Piety of John Calvin*, 20-21). Calvin wrote the first edition of the *Institutes* (1536) to provide a much-needed introduction to 'the Christian religion' for those, especially in Calvin's native France, who had embraced the Protestant faith, and for others who wanted to know more about it. Calvin's book presented to the king of France a clear statement of what Protestants believed. 'It seemed to me', Calvin wrote to the king, 'that I should be doing something worthwhile if I both gave instruction to [French Christians] and made confession before you' (1:9). Calvin set before the king an account of the beliefs of the persecuted Protestants in France, showing that they were not heretics but that it was their Catholic persecutors who had strayed from the true faith.

In his second edition of the *Institutes* (1539), Calvin stated an additional purpose: to offer a doctrinal introduction to Scripture. He wrote, 'If, after this road has, as it were, been paved, I shall publish any interpretations of Scripture, I shall always condense them, because I shall have no need to undertake long doctrinal discussions', thus sparing 'the godly reader ... great annoyance and boredom' (1:4-5).

'The *Institutes* had drifted on to the market in 1536 as a sailboat, but by 1559 it had grown into a cargo ship, increasing from six to eighty chapters ... It had ... also turned into a battleship with which Calvin wanted to defend God's glory' (Selderhuis, *John Calvin: A Pilgrim's Life*, 229).

Growth

Calvin's *Institutes* grew from 'a simple little handbook' of 1536, through several intermediate editions, into 'a bulky but compact and thoroughly organized textbook in theology' in 1559 (Warfield, *Calvin and Calvinism*, 7). Calvin did not rewrite and revise. Almost all of what he wrote in the 1536 edition and the later editions is incorporated into the 1559 edition. But he 'added, developed, defined' (Warfield, *Calvin and Calvinism*, 390). He also re-arranged, stating that he was not satisfied with his order of topics until the last edition (1:3).

'John Calvin to the Reader' in the final edition of the *Institutes* ends with a quotation from Augustine: 'I count myself one of the number of those who write as they learn and learn as they write' (1:5). As Calvin preached, lectured on Scripture, and wrote commentaries, his growing knowledge of the Bible was reflected in the successive editions of the *Institutes*. His continuing study of the church fathers added theological insights, quotations, and arguments. His pastoral experience in Geneva, Strasbourg, and again in Geneva developed his understanding of church life and practical theology. His controversies with Roman Catholics, Lutherans, Anabaptists, and others sharpened his polemics and greatly enlarged his *Institutes*.

French translations

To enable French people, most of whom, of course, did not know Latin, to read the *Institutes*, Calvin translated it into French. The first French edition appeared in 1541, translated from the 1539 Latin edition. Two English translations of Calvin's French edition of 1541 have appeared—one by Elsie Anne McKee (2009) and another by Robert White (2014). McKee writes that Calvin's French edition 'was more than a translation of the Latin 1539; it was a text of pastoral theology in the language of the common people and consciously directed to them' (x). Robert White hopes that readers of his translation 'will be touched by the Reformer's search for a language adequate to express the twin mysteries of God's great glory and of his goodness to the children of men' (xiii).

English translations

The *Institutes* was translated into English by Thomas Norton (1561), John Allen (1813), and Henry Beveridge (1845). In the introduction to a 1962 reprinting of Beveridge's translation, John Murray stated that 'a more adequate translation of Calvin's *Institutes* into English is a real desideratum'. Such a work would require 'linguistic skill of the highest order', continued Murray, 'thorough knowledge of Calvin's writings, and deep sympathy with his theology'. The translation of Ford Lewis Battles (1960), though subjected to occasional criticism, meets Murray's standards and brings us closer to Calvin's style and meaning.

Characteristics

'What made Calvin Calvin, and not another sixteenth-century writer, was his brilliance as a thinker and writer, and, above all, his ability to interpret the Bible. His coherent, penetrating and lucid vision of God's abiding love for humanity, expressed in some of the most exquisite prose of his age, has continued down the centuries to instruct and to inspire' (Gordon, *Calvin*, viii).

Calvin's *Institutes* may be described as biblical, systematic, polemical, pastoral, and devotional.

1. Biblical

> 'In his commentaries on Scripture, [Calvin] scarcely slights a verse, or
> fails to pause over any issue of interpretation of the Hebrew or Greek.
> By dint of unimaginable labour he creates a body of interpretation that
> is not allegorical, nor analogical, and not offered by him as certainly
> true. Where he is uncertain, he offers alternative interpretations and tells
> the reader to decide among them. He tries to avoid forced readings, and
> he is carefully attentive to the immediate context of a phrase or passage.
> He is sometimes called the father of modern exegesis' (Robinson, *The
> Death of Adam*, 191).

In the *Institutes* Calvin attempts to maintain what he called 'a settled
principle'—'that there is no word of God to which place should be given
in the church save that which is contained, first in the law and prophets,
and secondly in the writings of the apostles, and that the only right
method of teaching in the church is according to the prescription and
rule of the word' (IV.8.5).

There are almost seven thousand references to the Bible in the final
edition of the *Institutes*. (An index of biblical references is provided on
pages 1553-1592 in the second volume of the McNeill-Battles *Institutes*.)
Calvin described his goal in biblical interpretation as 'not subtle, not
forced, not distorted; but natural, fluent, plain' (IV.11.1). His ability to
use all parts of the Bible, and to use them well, has perhaps never been
equaled in the history of theological writing. R. C. Reed called Calvin 'a
wholesale plagiarist ... from Moses and David, Isaiah and Ezekiel, Jesus
and John, Peter and Paul' (*The Gospel as Taught by Calvin*, 14).

Calvin's *Institutes* is not only biblical in its content, it is biblical in its
intent. John Leith writes, 'The reformer sought not merely to take the
materials of his theology out of the Bible, but also to make his theology
a complete and consistent representation of the Bible' (*Pilgrimage
of a Presbyterian*, 174). Calvin intended his book to be a guide and a

theological companion to the Bible. The *Institutes* sends us to the Bible (and to commentaries on the Bible), and Bible study sends us back to the *Institutes* to find the Bible's content summarized and organized.

'The 1559 *Institutio* is great theology, and it is uncanny how often, as we read and re-read it, we come across passages that seem to speak directly across the centuries to our own hearts and our own present-day theological debates. You never seem to get to the book's bottom; it keeps opening up as a veritable treasure trove of biblical wisdom on all the main themes of the Christian faith' (Packer, *A Theological Guide to Calvin's Institutes*, xiii).

2. Systematic

'Calvin's true legacy is ... not a system but a method, the method of striving to see everything—man, Christ, faith, the world, the Bible, religion, life—not from man's point of view but from the viewpoint of God' (Fuhrmann, *God-Centered Religion*, 23).

Calvin's theology has been described as a logically self-consistent system, by some to denounce the *Institutes* and by others to praise it. Will Durant wrote that Calvin's 'genius lay not in conceiving new ideas but in developing the thought of his predecessors to ruinously logical conclusions' (*The Reformation*, 465). Abraham Kuyper saw Calvin's theology as superior to Augustine's because of its 'thoroughgoing logical consistency' (*The Presbyterian and Reformed Review*, July 1891, 377).

God has 'given us the light of understanding and reason', Calvin wrote, and he valued logic as one of 'the learned and exalted sciences'

(Comm. Psa. 119:73; Comm. Isa. 28:29). He occasionally appeals to logic in the *Institutes*, but only when it can be used to support what the Bible teaches. Human philosophy is based on reason alone, but 'the Christian philosophy bids reason give way to, submit and subject itself to, the Holy Spirit' (III.7.1). 'In the mysteries of the faith common sense is not our advisor, but with quiet teachableness and the spirit of gentleness … we receive the doctrine given from heaven' (IV.17.25).

In our study of the Bible, Calvin insisted that 'we should not investigate what the Lord has left hidden', and that 'we should not neglect what he has brought into the open'. We must avoid 'excessive ingratitude' by not going as far as the Bible goes and 'excessive curiosity' by going beyond what the Bible says (III.21.4). 'Whither the Bible took him, thither he went', wrote Warfield, 'where scriptural declarations failed him, there he stopped short' (*Calvin and Augustine*, 481).

Calvin warned that any attempt to search out doctrine beyond what the Bible reveals will lead us into a 'labyrinth' or 'maze'. When someone seeks to know everything about predestination, for example, he will find himself in 'a labyrinth from which he can find no exit' (III.21.1). Calvin preached, 'Let us be content to know what God tells us and to wait on the day of full revelation for knowing the rest … Let us ignore what God does not will to explain. For such ignorance transcends all the wisdom of the world' (*Sermons on the Ten Commandments*, 247). In another sermon Calvin warned that 'we must not measure God by our own yardstick', but reverence 'God's secrets which are incomprehensible to us' (Sermon on Eph. 1:3-4).

The reader of the *Institutes* quickly learns that Calvin does not solve all theological problems and answer all our questions. He is quite willing to allow seemingly competing biblical truths to stand side by side without forcing them into an artificial harmony. Edward Dowey writes that 'a hallmark of Calvin's theology' is 'clarity of individual themes' and 'incomprehensibility of their inter-relations' (*The Knowledge of God in Calvin's Theology*, 40). Calvin embraces and teaches doctrines of Scripture that seem incompatible, such as the goodness of God and the existence of evil; God's love and his wrath; gratitude for earthly life and a longing for heaven; and divine omnipotence and human responsibility.

Calvin is content, Selderhuis concludes,

> to live with the paradoxes between the divine word and our daily reality, between God's *ordo* and this worldwide chaos, between the heavenly rest and our inward unrest, between God's mercy and his wrath, between God's promise of salvation and man's miserable experience, between God's '*praesentia realis*' and God's hiddenness, and between faithful trust in God and the 'whys' that scream out to us (*Calvin's Theology of the Psalms*, 290-91).

Noting that Calvin follows the chapter on prayer in the *Institutes* (III.20) with several chapters on predestination (III.21-24), Elsie McKee writes:

> Calvin was a pastor, not a philosopher; he was a devout student of the Bible, not willing to skip or add anything. Since the Bible has something to say about predestination, so does Calvin; since the Bible has something to say about prayer, so does Calvin. In his view, combining predestination and prayer works; if it does not satisfy a philosopher, so be it (*Interpretation*, April 2009, 130).

B. B. Warfield states that it is as a systematizer that Calvin 'makes his greatest demand on our admiration and gratitude' (*Calvin and Calvinism*, 22). Charles Partee holds that 'Calvin is a systematic thinker, but not a system builder' (*The Theology of John Calvin*, 27). His theology contains 'conflicting perspectives', writes Mary Potter Engel, but it is, nevertheless, 'a unified whole. Its unity, however, is not that of logical consistency. Rather, its unity is that of a complex ordering of parts, one that joins contradictory yet complementary perspectives in order to describe a complex reality' (*John Calvin's Perspectival Anthropology*, 193).

Even though the Bible is not a book of systematic theology, it encourages orderly thinking. 'The Spirit of God', writes Calvin, 'did not adhere ... exactly or continuously to a methodical plan' in giving the Scriptures, 'yet when he lays one down anywhere he hints enough that it is not to be neglected by us' (III.6.1). Calvin may have been thinking of the Epistle to the Romans when he wrote these words, as his arrangement of topics in the *Institutes* follows Paul's order in Romans. Calvin notes Paul's preaching to the Greeks and applies it to his own work.

We know that in teaching, the right order requires a beginning to be made from things that are better known. Since Paul and Barnabas were preaching to Gentiles, it would have been useless for them to attempt to bring them to Christ at once. Therefore they had to begin from some other point, not so remote from common understanding, so that, when assent was given to that, they could then pass over to Christ (Comm. Acts 14:15).

Alister McGrath states that 'the only principle which seems to govern Calvin's organization of his theological system is a concern to be faithful to Scripture on the one hand, and to achieve maximum clarity of presentation on the other' (*Christian Theology*, 64-65).

3. Polemical

The contents of the 1559 Institutes 'include not only a complete guide to Calvin's biblical theology (how to understand Scripture as a whole and how to practice the Christian faith in the church and the world), but also how to defend this teaching against heresy and schism in terms of sixteenth-century controversies' (McKee, *Institutes of the Christian Religion 1541 French Edition*, viii).

'All major Christian theology seems to have arisen in polemical contexts … Jesus himself disputed with the religious scholars of his time … Great theology can only be great for its substance, whatever its occasion. Regrettably, the tone of indignation or emergency is often alienating to readers who do not see past the passions of its moment to the conceptual grandeur of the vision proposed by it' (Robinson, *John Calvin: Steward of God's Covenant*, xviii-xix).

Ford Lewis Battles has described the *Institutes* as 'a book of antitheses' (*Analysis of the Institutes of the Christian Religion of John Calvin*, 23). Calvin believed that 'the theologian's task is … to strengthen consciences by teaching things true, sure, and profitable', and then to defend the truth of those things (I.14.4). You will find sections of the *Institutes*, sometimes large sections, in which Calvin attacks the views of Catholics, Anabaptists, and those who, like Servetus, denied the Trinity. After almost twenty-five pages presenting the orthodox doctrine of the Trinity, Calvin adds: 'Hitherto it has been my particular intention to lead by the hand those who are teachable, but not to strive hand to hand with the inflexible and contentious. But now the truth which has been peaceably shown must be maintained against all the calumnies of the wicked' (I.13.21).

Preaching on the ninth commandment, Calvin says:

> When I see truth oppressed, to the best of my ability, I must not tolerate it. Why? [Because] God calls me in his name to see to it that lies are suppressed. And above all this applies with respect to the doctrine of salvation ... Let us learn that when we live with men in such simplicity that people cannot reproach us for wanting to denigrate anyone, either by calumny, or lies, or slander, we ought also to maintain this same zeal with respect to God, that his truth abide in its fullness and that it may be maintained in order for his reign to be active in our midst (*Sermons on the Ten Commandments*, 218).

B. B. Warfield states that Calvin's 'fundamental aim was constructive, not destructive: he wished to rebuild the church on its true foundations, not to destroy its edifice. But, like certain earlier rebuilders of the holy city, he needed to work with trowel in one hand and the sword in the other' (*Calvin and Augustine*, 10).

Readers of Calvin, especially those who are reading him for the first time, will likely be disturbed by his strong language in attacking opponents. Sometimes this is excused by saying that Calvin's ferocious polemic was typical of his day. It is true that sixteenth-century writers commonly used language every bit as sharp as Calvin's, and much sharper in the writings of Martin Luther and Thomas More. In a footnote in his translation of Calvin's *Sermons on the Beatitudes*, Robert White notes that 'the demonizing of one's opponents, a procedure not unknown in our day, was common currency in sixteenth-century debate' (106). Karl Barth has written that 'those who live with smaller views of a smaller cause than Calvin's really find it much easier to be less severe than he was' (*The Theology of John Calvin*, 125). Certainly Calvin's strong language reflected his deep convictions about important things. Preaching on Ephesians 4:29-30, Calvin said that those who are 'poisoners of souls' do 'a thing much more heinous and detestable than if they had murdered their bodies'.

4. Pastoral

> B. B. Warfield maintains that Calvin did not write out of an abstract scientific impulse 'but with the needs of souls, and, indeed, also with the special demands of the day in mind' (*Calvin and Augustine*, 133).

Calvin composed the *Institutes*, not in an ivory tower as a scholar, but as a busy city pastor in a difficult time and place. 'Although he does not make explicitly personal remarks', writes Elsie McKee, 'it is clear that Calvin's words do not come from a pastor who has never felt the doubts and trials of life, but from one who is passing on what he has himself experienced' (*John Calvin: Writings on Pastoral Piety*, 32). According to Serene Jones, Calvin's theological discourse is marked by a double purpose: 'It seeks to witness to the revelation of God in scripture, and it seeks to do so in a language capable of moving the hearts, minds, and wills of its audience toward an ever-deepening life of faith' (*Calvin and the Rhetoric of Piety*, 187). In preaching, Calvin wrote, teaching and exhortation 'must never be separated' (Comm. 1 Tim. 4:12-13).

Calvin believed that exegetical accuracy, clear and orderly presentation, and alertness to error—the three characteristics of the *Institutes* that we have already noted—were essential to preaching. So was relevant application and persuasive language.

Calvin explains that 'Matthew and Luke tell how John's preaching was not repentance in a general sense, but was a call brought home to individuals. Indeed it will be an unattractive way of teaching, if the masters do not work out carefully what are the needs of the times, what suits the people concerned' (Comm. Matt. 3:7). Preachers must 'consider what questions each [person] is able to bear, and accommodate our doctrine to the capacity of the individual' (Comm. Rom. 14:1).

Calvin rejected the dry, technical method of the medieval scholastics. He described scholastic theology as 'so twisted, involved, tortuous, and puzzling' that it might well be described 'as a species of secret magic' (*Tracts and Treatises* 1:40). Calvin preferred a fresh way of writing theology, using 'rhetorical devices and effects not only to explain but also to convince, cajole, scold, challenge, and move his readers' (Steinmetz, *Protestant Scholasticism*, 24). He frequently uses repetition, illustration, proverbs, and rhetoric. He defended his use of figurative language by giving, as he put it, 'the only answer becoming to a theologian'. Even though a figurative expression is less precise, 'it expresses with greater significance and elegance what, said simply and without figure, would have less force'. Figurative language wins attention and arouses the mind and 'enters more effectively into the heart' (*Calvin: Theological Treatises*, 319).

Calvin often moves us by the force and beauty of his language. A striking example is found as early as his 'Prefatory Address' attached to the *Institutes*:

> For what is more consonant with faith than to recognize that we are naked of all virtue, in order to be clothed by God? That we are empty of all good, to be filled by him? That we are slaves of sin, to be freed by him? Blind, to be illumined by him? Lame, to be made straight by him? Weak, to be sustained by him? To take away from us all occasion for glorying, that he alone may stand forth gloriously and we glory in him (1:13).

5. Devotional

'It is not the head but the heart which made [Calvin] a theologian and it is not the head but the heart which he primarily addresses in his theology ... His theology, if ever there was a theology of the heart, was distinctively a theology of the heart, and in him the maxim that "It is the heart that makes the theologian" finds perhaps its most eminent illustration' (Warfield, *Calvin and Augustine*, 23, 482-83).

Calvin's *Institutes*, writes Charles Partee, represents a reflection on loving 'God with all your heart, and with all your soul, and with all your strength, and with all your mind' (*The Theology of John Calvin*, 12-13). Rather than one topic among many, encouragement of piety—trust, obedience, and love for God—was Calvin's goal in the *Institutes*. Heiko Oberman asserts that 'Calvinistic pietism' is 'the precious core of the Reformed tradition' (*The Dawn of the Reformation*, 264). William A. Dyrness writes: 'The ordered structure which was so important to his understanding of truth and which shaped his *Institutes* was to be carried out consistently in the worshiping life of the people. But beyond that it was to be lived out in the homes and workplaces of Geneva' (*Reformed Theology and Visual Culture*, 82). Oberman distinguishes Calvin's understanding of 'piety' from late medieval 'spirituality', in that Calvin 'represents the life of sanctification through intensive involvement in this world', rather than 'contempt toward the world' (*The Dawn of the Reformation*, 265).

Calvin began his letter to Francis I, attached to his 1536 edition of the *Institutes* (and appearing in all subsequent editions), by explaining to the king that his 'purpose was solely to transmit certain rudiments by which those who are touched with any zeal for religion might be shaped to true godliness' (1:9). The full title of the first edition was *Institutes of the Christian Religion embracing almost the whole sum of piety and whatever is necessary to know of the doctrine of salvation: a work most worthy to be read by all persons zealous for piety.* These words may have been written by the publisher rather than Calvin himself but most likely received Calvin's approval and are indicative of the content of his book. In his prefatory note to the final edition of the *Institutes*, Calvin repeats that he had 'no other purpose than to benefit the church by maintaining the pure doctrine of godliness' through his 'zeal to spread [God's] kingdom and to further the public good' (1:4).

In the preface to his commentary on the Psalms, Calvin wrote about his conversion and its effect on his life. 'Having therefore received some taste and knowledge of true piety, I was suddenly fired with such a great desire to advance that even though I had not forsaken the other studies entirely I nonetheless worked at them more slackly' (Battles, *The Piety of John Calvin*, 31). His writing of the *Institutes* was driven by his passion to pass on to others the 'taste and knowledge of true piety' that he had received by God's grace. In the subject index of the McNeill-Battles *Institutes* there are seventy-seven entries under the word 'piety', but on almost every page of the *Institutes* one finds Calvin's concern for devotion to God and godly living. 'The whole life of Christians', he writes, 'ought to be a sort of practice of piety' (III.19.2).

What did Calvin mean by piety? In his first catechism, he wrote, 'True piety consists in a sincere feeling which loves God as Father as much as it fears and reverences him as Lord, embraces his righteousness, and dreads offending him worse than death' (Catechism of 1538, section 2). At the very beginning of the *Institutes* Calvin explains, 'I call "piety" that reverence joined with love of God which the knowledge of his benefits induces. For until men recognize that they owe everything to God, that they are nourished by his fatherly care, that he is the author of their every good, that they should seek nothing beyond him—they will never yield him willing service' (I.2.1). Throughout the *Institutes* and in his commentaries and sermons, Calvin describes piety and emphasizes its importance. Preaching on Ephesians 5:3-5, he asked, 'What is meant by holiness?' He answered, 'It is as much as to say that we must … offer ourselves to God, that he may enjoy us and mould us, so that we may be wholly his.'

'If we take doctrine and piety as belonging to two separate fields, one academic and the other pastoral, we will never understand John Calvin', writes Ellen Charry (*By the Renewing of Your Minds*, 199). Throughout the *Institutes* Calvin links theology and piety or devotion. He follows a chapter on the doctrine of providence with one titled 'How we may apply this doctrine to our greatest benefit' (I.17). Writing about justification, Calvin states that 'unless you first of all grasp what your relationship to God is, and the nature of his judgment concerning you, you have neither a foundation on which to establish your salvation nor one on which to build piety toward God.' He calls the doctrine of justification by faith 'the sum of all piety' (III.15.7). In his discussion of sanctification Calvin treats doctrinal matters and then moves to four chapters on the Christian life. He explains: 'We have given the first place to the doctrine in which our religion is contained, since our salvation begins with it. But it must enter our heart and pass into our daily living, and so transform us into itself that it may not be unfruitful for us' (III.7.4).

Throughout his commentaries Calvin stresses that correct doctrine is necessary for true piety.

- 'Piety is always built on knowledge of the true God and knowledge requires instruction' (Comm. Dan. 3:28).

- 'Let us realize that the truth and sound teaching of the word of God is the rule of piety, so that there may be no religion without the true light of understanding' (Comm. Acts 17:4).

- 'When there is no progress, and no edification in the doctrine itself, there is already a departure from the ordinance of Christ … for the "doctrine" will not be consistent with "piety" if it does not instruct us in the fear and worship of God, if it does not edify our faith, if it does not train us to patience, humility, and all the duties of that love which we owe to our fellow men' (Comm. 1 Tim. 6:3).

- 'That which can educate a man's piety demands a sane doctrine' (Comm. Titus 2:1).

- 'In doctrine … we should always have regard to usefulness, so that everything that does not contribute to piety shall be held in no estimation' (Comm. Titus 3:10).

Knowing God and ourselves

Elsie McKee speaks of 'the intensity and practicality, the biblical and all-encompassing character, the active and social manifestations' of Calvin's 'pastoral piety'. She describes it as

> intensely personal but never individualistic. Woven through with the great doctrines of justification by faith and regeneration of life, the glory of God and providence. Undergirded with prayer, proclaimed in word and shared in sacraments, sung in psalms. Embodied in action and demanding respect for the neighbour and solidarity with those who suffer in spirit, mind, or body. Not an easy or comfortable piety; it asks for one's all. Sturdy and down to earth, lived in the mundane context of daily work, yet always conscious of the presence of the transcendent God and the high calling of living before God. An energizing, lifelong response to God's liberating claim, God's righteous mercy, God's compelling love, a belonging that is all our joy. 'We are not our own ... We are God's!' (*John Calvin: Writings on Pastoral Piety*, 34-35).

1. Knowing God in Creation— 'The Mirror of Divinity'

'The world therefore is rightly called the *mirror of divinity*, not because there is enough clarity for men to know God by looking at the world, but because he makes himself clear to unbelievers in such a way that they are without excuse for their ignorance' (Comm. Heb. 11:3).

'The first five chapters of Calvin's *Institutes* are a gold mine for Christian theology generally, and for Christian apologetics more specifically. Given that Calvin's choice of topics follows closely the topics that Paul gives us in Romans, there can be little question that Calvin's initial concern was the relation of God to man generally, a relationship that has at its core the fact of man as God's image, and of God as constantly confronting man by way of his clear, and clearly understood, revelation in and through all of creation. The commonality that all of us share, as God's creatures, is that we all will never, because we can never, escape the presence (and knowledge of that presence) of God' (Oliphant, *A Theological Guide to Calvin's Institutes*, 40-41).

Read: *Institutes* I.1-5. [*1541* ch.1, pp. 1-16.]

Scripture Text: 'For the wrath of God is revealed from heaven against all ungodliness and unrighteousness of men, who by their unrighteousness suppress the truth. For what can be known about God is plain to them. For his invisible attributes, namely his eternal power and divine nature, have been clearly perceived, ever since the creation of the world, in the things that have been made. So they are without excuse. For although they knew God, they did not honour him as God or give thanks to him, but they became futile in their thinking, and their foolish hearts were darkened' (Rom. 1:18-21).

Notable Quote: 'For how can the thought of God penetrate your mind without your realizing immediately that, since you are his handiwork, you have been made over and bound to his command by right of creation, that you owe your life to him?—that whatever you undertake, whatever you do, ought to be ascribed to him?' (I.2.2).

Prayer

Grant, Almighty God, that as we enjoy the light of the sun by day and of the moon by night, we may learn to raise our eyes higher and not be like the unbelieving, who have this benefit in common with us, but may we look forward in hope of our eternal salvation.

Nor let us doubt but that as you set before our eyes a proof of your immovable constancy in these created things, so also secure and certain shall be our salvation, which is founded on your most certain truth, which renders sure all things, until at length we come into that blessed kingdom that has been obtained for us by the blood of your only begotten Son. Amen.

(Lifting Up Our Hearts, 135.)

Knowing God in creation

The title of the first chapter of the *Institutes* is not 'God the Creator' but 'The Knowledge of God the Creator.' Calvin does not begin with arguments for the existence of God. He does not pause, writes Marilynne Robinson, 'to dignify the question of the existence of God. To him God is simply manifest' (*John Calvin: Steward of God's Covenant*, xx). And so he plunges directly into the practical and all-important matter of how we can *know* God. 'Nearly all the wisdom we possess, that is to say, true and sound wisdom, consists of two parts: the knowledge of God and of ourselves' (I.1.1). The two-fold knowledge of God and ourselves, set forth in this famous opening sentence, will be expanded into a four-fold knowledge in Books I and II: knowledge of God as Creator and as Redeemer, and knowledge of ourselves as created and as redeemed.

Knowledge of God and knowledge of ourselves are 'joined by many bonds ... which one precedes and brings forth the other is not easy to discern' (I.1.1). No one can truly know God without knowing himself. No one can rightly know herself without knowing God. Calvin says that we can begin with either knowledge of God or knowledge of ourselves, but that the 'order of right teaching' leads him to begin with knowledge of God (I.1.13). This may reflect his desire to follow Paul's arrangement of topics in the Epistle to the Romans. The 'order of right teaching', however, is not necessarily the order in which we come to knowledge of God. Knowing ourselves as finite and sinful human beings can lead us to know God as infinite and merciful.

Knowing God is much more than information about God—a kind of theoretical knowledge 'that merely flits in the brain' (I.5.9). 'We shall not say that, properly speaking, God is known where there is no religion or piety' (I.2.1). One who knows God 'loves and reveres God as Father' and 'worships and adores him as Lord' (I.2.2).

Calvin describes 'the primal and simple knowledge to which the very order of nature would have led us if Adam had remained upright' (I.2.1).

There are two sources of the revelation of God in creation—internal and external.

Internal revelation

An internal knowledge of God from creation is 'naturally inborn in all ... of which each of us is master from his mother's womb' (I.3.3). This implanted knowledge of God is an 'awareness of divinity' or 'a certain understanding of [God's] divine majesty' (I.3.1). '"God" is a word, however problematical, we do not have to look up in the dictionary. We seem to have its acquaintance from birth', writes John Updike (*Self-Consciousness*, 40). In addition to knowledge of God's existence and divine majesty, there is also within human beings some understanding of his will, which Calvin describes as the 'seed of religion'. People know that God is to be worshipped, and that certain acts are pleasing to him and others are not.

> Gerald May writes that 'after twenty years of listening to the yearnings of people's hearts, I am convinced that all human beings have an inborn desire for God. Whether we are consciously religious or not, this desire is our deepest longing and most precious treasure' (*Addiction and Grace*, 1).

Nature itself permits no one to forget that there is a God, 'although many strive with every nerve' to do so (I.3.3). The Roman emperor Caligula hid under his bed in a lightening storm to escape the anger of the God he said he did not believe in. Those who claim to be atheists, Calvin writes, 'from time to time feel an inkling of what they desire not to believe' (I.3.2).

The internal knowledge of God, which 'can in no wise be uprooted', does not lead, however, to a true knowledge of God (I.4.4). God has 'sown a seed of religion in all men. But scarcely one man in a hundred is met with who fosters it ... and none in whom it ripens' (I.4.1). Why is this true? It is because of human sin, Calvin says. People 'deliberately befuddle themselves' (I.4.2).

> In *The Magician's Nephew*, C. S. Lewis tells how Uncle Andrew had heard the Lion singing 'long ago when it was still quite dark [and] he had realized that the noise was a song. And he had disliked the song very much'. When the sun rose and 'he saw that the singer was a lion ("*only* a lion", as he said to himself). Uncle Andrew tried his hardest to make himself believe that it wasn't singing and never had been singing—only roaring as any lion might in a zoo in our own world ... And the longer and more beautifully the Lion sang, the harder Uncle Andrew tried to make himself believe that he could hear nothing but roaring. Now the trouble about trying to make yourself stupider than you really are is that you very often succeed. Uncle Andrew did. He soon did hear nothing but roaring in Aslan's song. Soon he couldn't have heard anything else even if he had wanted to.'

Because of human sin God's witness within human beings fails to lead them to a true knowledge of God. Instead, it 'is so corrupted that by itself it produces only the worst fruits' (I.4.4). The result is not the absence of religion, but false religion, marked by superstition and hypocrisy. Timothy Keller explains: 'While everyone may have a *sensus divinitatis*, Calvin observed that we all refashion that sense of deity to fit our own interests and desires unless through the Spirit and the Scripture our view of God is corrected and clarified' (*Prayer: Experiencing Awe and Intimacy with God*, 45).

External revelation

Not only has God revealed himself *in* humanity (internal revelation) but he also has revealed himself *to* humanity (external revelation). People 'cannot open their eyes without being compelled to see him' (I.5.1).

> Marilynne Robinson writes that 'the beauty of what we see is burdened with truth. It signifies the power of God and his constant grace toward the human creature' (*John Calvin: Steward of God's Covenant*, xxii-xxiii).

The universe, Calvin writes, is 'a sort of mirror in which we can contemplate God' (I.5.1). It is a painting in which we can view his greatness (I.5.10). The study of the liberal arts enables us to 'penetrate with their aid far more deeply into the secrets of the divine wisdom' (I.5.2). Astronomy 'is not only pleasant, but also very useful to be known; it cannot be denied that this art unfolds the admirable wisdom of God' (Comm. Gen. 1:16). Preaching on God's questions to Job about the hawk and the eagle in Job 39:26-30, Calvin said, 'If we compare a hawk with the residue of the whole world, it is nothing. And yet if so small a portion of God's works ought to ravish us and amaze us, what ought all his works do when we come to the full numbering of them?'

We can also 'descend' within ourselves to find the wisdom of God displayed in our bodies, including even our toenails! The amazing activity of the human mind is an illustration of God's existence and presence with us (I.5.3-4).

God's work in history is another form of external revelation—a 'second kind of works, which are outside the ordinary course of nature' (I.5.7). The providence of God in human history, like creation itself, is 'a dazzling theatre' (I.5.8). Calvin knows, however, that the events of history do not give a complete picture of God's 'clemency' and his 'severity'. The incomplete nature of what happens in this world points to the future life when 'iniquity is to have its punishment, and righteousness is to be given its reward' (I.5.10). There will be a balancing of the books.

Just as people suppress the internal revelation of God, they also deny the external 'signs of divinity' (I.5.4). They do not see God in the wonders of creation, and they attribute history to a 'blindly indiscriminate fortune' (I.5.11). All are 'struck blind in such a dazzling theatre' (I.5.8), including 'the whole tribe of philosophers' (I.5.11). Every person's mind is a 'labyrinth'" (I.5.12), full of confusion and error. There is, therefore, 'no pure and approved religion, founded upon common understanding alone' (I.5.13). Left to its own devices, humanity's knowledge of God is finally confusion, superstition, error, and idolatry.

General revelation would have been the source of a sound knowledge of God, however, 'if Adam had remained upright' (I.2.1). The problem is not a lack of light but the corruption of the human heart. Calvin uses the illustration of blindness to make this point, but a little later changes it to 'old or bleary-eyed men and those with weak vision' who can 'scarcely construe two words' of 'a most beautiful volume' (I.6.7). By this change Calvin clarifies his main point: people do not see what they ought to see, and, therefore, they are inexcusable. 'We are not so blind that we can plead ignorance without being convicted of perversity … We see just enough to keep us from making excuse' (Comm. Rom. 1:20). People do not see clearly enough to give them a true knowledge of God, but they see enough to keep them from claiming to be innocent when faced with God's judgment.

Calvin writes that people will take refuge 'in the excuse that no blame ought to be laid on them, but rather that God was cruel when he did not think it worthwhile to give even a whistle to call back those whom he saw to be perishing' (Comm. Acts 14:17). But God did much more than 'give a whistle'. Michael Williams, professor of theology at Covenant Seminary, uses this illustration: 'Radio Yahweh is always on, always playing, loud and clear. But we refuse to listen. We keep changing the station.' We avoid and reject the revelation that God so generously and continually gives us. The immensity of God's positive revelation in creation and mankind's persistent refusal to receive such a rich message emphasize the magnitude of our guilt.

God has put into all people and before all people graphic evidence of his existence and character. In one of John Updike's novels, a woman says, 'I know you and your generation will think me quite mad, but God's non-existence is something I can't get used to, it seems unnatural' (*Seek My Face*, 206). According to Calvin, it *is* unnatural.

Knowing God and ourselves

What have we learned about God and ourselves from these opening chapters of the *Institutes*? 'From the feeling of our own ignorance, vanity, poverty, infirmity, and what is more—depravity and corruption—we recognize that the true light of wisdom, sound virtue, full abundance of every good work and purity of righteousness rest in the Lord alone' (I.i.i). We see ourselves as we really are and God as he really is. We are needy in every way, and must turn to God for everything. This lesson of human need and divine sufficiency will be repeated and reinforced throughout the whole of the *Institutes*.

2. Knowing God in Scripture— 'Spectacles'

'Just as old or bleary-eyed men and those with weak vision, if you thrust before them a most beautiful volume, even if they recognize it to be some sort of writing, yet can scarcely construe two words, but with the aid of spectacles will begin to read distinctly; so Scripture, gathering up the otherwise confused knowledge of God in our minds, having dispersed our dullness, clearly shows us the true God' (I.6.1).

'The Scriptures ... not only reveal the God of nature more brightly to the sin-darkened eye; they reveal also the God of grace, who may not be found in nature. Calvin does not overlook this wider revelation embodied in them: he particularly adverts to it (I.6.1). But he turns from it for the moment as less directly germane to his present object, which is to show that without the "spectacles" of Scripture, sinful man would not be able to attain to a sound knowledge of even God the Creator' (Warfield, *Calvin and Augustine*, 68).

Read: *Institutes* I.6-9. [*1541* ch.1, pp.16-26.]

Scripture Text: 'My Spirit that is upon you, and my words that I have put in your mouth shall not depart out of your mouth ... from this time forth and forevermore' (Isa. 59:21).

Notable Quote: 'Now, in order that true religion may shine upon us, we ought to hold that it must take its beginning from heavenly doctrine and that no one can get even the slightest taste of right and sound doctrine unless he is a pupil of Scripture' (I.6.2).

Prayer

Grant, Almighty God, that as you shine on us by your word, we may not be blind at mid-day, nor wilfully seek darkness, and thus lull our minds asleep. May we be roused daily by your words, and may we stir up ourselves more and more to fear your name and thus present ourselves and all our pursuits as a sacrifice to you, that you may peaceably rule, and perpetually dwell in us, until you gather us to your celestial habitation, where there is reserved for us eternal rest and glory through Jesus Christ our Lord. Amen.

(Devotions and Prayers of John Calvin, 21.)

A look back and a look ahead

'God has not left himself without a witness' (Acts 14:17). He has placed *within* every person a sense of his existence and an impression of his will. All people instinctively know that there is a God and that he is holy. Also God has placed *before* every person a witness to himself in creation, from the stars high above us to the depths of our own being. In the flow of history we see his purposes being worked out in judgment and in mercy. But because of Adam's sin (which we have inherited) and because of our own sin, our eyes are (almost) blinded and our minds have become a labyrinth of confusion and frustration. There is, therefore, 'no pure and approved religion, founded upon common understanding alone' (I.5.13) and 'all excuse is cut off because the fault of dullness is within us' (I.5.15). To know God, sinful people need a supernatural revelation and supernatural illumination. This is exactly what God has given in his word and by his Spirit.

Knowing God in Scripture

Calvin has quoted Scripture abundantly in I.1-5 to describe and illustrate the reality and the extent of natural revelation and the persistent rejection of that revelation by sinful people, but he introduces his formal teaching about the Bible in I.6. God 'not merely uses mute teachers' in the wonders of creation, he 'also opens his own most hallowed lips' in the Bible. The Bible is 'another and better help' and 'a more direct and more certain mark' (I.6.1). General revelation is not set aside but recovered in the Bible. The Bible, however, gives us far more than creation shows us. As Warfield puts it, the Scriptures 'reveal the God of nature more brightly to the sin-darkened eye; they also reveal the God of grace' (*Calvin and Augustine*, 68).

Calvin sets forth his doctrine of Scripture in five main points.

1. The Bible is the inspired word of God

God, Calvin says, is 'the author of the Scriptures' (I.9.2). The Bible 'has flowed to us from the very mouth of God' (I.7.5). 'For Calvin the Bible, the whole Bible and every nook and cranny of the Bible, is the word of God as completely as if God himself had spoken the actual words' (Parker, *Calvin's Old Testament Commentaries*, 66).

Did Calvin hold to the 'inerrancy' of Scripture? This word was not used about the Bible in the sixteenth century, but in his commentary on Psalm 119:130 Calvin describes the Bible as 'the certain and *unerring* rule' by which we regulate our lives. Calvin believed that the Bible was God's word, and, therefore, it is completely accurate and trustworthy. 'We owe to the Scripture the same reverence as we owe to God, since it has its only source in him and has nothing of human origin mixed with it' (Comm. 2 Tim. 3:16).

Some have argued that Calvin did not hold to inerrancy of Scripture since he acknowledges problems in the Bible. John T. McNeill gives a list of some of these problem texts and states that Calvin 'is frank to recognize that some passages do not admit of the claim of inerrancy on the verbal level' (1:lv).

Calvin does recognize problem passages, but never suggests that these make it impossible to claim that the Bible is less than the perfect word of God. He notes the possibility of copyist errors in the available texts. He points out that the Bible does not give precise or scientific data, but sometimes speaks 'inaccurately', not falsely but in popular and ordinary language, that is, in 'everyday ways of speaking' (Comm. Zeph. 3:7). He defends the free quotation of the Old Testament by New Testament writers and what may appear to be a misapplication of an Old Testament text in the New Testament. Commenting on Paul's use of Isaiah 64:4 in 1 Corinthians 2:9, Calvin says, 'Where shall we find a surer and more faithful interpreter than the Spirit of God of this authoritative declaration, which he himself dictated to Isaiah—in the exposition which he furnished by the mouth of Paul?' In a sermon Calvin noted that Paul in Ephesians 4:26 probably quotes from Psalm 4:4 when he writes 'be ye angry and sin not'. Calvin went on to say, 'Not that he quotes the psalm to report the natural sense of it, but to apply it to his own purpose.

For we may take many texts of Scripture and apply them to this and that without altering anything in them, while nevertheless they still keep their natural sense' (Sermon on Eph. 4:23-26). Calvin was critical of certain Old Testament laws that he felt were too strict or even savoured of barbarism, but he did not believe that the Scripture was in error. Appealing to God's accommodation, he wrote 'let us recollect that he designedly deviated from the more perfect rule, because he had to do with an intractable people' (Comm. The Last Four Books of Moses 3:40, 62-64).

Calvin insists that since the Bible in its entirety is the word of God, it reflects 'the character of the divine speaker' (I.7.4). Gerard Manley Hopkins reflects Calvin's point in a line of one of his poems:

> What God's Son has told me, take for truth I do;
> Truth himself speaks truly, or there's nothing true.
> > 'S. Thomae Aquinatis Rhythmus'

The word of God is 'pure and undefiled like gold seven times refined … The word of God is therefore certain truth … We have strong encouragement in that God who cannot lie when he speaks is not content merely to promise but gives his sworn word' (Comm. Heb. 6:18). B. B. Warfield concludes, 'Nothing is more certain than that Calvin held both to "verbal inspiration" and to "the inerrancy of Scripture," however he may have conceived the action of God which secured these things' (*Calvin and Augustine*, 61).

2. *The Bible is the inspired word of God revealed in human language*

Calvin states that the Scripture has 'flowed to us from the very mouth of God by the ministry of men' (I.7.5). He was perfectly at ease with the human authorship of the Bible. He notes the 'humanness' of Scripture in its diverse literary styles—both 'eloquence' and 'a rude and unrefined style' (I.8.2).

Calvin's statement that the Scriptures are not 'produced by men's minds … but are dictated by the Holy Spirit' (Comm. 2 Tim. 3:16) appears to indicate that he has no place for the human element in the Bible. Warfield comments: 'It is not unfair to urge … that this language is figurative and that what Calvin has in mind is not to insist that the mode of inspiration was dictation, but that the result is as if it were by dictation, viz., the production of a pure word of God free from all human admixtures' (*Calvin and Augustine*, 63-64).

Calvin often speaks of God's accommodation to our human limitations in the Bible. 'As nurses commonly do with infants, God is wont in a measure to "lisp" in speaking to us' (I.13.1). God's accommodation, however, does not mean that what God speaks in the Bible is something less than full truth. The Bible is accommodated truth, but it is absolutely true and trustworthy. 'We can safely follow scripture', Calvin writes, 'which proceeds at the pace of a mother stooping to her child, so to speak, so as not to leave us behind in our weakness' (III.21.4).

> 'And here let me remind you of the delightful familiarity of Scripture in this respect that *it speaks in the language of men*. If God had written us a book in his own language, we could not have comprehended it … As men conversing with babes use their broken speech, so doth the condescending word. It is not written in the celestial tongue, but in the *patois* of this lowland country, condescending to men of low estate' (C. H. Spurgeon, *The Metropolitan Tabernacle Pulpit* 17:595).

3. The authority of the Bible is confirmed to us by the testimony of the Holy Spirit

'Credibility of doctrine is not established until we are persuaded beyond doubt that God is its author' (I.7.4). How can we know for sure that the Bible is the word of God?

Our acceptance of the Bible as the word of God does not rest on the authority of the church. Neither does it come from rational proofs. Rather, it is given through 'the testimony of the Holy Spirit'. Because of our sin we do not receive the revelation of God given in creation. The *objective* cure for our condition is the Bible, 'the spectacles'. But we need more than the Bible. Since our minds and hearts are darkened by sin, we cannot see through the spectacles unless God provides the *subjective* cure by opening our eyes through 'the testimony of the Holy Spirit'. 'The same Spirit ... who has spoken through the mouths of the prophets must penetrate into our hearts to persuade us that they faithfully proclaimed what had been divinely commanded' (I.7.4). 'The word of God is like the sun, shining upon all those to whom it is proclaimed, but with no effect among the blind. Now all of us are blind by nature in this respect. Accordingly, it cannot penetrate into our minds unless the Spirit, as the inner teacher, through his illumination makes entry for it' (III.2.34).

'Scripture exhibits fully as clear evidence of its own truths as white and black things do of their colour, or sweet and bitter things do of their taste' (I.7.2). Scripture is 'self-authenticated ... it is sealed upon our hearts through the Spirit' (I.7.5). In his French translation of the *Institutes*, Calvin's expression for 'self-authenticated' is that the Bible 'carries within itself its own credentials'. The work of the Holy Spirit with respect to scripture is twofold: it is an illumination and a sealing—an illumination to our minds and a sealing upon our hearts.

4. *The authority of the Scripture, established by the testimony of the Holy Spirit, is supported by 'sufficiently firm proofs'*

The God-given conviction that the Bible is God's authoritative word 'requires no reasons', but, Calvin adds, it is 'a knowledge with which the best reason agrees' (I.7.5). Seven of the 'sufficiently firm proofs' that Calvin supplies are primarily from the Bible itself—its great antiquity, the miracles, fulfilled prophecy, its preservation, its heavenly character, its simplicity, and its authority (I.8.3-11). Two proofs are from church history—the testimony of the church, and the testimony of the martyrs (I.8.12-13).

The Holy Spirit directly creates belief in the authority of Scripture in the believer's heart. The 'proofs' serve 'to fortify' and 'to confirm' what is already accepted (I.8.1). They are, Calvin says, 'secondary aids to our feebleness' (I.8.13). We can do without them, but because of our weak faith, we may need them to help us preserve and, possibly at times, recover what we already believe—that the Bible is the word of God. Furthermore, these proofs, Calvin believed, give us arguments that we can use to vindicate the Bible against its disparagers. The effectiveness of some of the proofs may appear doubtful in our time, but remember that these are secondary proofs. Our conviction about the authority of the Bible does not ultimately depend on them but comes to us directly by the testimony of the Holy Spirit.

5. *The Bible and the Spirit belong together*

The word without the Spirit is dead—and deadly—Calvin maintains. He writes: 'The letter, therefore, is dead, and the law of the Lord slays its readers where it both is cut off from Christ's grace and, leaving the heart untouched, sounds in the ears alone' (I.9.3).

The Spirit without the word is a delusion. The Holy Spirit does not invent 'new and unheard of revelations' but seals 'our minds with that very doctrine which is commended by the gospel' (I.9.1). Because the Holy Spirit is 'the author of Scripture', he 'cannot vary and differ from himself. Hence he must ever remain just as he once revealed himself there [in the Scripture]' (I.9.2). The Holy Spirit does not release us from the word, but creates understanding and obedience to the word. Calvin explains that 'such as are truly taught of God are not led away from the law and the Scriptures by secret revelations, like some fanatics who think that they linger still at their ABCs unless disdainfully trampling under foot the word of God, they fly away after their own foolish fancies' (Comm. Psa. 119:171).

George Stroup sums up Calvin's point. 'The word without the Spirit is mere information and neither transformative nor redemptive; and the Spirit without the word invites self-deception and idolatry' (*Calvin*, 22). Anthony Lane writes, 'The Spirit without the word is dangerous; the word without the Spirit is deadly; the word with the Spirit is dynamite' (*A Reader's Guide to Calvin's Institutes*, 48).

Knowing God and ourselves

'For when [God] has spoken, it is once for all. And his intent is for us to adhere to what he has said … Our Lord wills for us to be wholly attached to him … This will be accomplished when we are simply confined between the boundaries of his word, when we permit no access to human inventions, when we forbid our minds to stray. It will come to pass only after we have listened to what the holy Scripture contains, promptly saying amen, not simply with our mouth, but when our faith has fully relied upon what has proceeded from the mouth of our God' (*Sermons on the Ten Commandments*, 242, 306-307).

Let the church say Amen,
Let the church say Amen,
God has spoken,
So let the church say Amen.

Andrae Crouch

3. God—
'Three Persons in One Essence'

'God is not truly known, unless our faith distinctly conceives *three Persons in one Essence*' (Comm. Matt. 28:19).

'Having expounded in the opening chapters of the *Institutes* the sources and means of the knowledge of God, Calvin naturally proceeds in the next series of chapters to set forth the nature of the God who, by the revelation of himself in his word and by the prevalent internal operation of his Spirit, frames the knowledge of himself in the hearts of his people' (Warfield, *Calvin and Augustine*, 133).

Read: *Institutes* I.10-13. [*1541* ch.1, pp.26-28; ch.3, pp.126-132; ch.4, pp.208-229.]

Scripture Text: 'The LORD passed before him and proclaimed, "The LORD, the LORD, a God merciful and gracious, slow to anger, and abounding in steadfast love and faithfulness, keeping steadfast love for thousands, forgiving iniquity and transgression and sin, but who will by no means clear the guilty, visiting the iniquity of the fathers on the children and the children's children, to the third and fourth generation"' (Exod. 34:6-7).

Notable Quote: 'Moreover, we said at the beginning that the knowledge of God does not rest in cold speculation, but carries with it the honouring of him' (I.12.1).

Prayer

Grant, Almighty God, that as you have shown to us by evidences so remarkable that all things are under your command, and that we, who live in the world through your favour are as nothing ... O grant that being conscious of your power, we may reverently fear your hand and be wholly devoted to your glory.

And as you kindly offer yourself to us as a father, may we, drawn by this kindness, surrender ourselves wholly to you by a willing obedience, and never labour for anything through life but to glorify your name, as you have redeemed us through your only begotten Son, that so we may also enjoy through him that eternal inheritance that is laid up for us in heaven. Amen.

(*Lifting Up Our Hearts*, 35.)

❦

A look back and a look ahead

The knowledge of God from creation is 'more intimately and also more vividly revealed' in the Bible (I.10.1). By looking at the splendour of the heavens, we see the glory of God. By reading in the Bible that 'the heavens declare the glory of God, and the sky above proclaims his handiwork' (Psa. 19:1) we are assured that what we see in creation is indeed true. With the Bible in our hands and the Holy Spirit in our minds and hearts, we can come to a fuller knowledge of God. We learn what we could not learn from creation alone. We learn that the one God is three persons—Father, Son, and Holy Spirit. We are given a more complete understanding of the 'time and manner' of creation and the full scope of God's particular providence. Calvin tells us that in I.10-13 he will focus on 'the knowledge [of God] that stops at the creation of the world and [will] not ascend to Christ the mediator' (I.10.1). That will come in Book II.

Doctrine of God

In I.11-12 John Calvin rejects what he sees as idolatry in the Roman Catholic use of images in worship. In I.13 he sets forth the orthodox doctrine of the Trinity and defends it against past and present heresies.

There are two notable characteristics of Calvin's treatment of the doctrine of God.

First, Calvin insists that true knowledge of God comes from Scripture alone. 'Let us not take it into our heads either to seek out God anywhere else than in his sacred word, or to think anything about him that is not prompted by his word, or to speak anything that is not taken from that word' (I.13.21). In other words, we must not go beyond what the Bible tells us about God. In an important sentence Calvin writes that in the Bible God is 'shown to us not as he is in himself, but as he is toward us' (I.10.2). There is a hidden depth in God that we cannot plumb. We can know God truly but we cannot know him exhaustively. We can be assured, however, that what God is 'toward us' is consistent with all that God is 'in himself'. Especially in thinking about the Trinity, we 'ought to play the philosopher soberly and with great moderation' (I.13.21). Calvin avoids setting forth proofs or illustrations of the Trinity from metaphysical reasoning or natural analogies. All 'comparisons from human affairs' fall far short (I.13.18).

Second, Calvin treats the true worship of God before he deals with the doctrine of God. For Calvin, true and acceptable worship is a necessary part of knowing God. Knowledge of God 'invites us first to fear, then to trust in him. By this we can learn to worship him both with perfect innocence of life and with unfeigned obedience, then to depend wholly upon his goodness' (I.10.2).

Worship of God

In the Bible God teaches 'what worship he approves or repudiates' (I.11.1). Calvin rejects the Catholic practice of using images of God in worship, since the Bible says that the worship of a 'visible form' of God is not acceptable. He notes that the people of Lystra believed in many gods, until Paul and Barnabas told them that there is one God who is the creator of the world. 'With the removal of that fictitious crowd of deities the way was opened for the second step, to teach them what that God, the creator of heaven and earth, was like. Our argument with the Papists today is a different one. They confess the unity of God, and they give admittance to Scripture. Therefore it remains for us to prove to them out of the Scripture what God is like, and the kind of worship he requires of men' (Comm. Acts 14:15).

Calvin gives three reasons why we should not use images of God in worship.

- Images are not allowed, because God 'himself has forbidden it' (I.11.12). Calvin knows and rejects the 'foolish evasions of the papists' (I.11.11) who distinguish *dulia* (respectful service given to images) and *latria* (worship given to God alone).

- Images are not worthy, because they cannot be used 'without some defacing of [God's] glory' (I.11.12). The Old Testament 'symbols of his heavenly glory'—cloud, smoke, flames—do not tell us what

God looks like but strike us with a sense of his overwhelming glory.

- Images are not needed, because we have 'living and symbolic images' in the sacraments, baptism and the Lord's supper (I.11.13), and in the true preaching of the gospel, where 'Christ is depicted before our eyes as crucified' (I.11.7). Warfield comments: 'It is in the true preaching of the gospel that Christ is really depicted—crucified before our eyes openly, as Paul testifies [in Gal. 3:1]: and there can be no reason to crowd the churches with crucifixes of wood and stone and silver and gold, if Christ is faithfully preached as dying on the cross to bear our curse, expiating our sins by the sacrifice of his body, cleansing us by his blood and reconciling us to God the Father' (*Calvin and Augustine*, 181). When Christ is rightly preached, we 'see' the truth in a deeper and purer way than by looking at images of God.

Although Calvin disallows the use of images in worship, he by no means rejects all art. 'Sculpture and painting are gifts of God' (I.11.12). Warfield claims that Calvin was 'a lover and fosterer of the arts' (*Calvin and Augustine*, 183). At least we can be sure that he was not an enemy of the arts, as many believe. There is a 'pure and legitimate use' of art, according to Calvin, that sets forth those things which 'the eyes are capable of seeing' (I.11.12). These include pictures of historical events (for teaching and admonition) and 'forms of bodies' (for pleasure). The depiction of human bodies must be modest, however. Brothels, Calvin claims, show harlots 'clad more virtuously and modestly' than the Catholic churches show 'those objects which they wish to be thought images of virgins' (I.11.7).

Attributes of God

Calvin does not treat the attributes of God in a philosophical or technical manner. He devotes himself, rather, to awakening in the hearts of his readers a practical knowledge of God, a knowledge that leads to a fear (awe and reverence) of God and trust in him. For Calvin the attributes of God are simply the sum of what the Bible tells us about

God. He stresses that we know God 'as he is toward us', although he touches lightly on God 'as he is in himself' (I.13.1). There are two 'special marks' of God that point to his essence—infinity and spirituality. His infinity ought to make us afraid to try to measure him by our own senses. His spirituality forbids our imagining anything earthly or carnal of him. Rather than seeking to discover more about God 'as he is in himself', we should be satisfied with finding God 'as he is toward us' in his character and works. Calvin writes:

> The majesty, or the authority, or the glory of God does not consist in some imaginary brightness, but in those works which so necessarily belong to him that they cannot be separated from his very essence. It is what particularly belongs to God, to govern the world, and to exercise care over mankind, and also to make a difference between good and evil, to help the miserable, to punish all wickedness, to check injustice and violence (Comm. Zeph. 1:12).

Calvin sums up his words on this topic by saying, 'Let us then willingly leave to God the knowledge of himself' (I.13.21).

Calvin presents a brief Bible study of Exodus 34:6, 7 and Psalm 145 to illustrate God's attributes. These are presented, 'so to speak in solution rather than in precipitate', comments Warfield (*Calvin and Augustine*, 143). In other words Calvin gives a general description of God in his total person rather than a technical division with separate treatments of his different attributes. It is worth noting that Calvin with all his emphasis on the sovereignty of God (here and elsewhere) puts even stronger emphasis on God's love. Commenting on Psalm 74:12, where the Psalmist speaks of God as king, Calvin writes, 'It is quite clear that the title king, which is applied here to God, ought not to be restricted merely to his sovereignty' but also points to 'his fatherly love towards us'.

Warfield writes:

> The sense of the divine fatherhood is as fundamental to Calvin's conception of God as the sense of his sovereignty. Of course, he throws the strongest conceivable interest on God's lordship: the sovereignty of God is the hinge of his thought of God. But this sovereignty is ever conceived by him as the sovereignty of God our Father … With all his emphasis on the sovereignty of God, Calvin

throws an even stronger emphasis on his love: and his doctrine of God is preeminent among the doctrines of God given expression in the Reformation age in the commanding place it gives to the divine fatherhood. 'Lord and Father'—fatherly sovereign, or sovereign Father—that is how Calvin conceived of God (*Calvin and Augustine*, 175-76).

Calvin stresses the divine fatherhood, but he also speaks, as the Bible does, of God as mother, and makes the point that this in some ways is an even more appropriate picture of God.

> 'I [the Lord] will cry out like a woman in labour'—By this comparison [God] expresses an amazing warmth of love and the most tender affection. For he compares himself to a mother whose love for her baby, though she gave birth to it in intense pain, has no parallel. This may not seem to fit God, but only by such figures of speech can his passionate love for us be expressed (Comm. Isa. 42:14).

> [God] compares himself to a mother, whose love for her baby is so engrossed and anxious as to leave a father's love a long way behind … The affection a mother feels for her baby is amazing. She fondles it in her lap, feeds it at her breast, and watches so anxiously over it that she passes sleepless nights, continually wearing herself out and forgetting about herself (Comm. Isa. 49:15).

> When [God] assumes a mother's role, he comes a great way down from his glory; how much further when he takes the guise of a hen, and deigns to treat us as his chicks! (Comm. Matt. 23:27)

Preaching on Ephesians 3:9-12, Calvin said, 'We may approach into the presence of our God and come to him for refuge, just as a child throws himself into the lap of his father or mother, for it is certain that God surpasses all the fathers and mothers of the world in all kindness and favour.' B. A. Gerrish writes, 'Not the divine despot, but the Parent-God, who is goodness itself, was the object of Calvin's piety and therefore the main theme of his doctrine of God' (*Grace and Gratitude*, 41).

> 'The Creator is by [Calvin's] reckoning, utterly greater than any conception we can form of his creation, and at the same time free, present, just, loving, and intimately attentive to fallen humankind, collectively and one by one' (Robinson, *John Calvin: Steward of God's Covenant*, ix).

Trinity

Calvin next comes to the doctrine of the Trinity as 'another special mark' by which God distinguishes himself 'more precisely from idols' (I.13.2). Apart from the knowledge of God as Trinity, Calvin believes, we have no knowledge of God at all. Only through his self-revelation as Father, Son, and Holy Spirit do we truly know who God is.

In the 1536 *Institutes* Calvin gave the doctrine of the Trinity only the briefest mention. His early reluctance to subscribe to doctrinal formulations such as the Nicene Creed came from his conviction that Christians have a 'reverent freedom' to formulate doctrine directly from the Bible, independent of traditional statements. Even in the 1559 *Institutes* Calvin wishes that the creedal statements 'were buried', if 'only among all men' the orthodox doctrine of the Trinity was accepted. Since the words we use about the Trinity (as Augustine said) are 'not to express what is there', but only so that we will not 'be silent', we must not take to task, 'like censors, those who do not wish to swear to the words conceived by us, provided they are not doing it out of either arrogance or frowardness or malicious craft' (I.13.5). Warfield speaks of the 'purity of [Calvin's] Protestantism'; it was the word of God and not the word of Athanasius to which he submitted (*Calvin and Augustine*, 206).

Calvin, however, came to support the use of technical, non-biblical words, such as 'person' and 'essence', as found in the Nicene Creed. Since heretics use the exact words of Scripture to set forth their false teaching, Calvin says, we may, and indeed must, use words not found in the Bible to make 'the truth plain and clear' (I.13.3). The use of one expression for God's threeness ('person') and another for God's oneness ('essence' or 'substance') states accurately and defends New Testament teaching about the Trinity. Such terms are good and necessary, 'provided they draw out the implications of Scripture while at the same time safeguarding the mystery … and protecting us against false teaching about it' (Helm, *Calvin at the Centre*, 113).

The main point of Calvin's doctrine of the Trinity may be briefly stated: in the unity of the Godhead there is a distinction of persons. Or in Calvin's own words: 'When we profess to believe in one God, under the name of God is understood a single, simple essence, in which we comprehend three persons, or *hypostases*' (I.13.20). And again, 'Father and Son and Spirit are one God, yet the Son is not the Father; nor the Spirit the Son, but … they are differentiated by a peculiar quality' (I.13.22).

Calvin realized the depth of mystery surrounding the doctrine of the Trinity. He states it but does not attempt to explain it. For this he finds support in the church fathers.

> Hilary [of Poitiers, a fourth-century church father] accuses the heretics of a great crime, that by their wickedness he is forced to submit to the peril of human speech what ought to have been locked within the sanctity of men's minds; and he does not hide the fact that this is to do things unlawful, to speak things inexpressible, to presume things not conceded. A little later [Hilary] excuses himself at length for daring to put forward new terms; for when he has set forth the natural names—Father, Son, and Spirit—he adds that whatever is sought besides these is beyond the meaning of language, above the reach of sense, above the capacity of understanding (I.13.5).

A little later Calvin quotes a passage from another church father, Gregory of Nazianzus, that, he writes, 'vastly delights me': 'I cannot think on the one without quickly being encircled by the splendour of the three; nor can I discern the three without being straightway carried back to the one' (I.13.17).

Calvin carefully uses the biblical texts in presenting the doctrine of the Trinity. He considers weak or spurious such frequently used arguments for the doctrine of the Trinity as the plural form of God (*Elohim*), the thrice-repeated adulation of the seraphim in Isaiah 6, and Jesus' statement in John 10:30—'I and my Father are one.' Calvin does see plurality in the Godhead, however, in the words of Genesis 1:26—'Let us make man in our own image.'

The Bible often calls the *Father* God, but Calvin insists that 'whenever the name of God is mentioned without particularization, there are designated no less the Son and the Spirit than the Father; but where the Son is joined to the Father, then the relation of the two enters in' (I.13.20).

In I.13.7-13, Calvin presents biblical evidence that the *Son* is God.

- Proverbs 1 and John 1 state that the Son is the Eternal Wisdom or the Eternal Word who is with God and who is also God.

- Christ is called God in the Old as well as in the New Testament.

- Works and miracles ascribed to Christ prove that he is God.

- In the Bible we are called upon to believe in Christ, pray to him, and worship him as God.

Calvin connects doctrinal knowledge of the deity of Christ with 'practical knowledge', in which 'the pious mind perceives the very presence of God, and almost touches him, when it feels itself quickened, illumined, preserved, justified, and sanctified' (I.13.13).

In I.13.14-15, Calvin shows that the *Holy Spirit* is God, adapting the arguments used for the deity of the Son to prove the deity of the Spirit.

- Works that can only be ascribed to God are ascribed to the Holy Spirit.

- Some Bible passages state that the Holy Spirit is God.

Having presented the oneness of God and the deity of each of the three persons, Calvin says that there is 'a distinction, not a division' in the Godhead (I.13.17). Nothing can obscure the unity of God, but at the same time it is 'not fitting to suppress the distinction' made by Scripture (I.13.18). Calvin asserts that in each of the persons of the Trinity 'the whole divine nature is understood, with this qualification—that to each belongs his own peculiar quality' (I.13.19). The Father, Son, and

Holy Spirit have always existed as distinct persons, with a significant and irreversible order. Calvin explains that 'to the Father is attributed the beginning of action, the fountain and source of all things; to the Son, wisdom, counsel, and arrangement in action; while the energy and efficacy of action is assigned to the Spirit' (I.13.18). Warfield states Calvin's view: 'The Father is conceived as the source, the Son as the director, the Spirit as the executor of all the divine activities; the Father as the fountain, the Son as the wisdom emerging from him, the Spirit as the power by which the wise counsels of God are effectuated' (*Calvin and Augustine*, 229). Julie Canlis describes Calvin's view as 'the fatherhood of God, the mediation of the Word, and the "tending" of the Spirit' (*Calvin's Ladder*, 5). Michael Horton writes, 'This formulation—"from the Father, in the Son, and through the Spirit"—reappears across the whole scope of Calvin's thinking ... Every topic that Calvin considers is therefore framed by this dynamic exchange and cooperation between the divine persons. In short, the Trinity is for Calvin not a dogma to which we yield assent, but the heart of reality in which we live and move and have our being' (*Calvin on the Christian Life*, 62-63).

Calvin is careful to emphasize that each of the three members of the Trinity is fully God. 'The Father', he writes, 'is the fountain of deity, with respect, not to being, but to order' (I.13.26). Any hint of causality or subordinationism latent in the Nicene terms of 'begetting' (the 'Lord Jesus Christ, the only-begotten Son of God, begotten of his Father before all worlds') and 'proceeding' ('the Holy Spirit ... who proceeds from the Father and the Son') must be rejected—not the words themselves, but an unbiblical interpretation of these words. Calvin will not allow any sense of derived deity for the Son and the Spirit—the idea that the Father, who alone is truly and properly God, poured his own deity into the Son and the Spirit. Whatever the Father is as God, that the Son is as God, and that the Holy Spirit is as God. The deity of the Son and Spirit is not derived from the person (*hypostasis*) of the Father but from the being or essence (*ousia*) of the Godhead. The Son is not God because of the Father but the Son is the Son because of the Father.

Calvin questions two of the Nicene expressions that he believed could be misunderstood or misused—'God of God' and 'eternally begotten'.

He does not reject the phrase 'God of God', as long as it does not imply that the Father gives deity to the Son. Calvin was willing to accept the words that the Son was 'begotten' of the Father before all time. He had trouble, however, with the idea of 'eternal generation' because it seemed to imply something that was continually occurring. Calvin found this conception difficult, if not meaningless. He ends I.13 with the words:

> While I am zealous for the edification of the church, I felt that I would be better advised not to touch upon many things that would profit but little, and would burden my readers with useless trouble. For what is the point in disputing whether the Father always begets? Indeed, it is foolish to imagine a continuous act of begetting, since it is clear that three persons have subsisted in God from eternity (I.13.29).

Douglas Kelly explains:

> Calvin's criticisms of certain interpretations of ancient terms from the Christian theological tradition is only intended to strengthen the biblical doctrine of the church that the one true God exists eternally as three coequal persons in one infinitely spiritual being. To know this God is to possess eternal life. And thus to seek to know, to speak of, and to love this God in humble and thoughtful accordance with his revealed word are worth the best efforts of our lives, as they have been worth the best efforts of God's saints through the ages (*A Theological Guide to Calvin's Institutes*, 89).

Warfield aptly states that the three 'notes' of Calvin's conception of the Trinity are 'simplification, clarification, and equalization'. Furthermore, Calvin's emphasis on equalization 'marks an epoch in the history of the doctrine of the Trinity' (*Calvin and Augustine*, 230).

Calvin sets forth the Bible's teaching about the doctrine of the Trinity, and then vigorously defends it against the anti-trinitarians of his time, one of whom was Servetus (I.13.21-29). Polemics are sometimes necessary, says Calvin, because 'the truth which has been peaceably shown must be maintained against all the calumnies of the wicked' (I.13.21).

Knowing God and ourselves

Warfield writes that Calvin 'closes every stage of consideration of God in the *Institutes* with an exhortation to the adoration of God or to the surrender of the heart to him' (*Calvin and Augustine*, 141-42). Look back over these chapters and find these exhortations. Read them again and mark them. Worship God and ask him to enable you more and more to surrender your heart to him.

4. Creation— 'A Spacious and Splendid House'

God 'has so wonderfully adorned heaven and earth with as unlimited abundance, variety, and beauty of all things as could possibly be, quite like a spacious and splendid house, provided and filled with the most exquisite and at the same time most abundant furnishings' (I.15.20).

> 'In developing his system, Calvin proceeds at once from the doctrine of God to an exposition of his works of creation and providence. That he passes over the divine purpose or decree at this point, though it would logically claim attention before its execution in creation and providence, is only another indication of the intensely practical spirit of Calvin and the simplicity of his method in this work. He carries his readers at once from what God is to what God does' (Warfield, *Calvin and Calvinism*, 287).

Read: *Institutes* I.14-15. [*1541* ch.2, pp.31-36, 39-52.]

Scripture Text: 'By faith we understand that the universe was created by the word of God, so that what is seen was not made out of things that are visible' (Heb. 11:3).

Notable Quote: 'It is evident that all creatures, from those in the heavens to those under the earth, are able to act as witnesses and messengers of God's glory … For the little birds that sing, sing of God; the beasts cry out for him; the elements of nature are in awe of him; the mountains echo his name; the waves and fountains cast their glances at him; and the grass and flowers laugh before him' (Calvin's Preface to the 1535 French Bible of Olivétan).

'Now the faithful, to whom he has given eyes, see sparks of his glory, as it were, glittering in every created thing. The world was no doubt made, that it might be the theatre of the divine glory' (Comm. Heb. 11:3).

In 'Pied Beauty', Gerard Manley Hopkins beautifully illustrates Calvin's thought.

> Glory be to God for dappled things—
> For skies of couple-colour as a brinded cow;
> For rose-moles in all stipple upon trout that swim;
> Fresh-firecoal chestnut-falls; finches' wings;
> Landscape plotted and pieced—fold, fallow, and plough;
> And all trades, their gear, tackle and trim.
> All things counter, original, spare, strange;
> Whatever is fickle, freckled (who knows how?)
> With swift, slow; sweet, sour; adazzle, dim;
> He fathers-forth whose beauty is past change:
> Praise him.

Prayer

God has set all things for our good and our salvation; in our very selves we feel his power and grace, his great, unnumbered benefits, freely conferred upon us.

What else can we then do but stir ourselves to trust, invoke, to praise and love him? For all God's handiwork is made for us. Even in the six days he shows a Father's care for his child as yet unborn.

Away, ingratitude, forgetfulness of him! Away with craven fear he may fail us in our need! For he has seen to it that nothing will be lacking to our own welfare.

Whenever we call on God, Creator of heaven and earth, we must be mindful that all he gives us is in his hand. Our every trust and hope we hang on him alone.

Whatever we desire, we are to ask of him and thankfully receive each benefit that falls to us. Let us then strive to love and serve him with all our hearts.

('Hymn to Creation'
adapted from the *Institutes* by Ford Lewis Battles,
The Piety of John Calvin, 169-70.)

❧

A look back and a look ahead

'God, the artificer of the universe, is made manifest to us in Scripture' (I.6.1). Fallen people see little or nothing of the splendid revelation of God in nature, but aided by the 'spectacles' of Scripture and with their eyes opened by the Holy Spirit, they come to a true knowledge of God the Creator. 'God by the power of his Word and Spirit created heaven and earth out of nothing' (I.14.20). God who made all things keeps and preserves all things, as we will see in Calvin's doctrine of providence, which comes next.

Creation

Creation is not 'the chief evidence for faith'—that will come in Book II with 'God the Redeemer in Christ'—but 'it is the first evidence in the order of nature, to be mindful that wherever we cast our eyes, all things they meet are works of God' (I.14.20). The beautiful works of God portray the power and wisdom of God as in a painting (I.5.10). The splendour and magnificence of the heavenly bodies preach 'the glory of God like a teacher in a seminary of learning' (Comm. Psa. 19:4). Indeed, all created things may be called 'the alphabet of theology' by which we learn the wisdom, power and goodness of God (Comm. Jer. 10:1-2).

Calvin's 'commentary on Genesis, completed the year before his death, is a joyful and effusive work, in which he relaxes the discipline of brevity which so strongly marks his earlier exegetical writing. It is touching to find this sick and weary man so eager to call Creation good' (Robinson, *The Death of Adam*, 184).

John Calvin's treatment of creation is practical, personal, and devotional. The object of Scripture in giving us 'the history of creation' is not to answer all our questions but to strengthen our faith in God that we 'might seek no other God but him who was put forth by Moses as the maker and founder of the universe' (I.14.1). Calvin wants to quicken 'in our hearts a sense of the glory and perfections' of God, 'whose wisdom, power, justice and goodness are illustrated by [the creation]', and to raise 'our hearts in gratitude to him for his benefits to us' (Warfield, *Calvin and Calvinism*, 306).

The Bible does not give us an account of creation in scientific and technical language. Calvin writes:

> The Holy Spirit had no intention to teach astronomy; and, in proposing instruction meant to be common to the simplest and most uneducated persons, he made use by Moses and the other prophets of language, that none might shelter himself under the pretext of obscurity, as we will see men sometimes very readily pretend an incapacity to understand, when anything deep or recondite is submitted to their notice. Accordingly ... the Holy Spirit would rather speak childishly than unintelligibly to the humble and unlearned (Comm. Psa. 136:7).

We have already noted that Calvin's doctrine of God's accommodation does not weaken his high view of biblical infallibility; speaking childishly and speaking erroneously are quite different matters. The Bible's story of creation is both accommodated and true.

Why did the omnipotent God take six days to create the heavens and the earth? Calvin answers that it was for our benefit—so that our minds would not be over-taxed by having to take in so much at once, and to show his love in so carefully preparing this world for us. Therefore, 'in the very order of things', we ought 'diligently to contemplate God's fatherly love toward' us (I.14.2).

Before he comes to the creation of man and woman, Calvin discusses angels and demons. His treatment is scriptural, practical, and restrained. The Bible does not clearly set forth the cause, manner, and time of the creation of the angels, nor of the fall of the devils. Calvin interprets Isaiah 14:12 as a reference to the king of Babylon, not to the fall of Satan.

Calvin calls the speculation of Dionysius (a late fifth-century work falsely attributed to the 'Areopagite' of Acts 17:34) about these matters 'foolish wisdom' (I.14.4).

Angels

Angels are real spirits characterized by 'perception and intelligence' (I.14.9). They are described in Scripture by such lofty titles as hosts, powers, principalities, dominions, and thrones, but like all of God's creatures their dependence on him is absolute. They are servants of God, indeed they are, as Calvin beautifully puts it, 'the hands of God … not which work instead of him, but by which he works' (I.14.12). God uses 'their ministry and service … to carry out all things he has decreed' (I.14.5). The work of the angels does not imply the absence of God; they are the agents of the presence of God. A preacher in Marilynne Robinson's novel *Lila* says, 'For Calvin, angels are the effective attention of God' (231).

As servants of God, the angels also serve God's people 'to comfort our weakness, that we may lack nothing at all that can raise up our minds to good hope or confirm them in security' (I.14.11). God works through the angels because he wishes not only to care for us but also to give us a sense of his protection. This comes when we know that there are angels who are sent by God to care for us—angels, not just one 'guardian' angel, because 'the care of each one of us is not the task of one angel only'. Indeed, Calvin says, all the angels 'with one consent watch over our salvation' (I.14.7). While the angels are watching over us, they 'lead us by the hand' straight to Christ 'that we may look upon him, call upon him, and proclaim him as our sole helper' (I.14.13).

Demons

Calvin examines the existence of evil here in his treatment of creation, and the existence of sin later in his doctrine of redemption. He deals with both sin and evil 'as present realities but final mysteries' (Partee, *The Theology of John Calvin*, 75).

The demons, Calvin writes, are 'God's adversary and ours' (I.14.15). He makes three main points about them.

1. The devils were created good by God, but 'they ruined themselves' (I.14.16). Satan was once in the truth but did not abide in it. The devils are good spirits gone wrong. We must be careful not to ascribe to God 'what is utterly alien to him' (I.14.16).

2. The devil stands under God's power. He 'can do nothing unless God wills and assents to it' (I.14.17). God uses the 'unclean spirits' to punish the wicked and to exercise and develop his children. Satan is behind those who trouble us, but behind Satan is God, who permits such trials to exercise, discipline and purify us (Comm. Psa. 44:13).

3. We are engaged in 'an unceasing struggle' against the devil (I.14.15). 'If we care about our salvation at all, we ought to have neither peace nor truce with him who continually lays traps to destroy it' (I.14.15). At the same time we must remember that in Christ our victory has 'always been full and complete'—although it is never fully complete in this life (I.14.18).

The world

In his treatment of the creation of the world Calvin asserts that God created all things out of nothing, that everything that God created was very good, and that he made and adorned the whole creation for the sake of human beings.

Calvin evidently believed that the six days of Genesis were ordinary days of twenty-four hours, but he does not discuss the issue in the *Institutes* nor in his commentary on Genesis. The creation of the heavens and the earth in Genesis 1:1 was perfected through a process of formation extending through the six days. Calvin describes God's work of creation in three stages: (1) God created heaven and earth out of nothing. (2) He brought forth living beings and inanimate things of every kind. (3) He provided for the preservation of each species 'until the last day' (I.14.20). All creation is, therefore, the direct work of God, creating something out of nothing, and then forming out of that something all things.

Human beings

Calvin follows his plan of developing a two-fold knowledge of ourselves—as created (which he discusses here in I.15) and as fallen (which comes in II.1-5). Human philosophy confuses created and fallen humanity and so looks 'in a ruin for a building' (I.15.18). To see human beings as God created them—'the noblest and most remarkable example of [God's] justice, wisdom, and goodness' (I.15.1)—produces in us wonder and gratitude. It also prevents our blaming God for our present 'sad ruin' (I.15.1) and thus trying to escape from our responsibility for that ruin. Our present ruin was caused by our sinful rebellion, so 'every escape route is blocked', declares Calvin (I.15.1).

> 'Humanity is a highly dangerous element in Creation, but it also has the capacity to protect and guarantee justice … The most eloquent statement of this double-edged character to human presence in the world is to be found in *Prince Caspian*. Prince Caspian has just discovered that his people are descended from a tribe of pirates … and he wishes that "he came of a more honourable lineage". "You come of the Lord Adam and the Lady Eve", said Aslan. "And that is both honour enough to erect the head of the poorest beggar, and shame enough to bow the shoulders of the greatest emperor on earth"' (Rowan Williams, *The Lion's World: A Journey into the Heart of Narnia*, 22-23).

There are three main points in Calvin's doctrine of the creation of man and woman.

1. Mankind was created body and soul

God's glory shines in the body or 'outer man' (I.15.2). The 'exquisite workmanship' of the human body contains 'enough miracles to occupy our minds, if we pay attention to them' (Comm. Gen. 1:26).

While he praises the wonder of the human body, Calvin also speaks of it as a 'frail lodging', a 'poor hut' (Comm. 2 Cor. 5:1), and an 'earthly prison' (I.15.2; III.6.5; III.25.1). Calvin's words may reflect his own experience of sickness. Sooner or later most people come to the place of seeing the body as more of a burden than a blessing. In a dramatic passage, Calvin writes, 'For if we reflect that this our tabernacle, unstable, defective, corruptible, fading, pining and putrid, is dissolved, in order that it may forthwith be renewed in sure, perfect, incorruptible, in fine, in heavenly glory, will not faith compel us eagerly to desire what nature dreads?' (III.9.5) What we desire, however, is not to get rid of our broken and feeble bodies, but to get better ones.

Some have seen in Calvin's language about the body the influence of Platonic theology. Mary Potter Engel argues that Calvin uses the common Platonic metaphor for the body as a prison house in two distinct ways: to refer to the sinful condition of human beings after the fall, and the transience of the temporal life which all people share. She notes that in many passages in Calvin 'the body appears similar to and in unity with the soul as worthy of God's creating, preserving and restoring grace' (*John Calvin's Perspectival Anthropology*, 169-71). Both in this life and in the life to come God provides for the body, which he deems 'worthy of such shining honour' (III.25.7). 'The spiritual union which we have with Christ is not a matter of the soul alone, but of the body also' (Comm. 1 Cor. 6:15). 'Since God created our bodies as well as our souls, and nourishes and maintains them, this is good enough reason why he should be served and honoured with our bodies. And furthermore, we know that the Lord honours us by calling not only our souls his temples, but also our bodies' (Comm. 1 Cor. 6:20). The body as well as the soul will be part of the new heaven and earth in the final restoration of all creation (Comm. 1 Cor. 15:53). For Calvin, then, 'the body is not in and of itself ... an unworthy element of human nature. All that is unworthy in it comes from sin' (Warfield, *Calvin and Calvinism*, 339, 341). Calvin writes: 'The whole man is overwhelmed—as by a deluge—from head to foot, so that no part is immune from sin and all that proceeds from him is to be imputed to sin' (II.1.9).

Calvin says that 'there lies hidden in man something separate from the body'—the soul, 'an immortal yet created essence' (I.15.2). Against those who claimed that the soul was merely a kind of power unable to exist without a body, Calvin asserts the real and substantial existence of the soul distinct from the body. He argues that 'many pre-eminent gifts' such as conscience, knowledge of God, marvellous agility of the human mind, and even dreams prove the separateness of the soul from the body. Calvin is on stronger ground, however, when he shows that the Bible from beginning to end assumes and states the distinctiveness, even the separability, of the soul from the body. Calvin denies that the soul is immortal in and of itself, as if it could subsist without God's care. The immortality of the soul is not the result of its distinct existence apart from the body. It is a gift, both at the time of its creation in the womb and at every moment of its preserved life. Calvin rejects traducianism (the idea that the soul is produced like the body through human generation). Each soul is a direct creation of God. It is not 'a derivative of God's substance', but is created out of nothing (I.15.5).

2. Mankind was created in the image of God

There are some 'sparks' of the image of God even in the body, for example, 'a face uplifted' which distinguishes people from animals (I.15.3). The image of God, however, is primarily located in the soul—in 'the integrity with which Adam was endowed', that is, 'the light of the mind … the uprightness of the heart … [and] the soundness of all the parts' (I.15.3-4).

For Calvin the image of God was not only the 'adornments' given to our first parents—'wisdom, virtue, holiness, truth, and justice'—but also their relationship with God. Adam was created in the image of God, 'thus suggesting that man was blessed, not because of his own good actions, but by participation in God' (II.2.1). B. A. Gerrish writes that for Calvin the image of God is 'a mode of personal existence rather than simply human nature as such, a relationship rather than simply a natural endowment' (*Grace and Gratitude*, 42-43). Michael Horton agrees. 'The image consists less than something in us than in a relationship between us (that is, with both God and fellow creatures)' (*Calvin on the Christian Life*, 64). The image of God is both a possession and a relationship. Michael Williams illustrates this with the analogy of a copier:

> A copier exists to make copies; that is both what it is and what it does. As image bearers of God, human beings are copying,

reflecting, imaging creatures. It tells us both what kind of creatures we are and why we exist in God's world ... We exist for the purpose of imaging God, reflecting him into the world, copying something of him into the lives of the people and societies around us. Of course, all of us can also imagine a malfunctioning copy machine, one that has run out of paper or toner, or is perhaps jamming paper. The copier is still a machine for the purpose of making copies, but now it is failing to do it properly. Just so, a human being may image well or poorly, but he or she is always—and at all times—a creature made for the purpose of imaging or reflecting God (*Presbyterion* 39/1:43-44).

In I.15.4 Calvin provides a sweeping summary of the image of God related to mankind's 'fourfold state':

1. 'Now God's image is the perfect excellence of human nature which shone in Adam before his defection' [the subject here in I.15].

2. 'But was subsequently so vitiated and almost blotted out that nothing remains after the ruin except what is confused, mutilated and disease-ridden' [this comes in II.1-5].

3. 'Therefore in some part it now is manifest in the elect, in so far as they have been reborn in the spirit' [the topic of much of Book III].

4. 'But it will attain its full splendour in heaven' [the last chapter of Book III].

3. Mankind was created with two faculties: understanding and will

Understanding is 'the leader and governor of the soul' and the will is the follower. Understanding distinguishes good from evil, and the will chooses to follow understanding (I.15.7). In his created integrity man possessed freedom of will and so 'had the power, if he so willed, to attain eternal life' (I.15.8). Calvin doesn't have here a separate category for the emotions, but he clearly believed that the emotions or passions were a part of understanding. He explains in his commentary on Exodus

32:19: 'For the principle which the Stoics assume, that all the passions are perturbations and like diseases, is false, and has its origin in ignorance; for either to grieve, or to fear, or to rejoice, or to hope, is by no means repugnant to reason.' Emotion, no less than reason and will, is a gift of God and essential to human nature. We cannot seek to eliminate emotions 'without insulting God himself'.

Knowing God and ourselves

Calvin writes that God 'distributed the creation of the world into successive portions, that he might fix our attention, and compel us, to pause and to reflect' (Comm. Gen. 1:5). 'This is ... the proper business of the whole life, in which men should daily exercise themselves to consider the infinite goodness, justice, power, and wisdom of God, in this magnificent theatre of heaven and earth' (Comm. Gen. 2:3). Review the six days of God's creation. Think about each day. Pause and reflect on the goodness of God in his loving and bountiful creation. Thank and praise him.

5. Providence—
'God's Ever-Present Hand'

'But anyone who has been taught by Christ's lips that all the hairs of his head are numbered … will consider that all events are governed by God's secret plan … [and] directed by *God's ever-present hand*' (I.16.2).

'Calvin's world, from stars to insects, from archangels to infants, is the realm of God's sovereignty. A reverent awe of God breathes through all his work. God, transcendent and unapproachable in majesty and unsearchable wisdom, but also immanent in human affairs, righteous in all his ways, and merciful to undeserving men, is the commanding theme to which Calvin's mind ever reverts. The flame of worship to the eternal God is ever on the altar of his thoughts' (McNeill, *The History and Character of Calvinism*, 209).

Read: *Institutes* I.16-18. [*1541* ch.4, pp.229-233; ch.8, pp.499-515.]

Scripture Text: 'Our God is in the heavens; he does all that he pleases' (Psa. 115:3). Preaching on what he called this 'lovely' text, Calvin said, 'It is true that we have not entered into his secret counsel to know how he has disposed everything, but he reveals to us sufficient for us to know as much as we have business knowing. We know that he wants to aid us! He has said it. He is not a deceiver. He "does what he wants"—He wants to aid us. He does not want to abandon us in our need' (*John Calvin: Writings on Pastoral Piety*, 164-65).

Notable Quote: God 'sustains, nourishes, and cares for, everything he has made, even to the least sparrow' (I.16.I).

Prayer

Grant, Omnipotent God, since our life is exposed to innumerable dangers, that we may flee to you and resign ourselves wholly to your will, that we may know that you are the guardian of our life, so that not a hair of our head can fall without your hidden permission. May we also learn to ask of you the spirit of wisdom and discretion, so that you yourself may guide our steps, as it is not in us to defend our life from those many intrigues by which we are on every side surrounded, the whole world being opposed to us, so that we may proceed in the course of our pilgrimage under your care and protection, until we shall be removed into that blessed rest laid up for us in heaven by Christ our Lord. Amen.

(*Lifting Up Our Hearts*, 57.)

❦

A look back and a look ahead

After setting forth God as the Creator of all things (I.14-15), Calvin comes to the doctrine of providence, which teaches that God is the sustainer and governor of all things (I.16-18). Calvin writes, 'We see the presence of divine power shining as much in the continuing state of the universe as in its inception' (I.16.1).

Note that providence and predestination are widely separated in Calvin's 1559 *Institutes* for reasons that we will consider later. Both concern what is sometimes called the decrees of God. Providence comes in Book I and treats God's work in preserving and governing his creation. Predestination, which is about God's work in salvation, comes in Book III.

Definition of providence

John Calvin carefully builds up a definition of providence in five points. As he does so he refutes two false views—Stoicism that traps God within creation, and Epicureanism that separates God from creation.

1. Providence is more than foreknowledge: it is government

God 'governs all events. Thus [providence] pertains no less to his hands than to his eyes' (I.16.4). God doesn't just see what is going to happen; he determines what is going to happen.

2. Providence is more than permission: it is purpose

Calvin notes that Augustine uses the word 'permission', but with a certain meaning: 'Nothing is done without God's will, not even that which is against his will. For it would not be done if he did not permit it; yet he does not unwillingly permit it, but willingly; nor would he, being good, allow evil to be done, unless being also mighty he could make good even out of evil' (I.18.3). Calvin uses permission in the same way: Satan 'carries out only those things which have been divinely permitted to him' (I.14.17). He rejects, however, what he calls 'bare permission'

(I.18.1) or 'indolent permission' (I.18.3) or 'mere permission' (I.23.8). 'Bare permission' weakens God's sovereignty without absolving him from responsibility. Paul Helm writes, 'The idea of "permission" reminds us that because the divine decree is intelligent and not the determinism of impersonal forces God is able to take up distinct intentional stances with respect to different kinds of occurrences' (*Calvin at the Centre*, 232). In other words, God chooses to bring about certain specific things, while he chooses to permit others. But nothing falls outside of his plan and purpose.

3. Providence is more than general: it is particular

The philosophers teach a general or universal providence, but Calvin insists that God's providence is definite and particular. Commenting on Psalm 135:6 ('Whatever the Lord pleases, he does, in heaven and on earth'), Calvin writes: 'The Psalmist expressly asserts every part of the world to be under the divine care, and that nothing takes place by chance.' A familiar spiritual makes the same point: 'He's got the whole world in his hands … He's got the wind and the rain in his hands.' Calvin says that 'not one drop of rain falls without God's sure command' (I.16.5). And 'no wind ever arises or increases except by God's express command' (I.16.7).

4. God's providence goes beyond nature and animal life: it includes human beings and their actions

The spiritual goes on to say, 'He's got the tiny little baby in his hands.' And he has 'the sinner man in his hands'. God governs the acts of people and even their 'plans and intentions' (I.16.8)—including their evil plans and intentions. Nothing falls outside God's control and government, not even sin and evil.

5. God's providence is not impersonal fate: it is God's personal ordering

The Stoics held that everything is governed by the necessity of nature, which contains within itself an intimately related, but ultimately inscrutable, fateful web of cause and effect. Fate, says Calvin, is a pagan word; it is an impersonal term. God is a personal God who, as creator and preserver, lovingly sustains and cares for the universe that he has made.

Calvin writes, 'Let the Stoics have their fate; for us the free will of God disposes all things' (*Concerning the Eternal Predestination of God*, 170).

We can now sum up Calvin's definition of providence: it is God's watchful, effective, active, ceaseless, total, detailed, personal, loving, wise, and holy governing of everything in this world and of everything that happens.

Application of providence

Having defined providence, Calvin applies the doctrine in several ways. We will examine Calvin's answers to four specific questions.

1. How does God's providence work?

Providence works 'sometimes through an intermediary, sometimes without an intermediary, sometimes contrary to every intermediary' (I.17.1). Calvin insists that when God works through an intermediary it is still God who works. Light existed before the sun was created. The sun is 'merely the instrument that God uses because he so wills' (I.16.2). The bread that we eat nourishes us, but only because of God's 'secret blessing' (I.16.7). Secondary causes are not independent causes, but they are real causes. It is chance that is banished from the universe by Calvin's doctrine of providence, not secondary causes.

2. Can we understand the reasons for God's providence?

Calvin answers this question in two ways. First, 'the order, reason, end, and necessity of those things which happen for the most part lie hidden in God's purpose, and are not apprehended by human opinion' (I.16.9). Second, God's 'fatherly favour and beneficence or severity of judgment often shine forth in the whole course of providence' (I.17.1). Providence is indeed mysterious but not totally so. In its broader outlines we can see God's blessing and judgment, but often the details, and even the bigger picture, are hidden from us. Even then we can know that God is wisely, righteously, and lovingly governing and controlling all things. Therefore, we 'do not try to make God render account to us' (I.17.1) but we 'reverently adore' him (I.17.2), while 'we wait in patience until our Lord puts things back into order, which will not be done in this age' (Sermon on Job 22:18-22).

God moves in a mysterious way
   His wonders to perform;
He plants his footsteps in the sea,
   And rides upon the storm.

Deep in unfathomable mines
   Of never-failing skill,
He treasures up his bright designs
   And works his sovereign will.

Ye fearful saints, fresh courage take;
   The clouds ye so much dread
Are big with mercy, and shall break
   In blessings on your head.

Judge not the Lord by feeble sense,
   But trust him for his grace;
Behind a frowning providence
   He hides a smiling face.

Blind unbelief is sure to err,
   And scan his work in vain;
God is his own interpreter,
   And he will make it plain.
               William Cowper

3. What are the practical results of the doctrine of God's providence in our lives?

Belief in God's providence does not lead us into an easy, superficial optimism—a 'God's in his heaven, all's right with the world' attitude. Calvin knows that all is not right with the world. It is not the way it is supposed to be. It is full of sin and evil, suffering and death. The tragedies of life are real calamities. We weep over the trouble of the world, just as Jesus wept at the tomb of Lazarus.

Furthermore, the doctrine of God's providence does not relieve us of responsibility and prudence. 'If the Lord has committed to us the protection of our life, our duty is to protect it; if he offers helps, to use them; if he forewarns us of dangers, not to plunge headlong; if he makes remedies available, not to neglect them' (I.17.4).

Following these two cautions, Calvin sets before us three positive results of the doctrine of God's providence in our lives.

(i) A true understanding of God's providence leads to 'gratitude of mind for the favourable outcome of things' (I.17.7). However good things come to us, we will know that it is God who sends them and be thankful to him.

(ii) A true understanding of God's providence enables us to exercise 'patience in adversity' (I.17.7). Preaching on Psalm 115 Calvin said, 'If God does not help us at first, let us wait on him; we will not be disappointed. Our God will come, and when? He knows when it will be time' (*John Calvin: Writings on Pastoral Piety*, 172).

(iii) The doctrine of providence brings 'incredible freedom of worry about the future' (I.17.7).

> 'We cannot be robbed of God's providence.' That was one of the sayings current in the household of Thomas Carlyle, apparently much on the lips of that brilliant woman, Jane Welsh Carlyle. In it, the plummet is let down to the bottom of the Christian's confidence and hope. It is because we cannot be robbed of God's providence that we know, amid whatever encircling gloom, that all things shall work together for good to those that love him. It is because we cannot be robbed of God's providence that we know that nothing can separate us from the love of Christ—not tribulation, nor anguish, nor persecution, nor famine, nor nakedness, nor peril, nor sword (*Selected Shorter Works of B. B. Warfield*, 1:110).

4. How can God's providence include sin and evil?

Calvin insists that 'nothing is done without God's will, not even that which is against his will' (I.18.3). At the same time, he maintains that

God is not the author of sin. How does he know that God is not the author of sin? Calvin points to what he calls the 'clear scriptural proofs' (I.18.4). God is not the author of sin because he says that he is not the author of sin!

Calvin presents four interrelated ideas in his treatment of this question.

(i) God works providentially in and through sin and evil, making use of both for his good purposes.

God 'knows right well how to use evil instruments to do good' (I.17.5). An example of this is Paul's 'thorn in the flesh' that was inflicted by 'a messenger of Satan'. Calvin writes, 'Satan's only intention, in accordance with his character and customs, was to kill and destroy ... so that it was a special act of mercy for the Lord to turn into a means of healing what was by nature the means of death' (Comm. 2 Cor. 12:7). This does not mean, however, that evil instruments are not evil. 'While God accomplishes through the wicked what he has decreed by his secret judgment, they are not excusable, as if they had obeyed his precept which out of their own lust they deliberately break' (I.18.4).

> In his book, *My Lady of the Chimney Corner*, Alexander Irvine told a story which illustrates this distinctively Calvinist perspective on providence. A starving Irish family is provided a good meal as a result of a wager made during a gambling game. Anna, the pious mother, thanks God for bringing them relief. Boyle, whose nefarious activity had won them the dinner, replies: 'Anna, if aanybody brought us here th' night, it was th' ould devil in hell.' 'Deed yer mistaken', Anna answers sweetly, 'When God sends a maan aanywhere, he always gets there, even if he has to be taken there by th' devil' (George, *Theology of the Reformers*, 208).

(ii) God works providentially in and through suffering 'to instruct his own people in patience, or to correct their wicked affections and tame their lust, or to subjugate them to self-denial, or to arouse them from sluggishness' (I.17.1).

(iii) Our miseries may function as occasions for God's glory to shine, as in Jesus' healing a man born blind (John 9:3).

(iv) Divine providence—especially when it comes to evil, sin, and suffering—is beyond human understanding. Beza heard Calvin say in the days before his death on May 27, 1564, 'Thou, O Lord, bruisest me; but it is enough for me that it is thy hand' (*Selected Works of John Calvin* 1:xcv). We cannot always understand the bruising but we can always know that it is 'God's ever-present hand'—and that is enough.

We cannot see how God can be omnipotent—governing and directing everything that happens—and, at the same time, good, hating and forbidding sin. Does this mean that God has two contrasting wills? No, answers Calvin. Although God's will appears 'manifold to us', there is but a single (or 'simple') will in God, even though there is a depth to that 'hidden will' which we cannot fathom (I.17.2). This is not a contradiction but a mystery. 'When we do not grasp how God wills to take place what he forbids to be done, let us recall our mental incapacity, but at the same time consider that the light in which God dwells is not without reason called unapproachable' (I.18.3). In a sermon, Calvin develops and illustrates this point:

> God's will is always one and single, and agreeable with itself, however much it seems diverse to us. It has many aspects to it, as if we saw a hundred different shapes which dazzled our eyesight or utterly dimmed it. When St Paul says [in Eph. 3:9-12] that God's wisdom is diverse in its many aspects, it is as if a picture had a thousand colours in it, so that a man could not distinctly distinguish one from another. Nevertheless St Paul, in so saying, did not mean that God's wisdom is so tortuous in itself that there is some contradiction or strife there. No, but he shows that God has always one uniform meaning, and keeps on in one course and direction (Sermon on Eph. 3:9-12).

The doctrine of providence for Calvin is not so much a matter of explanation of what happens as it is a confession of faith. It does not answer all our questions, but it enables us to live without answers until the time comes when we will live without questions. Horton Davies writes, 'I do not believe that those who seek a theodicy or a theoretical solution to the problem of evil will find it in Calvinism—or anywhere else for that matter ... Thus Calvinism responds to the problem of evil with an eschatology rather than a theodicy' (*The Vigilant God*, 2). Cowper's hymn ends with the words,

> God is his own interpreter,
> And he will make it plain.

A gospel song promises that 'we'll understand it better bye and bye'.

While some Christians will find Calvin's discussion of God and evil unacceptable or even preposterous, one can imagine the many questions Calvin would have about a Christian faith that has made its peace with sin and evil by placing these outside of God's sovereign control. Calvin writes, 'Our true wisdom is to embrace with meek docility, and without reservation, whatever the holy Scriptures have delivered. Those who indulge their petulance, a petulance manifestly directed against God, are undeserving of a longer refutation' (I.18.4).

We cannot properly know God until we see him as the God of providence. 'Hence we have then only the true knowledge of God, when we not only acknowledge him to be the creator of the world, but when we also fully believe that the world is governed by him, and when we further understand the way in which he governs it, that is, by doing mercy and judgment and justice' (Comm. Gen. 1:5).

> 'Any reader of the *Institutes* must be struck by the great elegance, the gallantry, of its moral vision, which is more beautiful for the resolution with which its theology embraces sorrow and darkness' (Robinson, *The Death of Adam*, 131).

Knowing God and ourselves

Calvin writes that 'gratitude of mind for the favourable outcome of things, patience in adversity, and also incredible freedom from worry about the future all necessarily follow' an understanding of the Bible's teaching about God's providence (I.17.7). Make three lists: the things that have worked out well for you, the troubles you are now facing, and the things you are worried about. Express your gratitude to God for the things in the first list. Ask God for patience for the things in the second list. Cross out the things in the third list, and enjoy the 'incredible freedom from worry about the future' that is yours as a Christian.

6. The Fall and its Consequences— 'The Curse ... A Burning Furnace'

'For, since it is said that we became subject to God's judgment through Adam's sin, we are to understand it not as if we, guiltless and undeserving, bore the guilt of his offense but in the sense that, since we through his transgression have become entangled in *the curse*, he is said to have made us guilty ... perversity never ceases in us, but continually bears new fruits ... just as *a burning furnace* gives forth flame and sparks, or water ceaselessly bubbles up from a spring' (II.1.8).

'Logically one's views of sin determine his views of redemption. Christ came to repair whatever ruin was wrought by Adam. To appreciate the work of the former we must understand the work of the latter. To know just how much we are indebted to Christ, we must know just how much we are indebted to Adam' (Reed, *The Gospel as Taught by Calvin*).

Read: *Institutes* **II.1-5.** [*1541* ch.2, pp.29-108.]

Scripture Text: 'For as in Adam all die, so also in Christ shall all be made alive' (1 Cor. 15:22).

Notable Quote: 'Our present condition is very short of the glory of God's children; for as to our body we are dust and a shadow, and death is always before our eyes; we are also subject to a thousand miseries, and the soul is exposed to innumerable evils; so that we find always a hell within us' (Comm. 1 John 1:2).

Prayer

O Lord God, eternal and almighty Father, we confess and acknowledge unfeignedly before your holy majesty that we are poor sinners, conceived and born in iniquity and corruption, inclined to do evil, useless for any good, and that in our depravity we constantly and endlessly transgress your holy commandments. By so doing we purchase for ourselves, by your righteous judgment, our ruin and perdition. Nevertheless, O Lord, we are grieved with ourselves to have offended you; and we condemn ourselves and our sins with true repentance, asking that your grace may relieve our distress.

O God and most gracious Father, you who are full of compassion, have pity upon us in the name of your Son, Jesus Christ, our Lord. By blotting out our sins and stains, magnify and increase in us day by day the graces of your Holy Spirit, so that as we acknowledge our unrighteousness with all our heart, we may be touched by the sorrow that brings true repentance, which causing us to die to all our sins, may produce in us the fruits of righteousness and innocence pleasing to you; through Jesus Christ, your Son, our Lord. Amen.

(John Calvin: Writings on Pastoral Piety, 217-18.)

A look back and a look ahead

Book II of the *Institutes* has the title: 'The Knowledge of God the Redeemer in Christ, First Disclosed to the Fathers under the Law, and then to Us in the Gospel.' The Father, the Son, and the Holy Spirit are active in Book I, 'God the Creator.' Likewise, the three persons of the Trinity are active in Book 2, 'God the Redeemer in Christ', as they are in Book III, 'The Way in which We Receive the Grace of Christ.' There is a special role, however, for each of the persons of the Trinity—the Father in creation (Book I), the Son in redemption (Book II), and the Holy Spirit in the application of redemption (Book III). Robert Peterson writes: 'Salvation was planned by the Trinity, especially the Father. Salvation was accomplished by the Trinity, especially the Son. Salvation was applied by the Trinity, especially the Spirit' (*Presbyterion*, Fall 2004, 81).

Before 'the Knowledge of God the Redeemer in Christ' in Book II there are five chapters about human sin and its consequences, setting forth clearly and vividly our need for a Redeemer. In Book I Calvin has presented God as creator and ourselves as his marvellous creation. In Book II he reverses the order and deals with ourselves as fallen and sinful creatures before coming to God's marvellous salvation in Christ. Calvin explains, 'Unless we realize our own helpless misery, we shall never know how much we need the remedy which Christ brings, nor come to him with the fervent love we owe him' (Comm. Isa. 53:6). According to Michael Horton, 'our age does not seem to know either the grandeur of creation or the tragedy of the fall' (*A Theological Guide to Calvin's Institutes*, 153).

Calvin begins Book II with a brief review of human beings as God made them. He sets before us again our 'primal worthiness'. He reminds us again of 'how great our natural excellence would be if only it had remained unblemished'. He now comes to a fuller discussion of the sad reality of 'the sorry spectacle of our foulness and dishonour' (II.1.1).

Adam's sin

Calvin believes, as Augustine did, that the nature of Adam's first sin was pride, but he sees it as also disobedience ('the beginning of the fall') and unfaithfulness ('the root of the fall'), all of which lead to ingratitude.

Why did God not prevent Adam's sin? The question, Calvin says, manifests 'inordinate curiosity'. It also has to do with 'the secret of predestination', which Calvin is not yet ready to discuss. He insists, however, that 'man's ruin is to be ascribed to man alone' (II.1.10). God is not to blame.

Transmission of Adam's sin

Adam's sin affected all his descendants. The church fathers called this 'original sin'. Calvin calls it 'inherited corruption' (II.1.5). 'Before we saw the light of this life, we were soiled and spotted in God's sight' (II.1.5). Through Adam's transgression, we have become 'entangled in the curse' (II.1.8), as has 'the whole order of nature' (II.1.5). Calvin admits that the early church fathers spoke obscurely on the matter of the transmission of Adam's sin, 'at least they explained it less clearly than was fitting' (II.1.5).

How is the sin of Adam passed on to all his descendants? Calvin rejects the idea that Adam's sin is transmitted biologically from parent to child. 'For the contagion does not take its origin from the substance of the flesh or soul' (II.1.7). Neither is Adam's sin 'propagated by imitation' (II.1.6), a view that Satan uses to cover up the disease and thus render it incurable (II.1.5). If our sin is caused by our imitation of the sinful acts of others, as Pelagius taught, it is not so serious, because we can reform by simply ceasing to do evil.

We are not sinners because we sin; we sin because we are sinners. 'Inherited corruption' comes to us from Adam, who is both the root of human nature and the representative of the human race. There is a natural relationship between Adam and all human beings. 'The beginning of corruption in Adam was such that it was conveyed in a perpetual stream from the ancestors into their descendants' (II.1.7). The relationship between Adam and the human race is also a matter of divine appointment. Adam was the representative of all people. 'It had been ordained by God that the first man should at one and the same time have and lose, both for himself and for his descendants, the gifts that God had bestowed upon him' (II.1.7).

Our guilt

By virtue of the fact that we are Adam's 'descendants' (II.1.7), and by God's 'ordinance' (Comm. John 3: 6), Adam's sin has become ours. Our sin is 'a hereditary depravity and corruption of our nature, diffused into all parts of the soul, which first makes us liable to God's wrath, then also brings forth in us those works which Scripture calls "works of the flesh"' (II.1.8). The 'contagion' imparted to us by Adam 'justly deserves punishment' (II.1.8). Many deplore Calvin's view of original sin as unjust. But the question is: 'Is it true? Not, is it palatable? A sinner's moral taste is no test' (Reed, *The Gospel as Taught by Calvin*, 35).

Our depravity

Not only are we born guilty, we are born depraved. Calvin explains this in two ways.

First, we are positively depraved. Our nature is not only 'destitute and empty of good' but it is also 'fertile and fruitful of every evil' (II.1.8). It is 'like a burning furnace, flaming and sparkling, or a spring endlessly gushing out water' (II.1.8). Medieval Catholic theologians taught that the fall of Adam meant the loss of the added 'gift of grace' that God gave Adam at his creation. But Calvin insists that fallen humanity is not merely deprived but also defiled.

Second, we are radically depraved. Catholic theologians limited our problem to one part of human nature, that is our 'concupiscence' (or sensuality). Calvin did not object to the use of the word 'concupiscence', but he did not limit it to our sensual nature. 'Whatsoever is in man, from the understanding to the will, from the soul even to the flesh, has been defiled' (II.1.8). Nothing less than 'the whole man is overwhelmed as by a deluge—from head to foot, so that no part is immune from sin' (II.1.9). From 'head to foot', we are sinners—from our minds now ruined by 'the fault of dullness', all the way down to our feet, 'wandering through various errors and stumbling repeatedly' (Comm. Rom. 1:20-21). Preaching on Ephesians 1:1-3, Calvin told the people, 'Man's heart is a pit of horrible confusion. We ourselves do not perceive it, but God has clearer eyes than me.'

Calvin's teaching, often called total depravity, is better described as radical depravity. Human beings are not totally depraved, because not every wicked trait appears in every person, and those sinful traits that do appear are not fully developed. Because of God's restraint, human wickedness is not as total as it could possibly be. Sin, however, does radically affect every part of every person's nature and life. Even the youngest child bears the 'hidden seed' of Adam (Comm. Psa. 69: 20).

'The Calvinist doctrine of total depravity ... was directed against casuistical enumerations of sins, against the attempt to assign them different degrees of seriousness. For [Calvin] we are all absolutely, that is equally, unworthy of, and dependent upon, the free intervention of grace' (Robinson, *The Death of Adam*, 155).

Our helplessness

We are guilty and radically depraved, and we are utterly unable to do anything about it. The title of II.2 asserts that human beings are 'deprived of freedom of choice' and are 'bound over to miserable servitude'. Captured by sin, we are totally dependent on God's liberating grace.

Calvin adopts Augustine's statement that 'the natural gifts were corrupted in men by sin ... the supernatural were altogether abolished' (II.2.12). The supernatural gifts—faith, love for God, and zeal for holiness—were completely lost in Adam's fall. The natural gifts—reason and will—were seriously impaired and radically perverted. Even so, fallen humanity 'does not cease still to be adorned with many of the gifts of God' (II.2.15).

Human reason, though fallen, still functions, and often functions very well. It produces truly amazing accomplishments in 'earthly things', such as law, science, art, medicine, and mathematics. Philosophers in all ages have enlightened the world with knowledge. Believers may use earthly philosophy to good advantage, as Calvin sometimes does in the *Institutes*, 'to confirm, illustrate, and elucidate the truth of heavenly philosophy' (Engel, *John Calvin's Perspectival Anthropology*, 97). The abilities of fallen human beings do not come from themselves. They are the result of God's 'special grace' (II.2.17), given by the Spirit of God who is 'the sole fountain of truth' (II.2.15). This 'special grace' is not regenerating grace (the subject of Book III of the *Institutes*) but what we sometimes call 'common grace'. 'Why is one person more excellent than another?' 'Is it not to display in common nature God's special grace, which, in passing many by, declares itself bound to none?' Calvin answers (II.2.17). The abilities and accomplishments of unregenerate men and women are the result of God's goodness to them—and are a blessing to everyone. Calvin writes in his commentary on Genesis 4:20 (concerning Jabal, 'the father of all such as dwell in tents') that 'the invention of arts, and of other things which serve to the common use and convenience of life, is a gift of God by no means to be despised'. He notes that the descendants of Cain 'excelled the rest of the posterity of Adam in rare endowments', and that the liberal arts and sciences 'have descended to us from the heathen'.

Mankind's understanding fails, however, when it comes to 'heavenly things'. 'Indeed, man's mind, because of its dullness, cannot hold to the right path, but wanders through various errors and stumbles repeatedly, as if it were groping in darkness, until it strays away and finally disappears' (II.2.12). Fallen people may, in Francis Schaeffer's phrase, understand 'bits and pieces' of spiritual truth but cannot put it together in any coherent way. Calvin says that man is like 'a traveller passing through a field at night who in a momentary lightning flash sees far and wide, but the sight vanishes so swiftly that he is plunged again into the darkness of the night before he can take even a step' (II.2.18).

To sum up, fallen men and women, by God's special help, learn and do many important and wonderful things, but they cannot come to a true knowledge of God. Calvin repeats this many times in his commentaries and sermons. Preaching on Ephesians 4:17-19, he said: 'God has poured out his gracious gifts in such a way that man's mind has shown itself most excellent in all branches of knowledge, except in the chief, that is to say, to know how to come to God' (Sermon on Eph. 4:17-19).

Turning to the human will, Calvin states that it is 'so deeply vitiated and corrupted in its every part that it can beget nothing but evil' (II.2.26). This point is fully developed in II.3—'Only damnable things come forth from man's corrupt nature.' But, as we have noted, not all 'wicked traits appear in every man' (II.3.2). Calvin compares Camillus, a noble Roman patriot, and Catiline, an evil man who conspired to assassinate Cicero and overthrow the Roman government. Does the noble Camillus have more righteousness than the evil Catiline? Calvin's answer is no. Does Camillus have as much sin? Again, the answer is no. Both men are lost— the good man and the bad man—but they are not equally sinful. Why? Because God's grace restrains when it does not cleanse (II.3.3).

Free will

Calvin next turns to what we could call a history of free will. The philosophers achieved some 'droplets of truth' (II.2.18), but in their conclusion that the will is free to follow reason they fell far short of the truth. Most of the church fathers (and Erasmus), in Calvin's opinion, followed the philosophers too closely. They did this to escape 'the jeers of the philosophers' and to avoid 'giving fresh occasion for slothfulness to a flesh already indifferent toward good'. The church fathers 'so differ, waver, or speak confusedly on this subject' (the Greek fathers above the rest, and Chrysostom, one of Calvin's favourite church fathers, among them) 'that almost nothing certain [about free will] can be derived from their writings' (II.2.4). Even so, Calvin maintains that the church fathers 'held human virtue in no or very slight esteem' and 'ascribed all credit for every good thing to the Holy Spirit' (II.2.9). Cyprian, for example, taught that 'we ought to glory in nothing, because nothing is ours'. Then came Augustine, the church father who for Calvin stood out far above all the rest. Calvin writes, 'I pretty much agree with that man whom the godly by common consent justly invest with the greatest authority' (II.3.8). The 'later writers', the medieval scholastic theologians, fell from bad to worse in their assertions of 'a perfectly unblemished reason and a will also largely unimpaired' (II.2.4). Calvin may unfairly stigmatize the whole medieval tradition here, but he is right in his understanding of the general direction of theology after Augustine.

Following his survey of the history of the doctrine of free will, Calvin comes to his understanding of the fallen human will. Mankind 'has not been deprived of will but of healthy will' (II.3.5). Fallen people can still choose but they cannot choose good. In that sense they do not have free will; their wills are bound by their sin. But in another sense, people's wills are 'free' because they act wickedly by their own choice and not because they are compelled to do so. They sin 'willingly, not unwillingly' (II.3.5). They sin 'of necessity, yet ... no less voluntarily' (II.4.1). Fallen people sin because of internal necessity not because of external constraint. They sin because they want to, not because they have to. The problem is that we cannot free ourselves from wanting to sin. In that sense our wills are bound. Calvin appropriated Augustine's insight that we are 'indeed free but not freed' (II.2.8). Calvin, however, preferred to avoid the expression 'free will' altogether, although he used it in a restricted sense. Humanity does have a 'free will' of a sort—we are 'willing slaves'. But Calvin asks, 'What purpose is served by labelling with a proud name such a slight thing?' (II.2.7).

To sum up Calvin's thought, we may say that fallen people can still think, but they cannot think correctly about God. They can still will, but they cannot will to obey God. In relation to 'things below', human nature, by virtue of God's 'special grace', is creative, perceptive, and capable of truly remarkable achievements. In relation to 'things above', human nature, by virtue of Adam's sin, is corrupt, depraved, and unable to take even the smallest step toward salvation. Calvin quotes Bernard: 'Simply to will is human; to will the bad belongs to corrupted nature; to will the good is of grace' (II.3.5).

Our need of God's grace

Our need for God's grace is 'the principal point' of this whole discussion about sin and its consequences (II.3.8). Calvin does not drag people down into the pit of their sinfulness in order to leave them there, but rather to prepare them to hear the good news of the gospel. 'No one is permitted to receive God's blessings unless he is consumed with the awareness of his poverty' (II.2.10). The Bible's description of human wickedness teaches us that we 'have all been overwhelmed by an unavoidable calamity from which only God's mercy can deliver us' (II.3.2). Preaching on Ephesians 1:7-10, Calvin said that we 'should not be so foolish as to bring, as it were, only a farthing when [our] needs run to a million crowns'. Julie Canlis writes, 'Calvin's emphasis on creaturely frailty and sin is not to stress the distance from God but to stress that it is God who takes the initiative with us—not we with him' (*Calvin's Ladder*, 65).

Calvin's doctrine of sin is 'bad news', but it is also 'good news', because the knowledge that we are sinners can lead us to the knowledge of God who is our Redeemer in Christ. About this Calvin makes two important points.

First, God is the author of our salvation. Medieval Catholic theology taught that people were sinners, certainly, but not such great sinners that they could not actively cooperate with God's grace to earn salvation. For Calvin, God is the author of our salvation 'from beginning to end'. 'Let us not divide between him and us what he claims for himself alone', he writes (II.3.6). And again, 'Nothing good can arise out of our will until it has been reformed and after its reformation, in so far as it is good, it is so from God, not from ourselves' (II.3.8). Our sin is far greater than we think, but so is God's grace.

Second, God enables us to respond to his message of salvation. 'He wills to work in us ... that [we] may actually so walk' (II.3.10). 'Man is not borne along without any motion of the heart, as if by an outside force; rather, he is so affected within that he obeys from the heart' (II.3.14). God's gracious action in us produces our human response. Much more on this topic will come in Book III of the *Institutes*.

How God works in men's hearts

In II.4 Calvin attempts to explain how the same work can be attributed to God, to Satan, and to human beings. Using the illustration of Job's troubles, Calvin states that 'the Lord's purpose is to exercise the patience of his servant by calamity; Satan endeavours to drive him to desperation; the Chaldeans strive to acquire gain from another's property' (II.4.2). Calvin repeats what he has already said in his treatment of providence that nothing stands outside God's control, even the sinful actions of human beings.

Refutation of the objections commonly put forward in defence of free will

Notice Calvin's apology for this polemical addition. 'It would seem that enough had been said concerning the bondage of man's will, were it not for those who by a false notion of freedom try to cast down this conception' (II.5.1). Heavily and gratefully dependent on Augustine, Calvin lists and answers four arguments defending free will.

1. Those defending free will say necessary sin is not sin; voluntary sin is avoidable. Calvin answers that it is because of the fall that sin is necessary, but it nonetheless remains voluntary. As Bernard teaches, 'We are the more miserable because the necessity is voluntary' (II.5.1).

2. They say that unless virtues and vices come from free choice, there can be neither punishment nor reward. Calvin answers that vices are punished because they are voluntary. God rewards our virtues, but they are his gifts to us. As Augustine says, 'Grace does not arise from merit, but merit from grace' (II.5.2).

3. They say that without free will, all distinction between good and evil would be obliterated, and human beings would be all bad or all good. Calvin answers, 'Though all of us are by nature suffering from the same disease, only those whom it pleases the Lord to touch with his healing hand will get well' (II.5.3).

4. They say that admonitions and exhortations are useless and foolish without the person's power to obey. Calvin answers that God uses admonitions and exhortations to help Christians to grow spiritually. 'God works in his elect in two ways,' Calvin writes, 'within, through his Spirit; without, through his Word' (II.5.5) For the 'reprobate' the same admonitions and exhortations serve another purpose—'today to press them with the witness of conscience, and in the Day of Judgment to render them the more inexcusable' (II.5.5).

Calvin next examines the biblical passages that are commonly used in defence of free will.

1. Defenders of free will point to 'God's precepts' in the Bible. They argue that 'ought' implies 'can'—that is, God's commands must imply human ability. Calvin answers that God's laws reflect his holy standards, not the capacity of fallen humanity. 'As soon as the law prescribes what we are to do, it teaches that the power to obey comes from God's goodness' (II.5.7).

2. Defenders of free will cite the 'promises' of the Bible 'in which the Lord makes a covenant with our will' (II.5.10). But the promises, like the precepts, Calvin answers, prompt us to call upon God's Spirit 'to direct us into the right path' (II.5.10).

3. Defenders of free will point to passages where 'God reproaches his ungrateful people that it was their own fault that they did not receive every sort of good thing from his tender mercy' (II.5.11). But 'we know that the pious ... attain victory by God's weapons alone', answers Calvin (II.5.11).

Calvin asks how our works can be ours when they are the result of God working in us. He answers that nothing 'prevents us from saying that we ourselves are fitly doing what God's Spirit is doing in us, even if our will contributes nothing of itself distinct from his grace' (II.5.15).

Knowing God and ourselves

The first sentence of the *Institutes* declares that almost the whole sum of wisdom consists in the knowledge of God and of ourselves. Earlier in the *Institutes* we learned by God's revelation in his word that we can know ourselves as created. We responded with gratitude to God for making us in such a wonderful way. This section of the *Institutes* describes in detail what we discover when we come to know ourselves as fallen. It is not a pretty picture, but it is a necessary one. Knowledge of ourselves as fallen produces humility and 'a new zeal to seek God, in whom each of us may recover those good things which we have utterly and completely lost' (II.1.1).

7. Redemption in Christ— 'The Only Door'

Scripture teaches that Christ is '*the only door* whereby we enter into salvation' (II.6.1).

Read: *Institutes* II.6-7. [*1541* ch.3, pp.168-181.]

Scripture Text: 'I am the door. If anyone enters by me, he will be saved and will go in and out and find pasture' (John 10:9).

Notable Quote: 'For herein shines forth more fully the unspeakable goodness of God, that he anticipated our disease by the remedy of his grace and provided a restoration to life before the first man had fallen into death' (Comm. 1 Pet. 1:20).

Prayer

And now we pray, most gracious God and merciful Father, for all people everywhere. Since you will be acknowledged as the Saviour of the whole world through the redemption wrought by your Son, Jesus Christ, grant that those who are still strangers to the knowledge of him, being in the darkness and captivity of error and ignorance, may be brought by the illumination of your Holy Spirit and the preaching of your gospel to the right way of salvation, which is to know you, the only true God, and the one whom you have sent, Jesus Christ. May those whom you have already visited with your grace and enlightened with the knowledge of your word daily grow in goodness, enriched by your spiritual blessings: so that all together we may worship you with one heart and one voice and may give honour and reverence to your Christ, our Master, King, and Lawgiver. Amen.

(*John Calvin: Writings on Pastoral Piety*, 177.)

❧

A look back and a look ahead

John Calvin begins this section of the *Institutes* with a quick review of the first five chapters of Book II.

- Fact of the fall—'The whole human race perished in the person of Adam' (II.6.1).

- Consequences of the fall—'Our eyes ... wherever they turn ... encounter God's curse' (II.6.1).

- Need for a Redeemer—'Therefore ... the whole knowledge of God the Creator that we have discussed would be useless unless faith also followed, setting forth for us God our Father in Christ' (II.6.1).

After setting forth our need for a Redeemer in II.1-5, the rest of Book II presents 'The knowledge of God the Redeemer in Christ.' In Book I Calvin 'orients theological knowledge toward ... the glorious grace of God clear in creation' and made available to us through the Scriptures. In Book II he turns to 'the merciful grace of God clear in Christ' (Boulton, *Life in God*, 80). It is in Christ that God's 'face shines, full of grace and gentleness, even upon us poor and unworthy sinners' (II.7.8).

The covenant

The full title of Book II is 'The knowledge of God the Redeemer in Christ, first disclosed to the fathers under the law, and then to us in the gospel.' Calvin begins his treatment of 'God the Redeemer in Christ" with covenant history (II.1-11) rather than with Christological doctrine (which follows in II.12-17). He is concerned first of all to locate Christ in the Bible's full story, to understand where Christ begins to act in human history. And so he begins with Eden rather than with Bethlehem. People in every generation since Adam find salvation in Christ, 'the only door' (II.6.1). Christ 'comprehends all ages' when he says, 'This is eternal life, to know the Father … and Jesus Christ whom he has sent' (John 17:3) (II.6.1). Therefore, all 'the Scriptures are to be read with the intention of finding Christ in them' (Comm. John 5:39). He is what the Bible is all about.

In II.6 Calvin begins with Christ ('Fallen man ought to seek redemption in Christ'), moves to a discussion of the Old Testament law in II.7-8, and comes again to Christ in II.9 ('Christ, although he was known to the Jews under the law, was at length clearly revealed only in the gospel'). Calvin's history of salvation is not 'law and grace' but 'grace and law and grace'. He surrounds law with grace. As we shall see, the law also sets forth God's grace, so we could better describe Calvin's 'history of salvation' as 'grace and grace and grace'! Indeed, 'whenever the word "covenant" appears in Scripture', Calvin tells us, 'we ought at the same time to call to remembrance the word, "grace"' (Comm. Isa. 55:3). This is the heart of Calvin's covenant theology. It is God's grace in Christ that reaches to all times and to every place.

In II.9-11 Calvin stresses the unity of God's plan for human salvation throughout all ages. In those chapters we find the fullest presentation of covenant theology in the *Institutes*. Although Calvin does not use the covenant theme to structure the *Institutes*, it is important to him, not only in Book II, but also in his treatment of election in III.21 and the sacraments, especially infant baptism, in IV.14-17.

The law

The Old Testament law is not merely a collection of commands; it is part of the ongoing revelation of God set in the larger context of the promise of the gospel. Moses was not the founder of a religion of law but the prophet of God's covenant of grace. The chief thing about the law is that it is an expression of the gospel. The gospel tells us that we ought 'to seek redemption in Christ', and the law preaches the same message. The law was not given 'to lead the chosen people away from Christ, but rather to hold their minds in readiness until his coming' (II.7.1). Of course, the word 'law' is sometimes used in the Bible 'in a narrow sense', such as Paul did in Galatians when he spoke of the law torn from the context of grace. Misused and misapplied, the law is no longer gospel.

The primary purpose of the law is 'to unite us to our God' (*Sermons on the Ten Commandments*, 39).

In II.7-8, we have Calvin's treatment of the Old Testament law under three main points.

1. Form of the law

God's giving of the law is an example of his 'accommodation'. The Old Testament people were 'like children', so God spoke to them in ways they could understand (II.7.2).

2. Types of the law

The law is expressed in three ways—ceremonial, civil, and moral laws. Calvin returns to this topic in III.19 and IV.20.

The ceremonial law in itself was worthless and empty, 'for what is more vain or absurd than for men to offer a loathsome stench from the fat of cattle in order to reconcile themselves to God?' (II.7.1) Since the ceremonial law pointed to the coming of Christ and indeed promised the presence of Christ, it was life-giving to the people of Israel. It constantly and powerfully presented the gospel of God's grace. The ceremonial laws were 'external representations of grace' that mirrored the 'spiritual effect' of Christ (Comm. Exod. 29:38). They were 'exercises of faith and repentance' (Comm. Exod. 25:8).

Christ by his life and death terminated the ceremonial laws, but in doing so he 'sealed their force and effect' (II.7.16). In other words, the ceremonial laws were terminated in their use and function but not in regard to their meaning. They still point to Christ as they always did—but now as written laws, no longer as religious acts. 'Although the rite of sacrificing is abolished, it yet greatly assists our faith to compare the reality of the types, so that we may seek in the one what the other contains' (Comm. 1 Pet. 1:19). As we study the Old Testament ceremonial laws, we can better understand how Christ fulfilled them. The ceremonial laws 'belonged to the doctrine of piety', but the laws were not themselves necessary for piety. The ceremonial laws ceased, but piety remains (IV.20.15).

The civil law contained rules and regulations for the nation of Israel. When the New Testament church replaced the Old Testament nation the civil laws were terminated in their specific details but not in their general principles—'love' and 'equity' and 'justice'. The civil law ceased, but 'the perpetual duties and precepts of love' remained (IV.20.15). Calvin explicitly rejected the 'false and foolish' notion that a modern state should be governed under 'the political system of Moses' (IV.20.14). He clearly set forth his views in a sermon:

> The gospel is not brought in to change the common politics of the world and to make laws that belong to the temporal state. It is true that kings, princes, and magistrates ought always to ask counsel at God's mouth and to conform themselves to his word, but yet for all that, our Lord has given them liberty to make such laws as they shall perceive to be fitting and suitable for the rule committed to them. They must call upon God to give them the spirit of wisdom and discretion, and because they are insufficient for this in and of themselves, they must take counsel from God's word (Sermon on Eph. 6:5-9).

Calvin states that the 'ceremonial and judicial laws pertain also to morals' (IV.20.14). Calvin's commentary on Exodus, Leviticus, Numbers, and Deuteronomy is arranged in the form of a harmony in which he places much of the content of these books under the outline of the ten commandments. He explores how the ceremonial and judicial laws reflected and spelled out the moral law in areas of worship and government for the people of Israel.

The moral law, says Calvin, is 'nothing else than a testimony of natural law and of that conscience which God has engraved upon the minds of men' (IV.20.16). In the written law, summarized in the ten commandments, God clarifies and codifies natural law. There are no chronological or national limitations with respect to the moral law as in the case of ceremonial and civil law. The moral law was prescribed for people of all nations and for all ages.

3. Uses of the moral law.

David Jones writes, 'On Calvin's analysis, the use or function of the moral law in its scriptural setting is threefold, which may be conveniently characterized as preparative, preservative, and restorative' (*A Theological Guide to Calvin's Institutes*, 302).

The first 'use' of the law is preparative. The law points out sin and leaves men and women inexcusable. It was given not to curse but to bless, but 'because observance of the law is found in none of us, we are excluded from the promises of life, and fall back into the mere curse' (II.7.3). This use or function of the law, however, is 'accidental'. Even as the moral law slays the sinner by exposing the exceeding sinfulness of sin, by it we are 'moved to seek and await help from another quarter' (II.8.1).

- Scripture text: 'Through the law comes the knowledge of sin' (Rom. 3:20).

- Illustration—a mirror: 'In [the law] we contemplate our weakness, then the iniquity arising from this, and finally the curse coming from both—just as a mirror shows us the spots on our face' (II.7.7).

The second 'use' of the law is preservative. It protects society and restricts the tendency of people to fall into ever more sinful acts, and so makes possible human life on earth. It also serves as a holding action whereby God preserves from utter ruin those whom he has decreed to bring to faith.

- Scripture text: 'The law is not laid down for the just but for the unjust' (1 Tim. 1: 9-10).

- Illustration—a halter: 'The law is like a halter to check the raging and otherwise limitlessly ranging lusts of the flesh' (II.7.10).

The third, and principal 'use' of the moral law is restorative. It gives Christians an understanding of God's will and moves them to full obedience. The moral law does not come between God and the Christian, substituting a legal for a personal relationship; it describes that relationship. We need the law to show us how we can love God. Christians 'must learn more thoroughly each day the nature of the Lord's will to which they aspire and be confirmed in their understanding of it. It is as if some servant, already prepared with all earnestness of heart to commend himself to his master, must search out and observe his master's ways more carefully in order to conform and accommodate himself to them' (II.7.12). Furthermore, obedience to the moral law greatly benefits the Christian. Left to ourselves we would not act in our own best interest. The one who made us and saved us knows what is best for us.

- Scripture text: 'Thy word is a lamp to my feet' (Psa. 119: 105).

- Illustrations—a lamp and a whip: By the law God teaches us and lights our journey, so that we see 'more thoroughly each day the nature of the Lord's will' (II.7.12) 'The law is to the flesh like a whip to an idle and balky ass, to arouse it to work' (II.7.12).

In most Lutheran liturgies the ten commandments come before the confession of sin to show us our need for forgiveness. Calvin placed the commandments after the confession as a guide for the grateful obedience of the forgiven Christian. 'While Luther emphasized the consolations of grace, Calvin dwelt upon the demands of grace' (Thompson, *Liturgies of the Western Church*, 194). Actually Calvin dwelt upon both.

Knowing God and ourselves

'Since [God] wishes to have and hold us in his house, let us walk as in his presence and in his sight, indeed in such a way that we worship him as our only God, not solely in ceremonies, or in external affirmation, but in our heart' (*Sermons on the Ten Commandments*, 64).

8. The Ten Commandments— 'The Law of Grace'

'To be Christians under *the law of grace* does not mean to wander unbridled outside the law, but to be engrafted in Christ, by whose grace we are free of the curse of the law, and by whose Spirit we have the law engraved upon our hearts' (II.8.57).

'For Calvin the law is "The Way", ... the infallible and therefore reliable directive toward the right relation with God and the neighbour.' The law is much more than 'a set of precepts ... its main point is faith and salvation. The core of the law teaches that God is the Father and Saviour of his people with whom he has made ... a covenant of grace. The law of Moses is therefore not just a way of living but the Way of Life' (Oberman, *Calvin Studies VI*, 4).

Read: *Institutes* II.8. [*1541* ch.3, pp.109-168.]

Scripture Text: 'But this is the covenant that I will make with the house of Israel after those days declares the Lord: I will put my law within them, and I will write it on their hearts. And I will be their God, and they shall be my people' (Jer. 31:33).

Notable Quote: 'In the same way ... that God wrote his law on two stones with his finger, that is, with his miraculous power, he must today write on our hardened hearts of stone by means of his Holy Spirit' (*Sermons on the Ten Commandments*, 250).

Prayer

Now let us kneel down in the presence of our good God with acknowledgement of our faults, praying to him to make us feel them better than we have done, so that we may submit ourselves wholly unto him. May he stretch out his hand, not allowing us to continue to be given to our fancies and affections, but that we may magnify his goodness which he extends toward us and yield him the obedience that he deserves, especially because he has promised to bring us his law and to teach it to us. By it he has not only shown us the way to live well, but also promised to adopt us as his children, and to show himself as our Father and Saviour for our Lord Jesus Christ's sake. Amen.

(*Sermons on the Ten Commandments*, 50.)

❖

A look back and a look ahead

Having introduced Christ the Redeemer, Calvin doesn't turn first to the New Testament to explain and describe the redemption that Christ wrought. He turns first to the Old Testament, and in II.8 to the ten commandments, which he calls 'the law of grace'.

Heiko Oberman writes that in Calvin

> for the first time in the history of the West the Jewish Scriptures are no longer presented as the 'Old' Testament. [They] are now seen as the ancient, i.e. original, testament in which the eternal and lasting covenant is proclaimed to the people of Israel for all times … The 'Old' or rather the 'Primary' Testament is not only Holy Scripture because of its prophetic witness to the future Messiah, but because it tells the story of God's care for his people, as relevant today as it was in the time of Moses and the prophets (*Calvin Studies VI*, 3-4).

The ten commandments

John Calvin says that God speaks directly and simply in the ten commandments so that we 'might realize that it is not necessary to be a great scholar in order to understand the law of God' (*Sermons on the Ten Commandments*, 154-55). He sets forth five general principles to help us interpret the ten commandments.

Principles for interpretation

1. The law is inward; it is 'concerned not so much with outward appearances as with purity of heart' (II.8.6). This is what Christ, the law's 'best interpreter', insists on in the Sermon on the Mount. Christ did not add to the law but 'only restored it to its integrity' (II.8.7). Since the law is not only outward but also inward, our obedience must be not only outward but also inward. Calvin says that law-keeping which involves only 'the feet, hands, and eyes' and not the heart is mere pretence (Comm. Psa. 40:8).

2. The purpose of each commandment determines its meaning. For example, the fifth commandment, that we are to honour our parents, points to the fuller purpose of the commandment—'that honour ought to be paid to those to whom God has assigned it' (II.8.8).

3. The positive opposite is included in each negative commandment or prohibition. The commandment that prohibits killing requires that 'we give our neighbour's life all the help we can' (II.8.9). The command that prohibits stealing requires that we give to those in need.

4. There are two tables or requirements of the law: love for God and love for people. In the same way that there are two great purposes for our lives, 'our Lord has divided his law into two tables, that is, that we might know how we are to govern ourselves toward [God] and how we ought to live with our neighbours' (*Sermons on the Ten Commandments*, 247). Each table involves the other. 'It is vain to cry up righteousness' (second table: love for people) 'without religion' (first table: love for God). 'Apart from the fear of God' (first table: love for God) 'men do not preserve equity and love among themselves' (second table: love for people) (II.8.11). The commandments are 'guides to love in action' toward God and people (*John Calvin: Writings on Pastoral Piety*, 32).

5. The law is complete. We must not add 'good works upon good works' (II.8.5). We must 'not become God's censors by adding bits and pieces to his word' (*Sermons on the Ten Commandments*, 242).

Preamble

'I am Jehovah, your God, who brought you out of the land of Egypt, out of the house of bondage' (Exod. 20:2-3). The preface or preamble to the ten commandments, writes David Jones, 'establishes the proper relationship between enabling grace and obedient love' (*A Theological Guide to Calvin's Institutes*, 310). Calvin states that God 'holds out the promise of grace to draw [the Israelites] by its sweetness to a zeal for holiness' (II.8.13). Our primary motive for obeying God's law is gratitude for his kind and merciful deliverance. Calvin describes God's generosity to us when he presents God as saying:

> Let us consider our situation. It is true that there is an infinite distance between you and me and that I should be able to

command of you whatever seems good to me … But behold, I set aside my right. I come here to present myself to you as your guide and saviour. I want to govern you. You are like my little family. And if you are satisfied with my word, I will be your king. Furthermore, do not think that the covenant which I made with your fathers was intended to take anything from you. For I have no need, nor am I indigent in anything. And what could you do for me anyway? But I procure your well-being and your salvation. Therefore, on my part, I am prepared to enter into covenant, article by article, and to pledge myself to you (*Sermons on the Ten Commandments*, 45).

Preaching on Ephesians 1:15-18, Calvin pointed out that in verse 15 Paul speaks of the faith and love of the Ephesians. Calvin said that, under these two words,

St Paul has comprehended the whole perfection of Christians. For the mark at which the first table of the law aims is that we should worship one God only and cling to him for all things, acknowledging ourselves to be so indebted to him, that we ought to flee to him alone for all refuge and endeavour to spend our whole life in his service. That is the sum of the first table of the law. The contents of the second are nothing else but that we should live together in equity and uprightness, and deal in such a way with our neighbours that we strive to help all men without hurting any man. And we are sure that God has set forth so good and perfect a rule of good life in his law that nothing can be added to it.

The first table

The first four commandments pertain 'to those duties of religion which particularly concern the worship of [God's] majesty' (II.8.11). He 'does not want us to worship him out of servile fear. Rather he wants us to come to him with a sincere and cheerful heart, so much so that we take pleasure in honouring him. That cannot be done unless we love him. Thus let us note that the beginning of obedience, as well as its source, foundation, and root, is this love of God; that we would not attempt to come to him unless we found in him our deepest pleasure' (*Sermons on the Ten Commandments*, 76).

1. 'You shall have no other gods before my face'

God commands us to worship him, and him alone, 'with true and zealous godliness'. We are not to give to anyone or anything what belongs to God—adoration, trust, invocation, and thanksgiving (II.8.16). 'We cannot have the true God unless we have him alone, that is, unless we do not [attempt] to add a companion to him, for as soon as we begin introducing little gods, we renounce the living God' (*Sermons on the Ten Commandments*, 305). 'Let us walk as in [God's] presence and in his sight, indeed, in such a way that we worship him as our only God, not solely in ceremonies, or in external affirmation, but in our heart … Let him possess our bodies and souls, in order that he might be glorified in all and by all' (*Sermons on the Ten Commandments*, 64). It is in the worship of God that our whole life finds direction and meaning: 'to contemplate, fear, and worship his majesty; to participate in his blessings; to seek his help at all times; to recognize, and by praises to celebrate, the greatness of his works—as the only goal of all the activities of this life' (II.8.16).

2. 'You shall not make yourself a graven image'

'The first commandment summons us to worship the correct God, the second commands us to worship this God correctly' (Horton, *Calvin on the Christian Life*, 174). God describes the kind of worship he requires—'a spiritual worship established by himself' (II.8.17).

Calvin rejects the practice of dividing the 'ten words' into three commandments in the first table and seven in the second table. He believes that this arrangement erased the commandment concerning images or at least hid it under the first. Why did Calvin consider it so important that the second commandment stand out? Because Roman Catholic 'images' were an issue in his day, Calvin insisted that God 'does not will that his lawful worship be profaned by superstitious rites' as prohibited by the second commandment (II.8.17). Commenting on the apostle Paul's preaching against the idolatry of the Athenians, Calvin writes that 'God cannot be represented by a picture or sculpture, since he has intended his likeness to appear in us' (Comm. Acts 17:29). In other words, the Christian is not to make images of God, but to be the image of God.

3. 'You shall not take the name of Jehovah your God in vain'

We are to 'hallow the majesty of [God's] name' and not to profane it 'by treating it contemptuously and irreverently' (II.8.22). 'All who take the name of God other than in sincerity and simplicity blaspheme him' (*Sermons on the Ten Commandments*, 85). Calvin connects the third commandment with the first petition of the Lord's Prayer, 'Hallowed be thy name.' 'Hallowed be thy name' is followed by 'thy will be done on earth as it is in heaven.' We hallow God's name not only by speaking correctly of him but also by living holy lives.

4. 'Remember to keep holy the Sabbath day'

God gave his people a special day for worship and rest. Calvin believed that the 'ceremonial part' of the commandment with its 'rigid scrupulousness' was abolished with the rest of the ceremonial laws, but that the fourth commandment continues as a rule for Christians today.

The main point of the Sabbath day is its representation of 'spiritual rest, in which believers ought to lay aside their own works to allow God to work in them' (II.8.28). 'This foreshadowing of spiritual rest occupied the chief place in the Sabbath' (II.8.29). And it pointed to 'the coming perfection of [God's] Sabbath in the last Day' (II.8.30). The 'Lord's Day' was substituted for the Sabbath in the early church because 'the purpose and fulfilment of that true rest, represented by the ancient Sabbath, lies in the Lord's resurrection' (II.8.34).

In the Sabbath God also provides a special day for believers to gather for instruction and worship 'to be trained in piety' (II.8.28). It is a day for 'the consideration of the beauty, excellence, and fitness' of all God's works (Comm. Exod. 20:8) and 'the consideration of the wisdom, power, and justice of God' in his providence (Comm. Num. 15:32, 35). The Sabbath day enables people to live well the rest of the week. 'And when we have spent Sunday in praising and glorifying the name of God and in meditating on his works, then, throughout the rest of the week, we should show that we have benefited from it' (*Sermons on the Ten Commandments*, 113).

The Second Table

The fourth commandment serves as a bridge between the two tables of the law. It is part of the first table and is therefore directed toward God, and points to our responsibility toward people, which is the theme of the second table. The first four commandments teach us to love God with all our hearts; the last six show us how to love our neighbours as ourselves. Preaching on Ephesians 5:8-11, Calvin said that 'it is the manner of holy Scripture, when it speaks of the serving of God, to send us back to our neighbours' (Sermon on Eph. 5:8-11).

Heiko Oberman states that the commandments of the second table of the law 'were, for Calvin, not arbitrary divine directives but remedies for social evil and the best protection of true humanism' (*Calvin Studies VI*, 6). The commandments, Calvin insists, are laws of grace, gifts of a loving father, to enable us to live and flourish as human beings. They are not barriers but guardrails, to help us to walk, to keep us from falling and hurting ourselves.

5. *'Honour your father and your mother'*

This is the first commandment of the second table of the law, 'seeing that the descending order from God is to honour those whom he has set over us'. 'Therefore, insofar as fathers and mothers, magistrates and all who exercise authority, are lieutenants of God and represent him, certainly if we despise and reject them, it's as much as if we should declare that we don't want to obey God' (*Sermons on the Ten Commandments*, 138, 151). This commandment also speaks to those in places of authority, reminding them 'that there is a master' over them, 'and that he truly must be obeyed, and that his right must be preserved in its entirety' (*Sermons on the Ten Commandments*, 143).

Preaching on Ephesians 6:1-4, Calvin noted that this is the only commandment with a specific promise attached—'that your days may be long in the land that the Lord your God is giving you'. Stating that some, however, who are disobedient to parents have a long life, and others who are kind and loving to mother and father die young, Calvin explained that 'things do not always fall out the same with respect to temporal promises'. God 'knows what is expedient for us, and therefore we must not take his [temporal] promises rigorously'. Rather 'we must always bear in mind that he knows what is for our profit and benefit'.

6. *'You shall not kill'*

The sixth commandment not only forbids murder but also requires that we concern ourselves with preserving life and with 'the safety of all' (II.8.39). 'Our Lord wants us to go to the trouble of helping each other, insofar as our neighbour's life ought to be as precious to us as it is to him' (*Sermons on the Ten Commandments*, 163).

While Calvin gave the least space in his *Institutes* to the sixth commandment, he devoted considerable attention to the practical application of the commandment in his commentaries and sermons. In his *Harmony of the Last Four Books of Moses*, he follows each of the ten commandments with a discussion of those passages that have to do specifically with that commandment. Under the sixth commandment, 'Thou shalt not kill', he treats various violations of that commandment, including abortion and slavery. 'The sum of this commandment', he says, 'is that we should not unjustly do violence to anyone' (III.20).

Preaching on Ephesians 6:5-9, Calvin explains the difference between the bondslaves of Paul's time and the servants of the present time and says, 'We have great cause to praise God for taking away such bondage from among men.' When Paul exhorts slaves to be obedient to their masters, it seems, says Calvin, that 'he thereby did wrong to the slaves, and that he should rather have cried out against this common abuse [of slavery] in order that such outrage might have been put down'. While clearly uncomfortable with this scripture, Calvin puts forth two principles to keep in mind. First, slavery was the 'fruit of disobedience and sin of our father Adam', but was allowed by God. Second, 'the gospel is not brought in to change the common politics of the world and to make laws that belong to the temporal state'. Paul, therefore, encourages slaves 'to bear patiently the state they are in' and masters to be 'gentle and benign'.

7. *'You shall not commit adultery'*

This commandment requires that we 'chastely and continently regulate all parts of our life'. 'Because God loves modesty and purity, all uncleanness must be far from us' (II.8.41). Calvin ends his sermon on the seventh commandment by saying that we must demonstrate morality and godliness in our lives, as we 'offer our bodies and souls as gifts and sacrifices to God, seeing that he has so costly redeemed them by our Lord Jesus Christ and has willed for them to be dedicated to him, that he might indwell them like his temples' (*Sermons on the Ten Commandments*, 183).

8. *'You shall not steal'*

We must not only refrain from taking what belongs to others, but also 'strive faithfully to help every man to keep his own possessions' (II.8.45). We are 'to refrain from every form of injurious activity and wrong' and 'at the same time, insofar as we can, let us not permit anyone to be wronged or injured' (*Sermons on the Ten Commandments*, 200).

There are subtle ways of breaking the commandment. 'All those arts whereby we acquire the possessions and money at the expense of our neighbours are to be considered as thefts. Although those who behave in this way often win their case before the judge, yet God upholds them to be none other than thieves. For he sees the intricate deceptions with which crafty people set out to snare those of simpler mind; he sees the rigour of the exactions which the rich impose on the poor to crush them' (II.8.45). Notice Calvin's impressive statements in II.8.46 in which he sets forth the implications of this commandment for people in general, rulers, ministers of churches, church members, parents, children, old people, young people, servants, and masters.

Calvin calls on the poor to trust God and be content. He calls on the rich to serve God and be generous. And 'above all, let us learn to wait upon the benediction of God for all that is necessary in this world. For if we would live by this rule, it is certain that all avarice and robbery and fraud … would be immediately corrected. This is the only medicine we need for healing these vices, for us to be able to lift our eyes to heaven and say, "God is our Father, he will provide all that we need; it is he in whom we must hope for all that sustains us in this present life; in sum it is his benediction that constitutes the fountain of all wealth"' (*Sermons on the Ten Commandments*, 196).

9. 'You shall not be a false witness against your neighbour'

The eighth commandment forbids harming others by stealing from them. The ninth commandment teaches us that our words can also harm others by bringing reproach or discredit upon them. 'If we speak ill of our neighbours, if we slander them—although in the world's eyes that sin isn't considered grievous—God disapproves of it as false witnessing' (*Sermons on the Ten Commandments*, 204).

This commandment, says Calvin, is rightly practised 'when our tongue, in declaring the truth, serves both the good repute and the advantage of our neighbours' (II.8.47). 'Now if we want to observe what this text contains, we need to consider a higher principle, that is, to consider why God created our tongues and why he gave us speech, the reason being that we might be able to communicate with each other. Now what is the purpose of human communication if it isn't our mutual support in charity?' (*Sermons on the Ten Commandments*, 216)

10. 'You shall not covet'

The last commandment may seem unnecessary since God has already condemned robbery and adultery. But this commandment goes further by requiring that we 'banish from our thoughts all desire contrary to love' (II.8.49). We ought to 'make the effort to call upon God in order that he might govern us by his Holy Spirit and ... so to restrain ourselves that Satan may have no entrance and be unable to make a breach and thus gain possession of our hearts. May we repulse him quite some distance. And if we are conscious of a wayward thought, may we head it off, and bar the gate, and remind ourselves: "It is imperative for your God to rule you completely; let him possess not only your heart, but also your entire senses"' (*Sermons on the Ten Commandments*, 227). In a sermon, Calvin said that 'not without cause' is covetousness called idolatry in Ephesians 5:5 'because it is certain that when a man once gives himself to it, he fixes his whole happiness in it' and fails to see that it is a grievous sin.

Summary

Following his sermons on the ten commandments, Calvin preached four more times on Deuteronomy 5:22-6:4. He makes three points in his sermon on Deuteronomy 5:22 (*Sermons on the Ten Commandments*, 237-39).

1. In publishing his law [God] willed that the doctrine it contains be announced loud and clear, indeed, not merely spoken to three or four, but to all the people, the great and small without exception. Moreover, he willed for the law to be written and preserved that it might not simply serve one age, but that it might retain its vigour and authority until the end of the world. And that is why it is said in this passage that God spoke in a loud voice.

2. God added nothing after these ten precepts. The brevity with which Moses admonishes the people ought to give us courage to receive what God says to us. For if he had set before us numerous volumes, we would be able to retort that all our life should not suffice for such a study. Therefore God used brevity when he gave us his word; there are no more than ten statements. We can count on our fingers all the instruction that is required for our life. Furthermore, Moses means that [God] did not intend for anything to be added to what he said. It is important for us to cling to that; it is unlawful for creatures to add anything to it.

3. In publishing his law, God spoke out of the midst of the cloud … the mountain was smoking … there were flames of fire and flashes of lightning all about. Now what is the meaning of all that? That the doctrine might possess more majesty; that men might be led to humble themselves before God in complete reverence; that they might fully yield themselves to his word to obey it.

Knowing God and ourselves

As we study the ten commandments we come to know ourselves as sinners. Calvin writes, 'In our discussion of the knowledge of ourselves we have set forth this chief point: that, empty of all opinion of our own virtue, and shorn of all assurance of our own righteousness—in fact, broken and crushed by the awareness of our own utter poverty—we may learn genuine humility and self-abasement' (II.8.1).

9. Old and New Testaments— 'Dawn ... Noonday'

'However much darkness there might be under the law, the [Old Testament] fathers were not ignorant of the road they had to take. The *dawn* may not be as bright as *noonday*, but it is sufficient for making a journey, and travellers do not wait until the sun is right up. Their portion of light was like the dawn; it could keep them safe from all error and guide them to everlasting blessedness' (Comm. Gal. 3:23-24).

In these chapters Calvin argues 'for a unitary narrative view of Scripture in which the Gospel fully reveals, completes, and so fulfils what was the substance of the law and the whole of the old covenant from the beginning—the mercy of God realized and manifested in Christ'. These chapters are like 'the book of Malachi or John the Baptist ... summarizing the substance of the Old Testament history from which we have tasted Christ, but in such a way that we cannot rest content there, but are driven on in hope and desire to find the full banquet laid before us in the gospel' (Edmondson, *Calvin's Christology*, 47).

Read: *Institutes* II.9-11. [*1541* ch.7, pp. 429-462.]

Scripture Text: 'Your father Abraham rejoiced that he would see my day. He saw it and was glad' (John. 8:56).

Notable Quote: 'For what is the law without Jesus Christ? It is a body without a soul' (*John Calvin: Writings on Pastoral Piety*, 187).

Prayer

Almighty God, since you have deigned in your mercy to gather us to your church, and to enclose us within the boundaries of your word, by which you preserve us in the true and right worship of your majesty, O grant that we may continue contented in this obedience to you. And though Satan may, in many ways, attempt to draw us here and there, and we be also ourselves inclined to evil, O grant, that being confirmed in faith and united to you by that sacred bond, we may constantly abide under the restraint of your word.

May we cleave to Christ, your only begotten Son, who has joined us forever to himself. May we never by any means turn aside from you, but be, on the contrary, confirmed in the faith of his gospel, until at length he will receive us all into his kingdom. Amen.

(Devotions and Prayers of John Calvin, 14.)

❧

A look back and a look ahead

John Calvin's title for II.9 is 'Christ, although he was known to the Jews under the law, was at length clearly revealed only in the gospel.' Calvin says that the 'law' was a 'shadowed outline' and the 'gospel' gave 'far more light' (II.9.1). By the 'law' Calvin means the Old Testament, and by the 'gospel', the New Testament. But note that Calvin uses 'gospel' in two ways.

(1) The promise in the law or 'those testimonies of mercy and fatherly favour which God gave to the patriarchs of old' (II.9.2). This describes the 'gospel' in the Old Testament.

(2) The fulfilment of the promise or 'the proclamation of the grace manifested in Christ' (II.9.2). This describes the 'gospel' in the New Testament. The gospel in the New Testament sense does not supplant the law, that is, the gospel in the Old Testament sense, but ratifies it (II.9.4). 'God had indeed promised a new covenant at the coming of Christ; but had, at the same time, showed that it would not be different from the first, but that, on the contrary, its design was, to give a perpetual sanction to the covenant, which he had made from the beginning with his own people' (Comm. Matt. 5:17).

> 'The whole of the OT is full of promise, full of Christ, so that the NT is in the OT. Conversely the NT does not set aside but confirms and purifies the law that the Pharisees had perverted. Both apostles and prophets preached the same unchangeable will of God both to judge and to save. Few thoughts were so much on Calvin's heart in his own time as that of the primary unity of the biblical revelation both with itself, and then further back, and less evident, with what God has said and still says to us in nature, history, and conscience' (Barth, *The Theology of John Calvin*, 165).

Similarity of the Old and New Testaments

Calvin discusses the similarity of the Old and New Testaments in four points.

1. Both testaments have the same goal: everlasting life

Even though much of the Old Testament is about earthly promises—land and nation, for example—the real goal of the Old Testament was not 'carnal prosperity and happiness' but the 'hope of immortality' (II.10.2). Servetus and some others regarded the Israelites, Calvin says, 'as nothing but a herd of swine' (II.10.1). To answer them he devotes II.10.7-22 to a 'history of salvation' from Adam to the prophets, proving that the Old Testament saints 'sought for everlasting life' (II.10.13). Their hopes, like ours, did not rely on earthly blessings alone but mainly on heavenly things. In their troubles and trials, the Old Testament saints 'lifted up their hearts to God's sanctuary, in which they found hidden' the spiritual and eternal blessing that did not appear so clearly 'in the shadows of the present life' (II.10.17). Calvin summarizes his argument: 'The Old Testament or Covenant that the Lord had made with the Israelites had not been limited to earthly things, but contained a promise of spiritual and eternal life ... Christ the Lord promises to his followers today no other "kingdom of heaven" than that in which they may "sit at table with Abraham, Isaac, and Jacob"' (II.10.23).

2. Both testaments have the same mediator: Christ

Earthly priests are prominent in the Old Testament, but believers at that time also 'had and knew Christ as mediator' (II.10.2). Hebrews 13:8, 'Christ remains, yesterday and today and forever', refers not only to his everlasting divinity, but to his power which is always available to believers in all times. The resurrection of the saints in Jerusalem at the time of the death of Christ is Christ's 'sure pledge that whatever he did or suffered in acquiring eternal salvation pertains to the believers of the Old Testament as much as to ourselves' (II.10.23). The Old Testament ceremonial laws were not only a prefiguration of Christ, but the representation of his pre-incarnate presence as mediator. The loaves set before the Lord in Leviticus 24 betokened 'no symbol of God's routine favour, since he descended [close] to them as though he were their table companion' (Comm. Lev. 24:5-9).

3. Both testaments have the same means: grace

Old Testament believers 'were covenanted to [God] by the same law and by the bond of the same doctrine as obtains among us' (II.10.1). The Old Testament appears to be full of 'works', but Old Testament believers were saved 'not by their own merits, but solely by the mercy of God who called them' (II.10.2).

4. Both testaments have the same sacraments: baptism and the Lord's Supper

'The Lord manifested his grace [to Old Testament saints] by the same symbols' as in the New Testament, although in different forms (II.10.5). The Israelites 'had the same benefits which we enjoy today. The church of God was in their midst, as in ours today. They had the same sacraments, to be testimonies to them of the grace of God' (Comm. 1 Cor. 10:1-4).

There is such great similarity between the Old and New Testaments that Calvin describes them as virtually identical. 'The covenant made with all the patriarchs is so much like ours in substance and reality that the two are actually one and the same' (II.10.2). 'The law is not at all superfluous, nor is the Old Testament, but it is a permanent thing, which must always retain its strength, even to the end of the world' (Sermon on 1 Tim. 4:12-13). Heiko Oberman writes, 'For the first time in the history of the West the Jewish Scriptures are no longer presented as the "Old" Testament. The Jewish Scriptures are now seen [by Calvin] as the ancient, original, Testament in which the eternal and lasting covenant is proclaimed to the people of Israel [the people of God] for all times' (*Calvin Studies VI*, 3).

Difference between the Old and New Testaments

Calvin makes such a strong case for the sameness of the Old and New Testaments that he is prompted to ask: 'Is no difference left between the Old and the New Testaments? What is to become of all the passages in Scripture where they are contrasted as quite different?' Calvin answers that there is a difference between the two testaments, but 'in such a way as not to detract from its established unity'. These differences pertain 'to the manner of dispensation rather than to the substance' (II.11.1).

1. Temporal blessings of the Old Testament and spiritual blessings of the New

There were earthly elements in the Old Testament covenant, but it was not a carnal, earthly covenant. The Lord, not the land, was the real inheritance of God's Old Testament people. God conferred earthly benefits on the Jews as a 'lower mode of training' because he 'determined to lead them by his own hand to the hope of heavenly things' (II.11.1). 'Though the law of the Lord be now the same as it ever was, yet it came out of Zion with a new garment' (Comm. Isa. 2:3).

2. The images and ceremonies in the Old Testament and 'the very substance of truth' (II.11.4) in the New Testament

The images and ceremonies were 'accidental properties of the covenant' (II.11.4), given because of Israel's 'childhood' (II.11.5). The ceremonies—in themselves meaningless—pointed beyond themselves to Christ and so were 'an introduction to the better hope that is manifested in the gospel' (II.11.4). 'The ancient prophets beheld Christ afar off, as he had been promised to them, and yet were not permitted to behold him present, as he made himself intimately and completely visible when he came down to men from heaven' (Comm. John 8:56).

3. The literal nature of the Old Testament and the spiritual nature of the New Testament

Calvin argues that this difference is not absolute but relative—'by way of comparison to commend the grace abounding, wherewith the same Lawgiver, assuming, as it were, a new character, honoured the preaching of the gospel' (II.11.8).

4. The bondage of the Old Testament and the freedom of the New Testament

The bondage of the Old Testament saints was bondage only 'in contrast to us' (II.11.9). When Old Testament believers were oppressed by their situation 'they fled for refuge to the gospel' (II.11.9). They 'so lived under the old covenant as not to remain there but ever to aspire to the new, and thus embraced a real share in it' (II.11.10).

5. One nation in the Old Testament and all nations in the New Testament.

The calling of the Gentiles in the New Testament is 'a notable mark of excellence of the New Testament over the Old' (II.11.12). Preaching on Deuteronomy 6:3, Calvin said:

> Now since the land promised to the Jews is mentioned here, let us note that today we ought to be far more inspired to serve God inasmuch as he has dedicated the whole earth to himself and wills for his name to be entreated everywhere, for the blood which our Lord Jesus shed has sanctified the whole earth … For we know [that at that time], Israel was the only land which God had reserved for himself and over which he willed to rule until the coming of his Son. But when our Lord Jesus Christ appeared, then he acquired possession of the whole world and his kingdom was extended from one end of it to the other, especially with the proclamation of the gospel (*Sermons on the Ten Commandments*, 299).

Calvin is 'quite ready to agree that the efficacy of the signs is at once richer and more abundant for us since the incarnation of Christ than it was for the fathers under the law. So the difference between us and them is only one of degree, or, as the common saying goes, one of "more or less", because what they had in small measure, we have more fully' (Comm. 1 Cor. 10:1-4). The main point, however, is not difference but similarity. 'When [God] says, "I will establish a covenant", we may explain it as though he said, "I will set it up again, or restore it to its former condition" … We see then that the difference which Jeremiah points out was really true and yet the new covenant so flowed from the old that it was the same in substance, while distinguished in form' (Comm. Ezek. 16:61).

Twice Calvin states that the differences between the two testaments can be explained by 'the mode of administration' (II.10.2 and II.11.1). God's mode of administration in the Old Testament was not the same as it is in the New. Why did God choose to reveal himself in different ways? Calvin gives two answers. First, God has done everything 'wisely and justly' (II.11.14). Second, God 'accommodated diverse forms to different ages, as he knew would be expedient for each' (II.11.13).

Knowing God and ourselves

As we study these chapters, we see God as a wise and careful teacher accommodating his truth to the level of understanding of his people in different ages. Because we live in the full daylight of the New Testament, we are challenged to live more fully for God who has so abundantly given us his truth.

10. The Person of Christ— 'The Bright Mirror'

'He is the *bright mirror* of God's wonderful and singular grace' (II.14.7).

> 'Bernard's admonition is worth remembering: "The name of Jesus is not only light but also food; it is also oil, without which all food of the soul is dry; it is salt, without whose seasoning whatever is set before us is insipid; finally, it is honey in the mouth, melody in the ear, rejoicing in the heart, and at the same time medicine. Every discourse in which his name is not spoken is without savour"' (II.16.1).

Read: *Institutes* II.12-14. [*1541* ch.4, pp.233-257.]

Scripture Text: 'For there is one God, and there is one mediator between God and men, the man Christ Jesus' (1 Tim. 2:5).

Notable Quote: : 'As the sun discovers to our eyes the most beautiful theatre of earth and heaven and the whole order of nature, so God has visibly displayed the chief glory of his work in his Son' (Comm. John 9:5).

Prayer

Grant, Almighty God, that as you not only invite us continually by the voice of your gospel to seek you, but also offer to us your Son as our Mediator, through whom an access to you is open, that we may find you a propitious Father.

O grant, that relying on your kind invitation, we may through life exercise ourselves in prayer, and as so many evils disturb us on all sides and so many wants distress and oppress us, may we be led more earnestly to call on you, and in the meanwhile be never wearied in this exercise of prayer; until having been heard by you throughout life, we may at length be gathered to your eternal kingdom where we shall enjoy that salvation which you promised to us, and of which also you daily testify to us by your gospel, and be forever united to your only-begotten Son of whom we are now members; that we may be partakers of all the blessings which he has obtained for us by his death. Amen.

(*Devotions and Prayers of John Calvin*, 39.)

A look back and a look ahead

The title of Book II is the 'Knowledge of God the Redeemer.' Calvin establishes the need for the Redeemer in II.1-5. He introduces the Redeemer in II.6 and spends six chapters discussing the relationship between the Old and New Testaments (II.6-11). The central message of both testaments is Christ and salvation through him. Everything before II.6 prepares for and leads up to Christ the Redeemer; everything that comes after II.6 flows from Christ the Redeemer. Note the titles of Books III and IV—'The Way in which We Receive the Grace of Christ' and 'The External Means or Aids by which God Invites Us into the Society of Christ.'

Calvin's doctrine of Christ is set forth in II.12-17. Calvin begins with a restatement of the human predicament. We are so estranged from God that we need an intermediary who is both human and divine. Calvin describes the person of Christ in II.12-14 and the work of Christ in II.15-17. He insists that these two topics be held together. We cannot understand who Christ is apart from what he does nor can we know what he does apart from who he is.

The person of Christ

John Calvin's treatment of the person of Christ has four main points.

- The Mediator must be God and man (II.12).

- Christ is God (I.13).

- Christ is man (II.13).

- Christ who is both God and man is one person (II.14).

The necessity of the incarnation

The incarnation of Christ is God's supreme accommodation. Calvin quotes Irenaeus, who wrote 'that the Father, himself infinite, becomes finite in the Son, for he has accommodated himself to our little measure lest our minds be overwhelmed by the immensity of his glory' (II.6.4). Calvin repeats this thought in his commentary on 1 Peter 1:20; he writes that we cannot believe in God except through Christ 'in whom God in a manner makes himself little ... in order to accommodate himself to our comprehension'.

Calvin argues that there was no 'simple' or 'absolute' necessity for Christ to become human. He refutes a Lutheran theologian named Osiander who taught that Christ was predestined to become incarnate whether or not Adam fell into sin. Christ, the image of God, was the model by which all humanity was created. In Osiander's view Adam's creation, therefore, necessitated Christ's incarnation. Calvin calls Osiander's view 'rubbish', and insists that the purpose of the incarnation is our redemption, as stated clearly in 1 Timothy 1:15, 'Christ Jesus came into the world to save sinners' (II.12.5). Calvin writes that Christ's incarnation 'stemmed from a heavenly decree'. While there was no 'absolute' necessity for the incarnation, 'it was of the greatest importance for us that the mediator be both true God and true man' (II.12.1).

Calvin suggests that God could have saved mankind in some other way. 'God could have redeemed us by a word or a wish, save that another way seemed best for our sakes: that by not sparing his own and only-begotten Son he might testify in his person how much he cares for our salvation' (Comm. John 15:13). Paul Helm writes that for Calvin, 'there may have been another way [for God] to pay the price of sin; or rather, not to pay the price of sin but to freely pardon it. But there was no other way of procuring those God-glorifying effects that evoke wonder and amazement at God's pardon ... The atonement is necessary, or is required, if (and only if) God wants, in pardoning us, to show his great love for us' (*Calvin at the Centre*, 179-80). Calvin simply says, 'Our most merciful Father decreed what was best for us' (II.12.1).

Calvin held that even before the fall man needed a mediator. 'Even if man had remained free from all stain, his condition would have been too lowly for him to reach God without a mediator' (II.12.1). A mediator was necessary to enable sinless but finite human beings to enjoy fellowship with God. The Reformed tradition has held that this function indeed belonged to Christ but has not usually described it as mediation. The Westminster Confession of Faith states that sinless man required God's 'voluntary condescension' to be sustained and blessed and that God was pleased to express this 'by way of covenant' (II.7.1).

If sinless man needed a mediator, how much more do sinful people need a mediator. The role of Christ as mediator between a holy God and fallen humanity began at the fall and extended through the Old Testament in the promise of the covenant of grace, under the signs and ceremonies of the law, and in the appearances from time to time of the angel of the Lord. At the fall Christ 'already at that time, as a sort of foretaste, began to fulfil the office of mediator. For even though he was not yet clothed with flesh, he came down, so to speak, as an intermediary in order to approach believers more intimately' (I.13.10). At the incarnation the mediator was 'manifest in the flesh', approaching us much more closely by becoming one of us.

In order to be restored to 'God's grace' (II.12.2), we must 'pay the penalties for sin' (II.12.3). This we cannot do, but Christ came in the flesh to do it for us. Calvin asks, 'Who could have done this had not the self-same Son of God become the Son of man, and had not so taken what was ours as to impart what was his to us, and to make what was his by nature ours by grace?' (II.12.2) 'In short, since neither as God alone could [Christ] feel death, nor as man alone could he overcome it, he coupled human nature with divine so that to atone for sin he might submit the weakness of the one to death; and that, wrestling with death by the power of the other nature, he might win victory for us' (II.12.3). 'The sin of Adam is overcome by the righteousness of Christ. The curse of Adam is overcome by the grace of Christ, and the life which Christ bestows swallows up the death which came from Adam' (Comm. Rom. 5:17). George Herbert expressed Calvin's thought in a few words in a poem called 'An Offering'—'In Christ two natures met to be thy cure' (*The Works of George Herbert*).

Calvin is concerned to state as clearly as possible the true nature of Christ, because, as he writes in his commentary on Matthew 22:42, 'Ever since Christ was manifested to the world, heretics have attempted by various contrivances … to overturn sometimes his human and sometimes his divine nature, that either he might not have full power to save us, or we might not have ready access to him.'

Christ is God

Calvin has already set forth the deity of Christ in his treatment of the Trinity (I.13.7-13).

Christ is man

Against the Manichees (who believed that Christ assumed a 'heavenly flesh'), the Marcionites (who held that Christ's body was not real but 'mere appearance'), and Menno Simons (who taught that Christ took his body 'out of nothing'), Calvin argues that Christ assumed real flesh. He became a human being—not disguised as human, not temporarily human, but really and truly human as we are.

The Virgin Mary was the source of Christ's authentic, true humanity. Mary was not merely 'a channel through which Christ flowed', but he was born of Mary (II.13.3). He was a man 'begotten of human seed [but not a human father] ... [and so] subject to hunger, thirst, cold and other infirmities of our nature' (II.13.1). 'How do groaning and trouble of mind belong to the person of the Son of God?' Calvin rejects Augustine's explanation that Christ, 'otherwise calm and free from all passion, summoned groaning and grief of his own accord'. 'When the Son of God put on our flesh', Calvin asserts, 'he also of his own accord put on human feelings, so that he differed in nothing from his brethren, sin only excepted' (Comm. John 11:33).

Not only is Mary the mother of Christ, the source of Christ's humanity, but she is also, Calvin says in a sermon on Luke 1:39-44, 'one of the first members of the church'.

She was of necessity blessed in the same way as all other believers—blessed therefore by grace, so that the praise belongs wholly to our Lord Jesus Christ, as is his right. There is no doubt, then, that she carried Jesus Christ by faith in her heart, just as she carried him in her womb. We will later see how greatly we may profit from her example, in that she let nothing pass which she did not carefully commit to memory, so as to have ever firmer confidence in God's goodness, and always be united to his Son, not by a physical bond, but by faith.

In II.13.3, Calvin speaks of 'the superiority of the male sex'. Despite this unfortunate comment, 'Calvin's view of women is actually notable in a positive sense', writes Herman Selderhuis (*John Calvin*, 173). Scattered throughout the *Institutes*, commentaries, and sermons there are passages that to some extent correct his statement in II.13.3. Concerning the genealogy of Christ, Calvin writes in this same place that if the Bible names only men, 'Must we say then that women are nothing? Why, even children know that women are included under the term "men".'

Christ is sinless.

Christ is sinless 'not just because he was begotten of his mother without copulation with man, but because he was sanctified by the Spirit that the generation might be pure and undefiled as would have been true before Adam's fall' (II.13.4). In other words, the sinlessness of Christ is not because he did not have an earthly father, but because of the work of the Holy Spirit. The virgin birth, or rather the virgin conception, of Christ testifies to, but does not create, a sinless human being. Calvin writes:

> Just as he had to be true man to expiate our sins and death, and overcome Satan in our flesh, all in all to be the true mediator, so it was necessary for him, in order to cleanse others, to be clear of all uncleanness or spot. Thus though Christ was born of the seed of Abraham, he drew no contagion from that blemished nature, for from the very first, God's Spirit kept him pure, not merely that he should abound in holiness unto himself alone, but rather that he should make others holy. The very mode of his conception testifies that he was set apart from sinners to be our mediator (Comm. Luke 1:35).

Christ is united to but not restricted to the flesh.

Christ is man—a true but sinless human being—and at the same time he is the eternal God, united to but 'not restricted to the flesh'. The second person of the Trinity became incarnate in Jesus but not in such a way that he had no existence also beyond the flesh. Calvin writes,

For even if the Word in his immeasurable essence united with the nature of man into one person, we do not imagine that he was confined therein. Here is something marvellous: the Son of God descended from heaven in such a way that, without leaving heaven, he willed to be borne in the virgin's womb, to go about the earth, and to hang upon the cross; yet he continuously filled the world even as he had done from the beginning (II.13.4).

Calvin later repeats the same idea in his discussion of the Lord's Supper.

There is a commonplace distinction of the schools to which I am not ashamed to refer: although the whole Christ is everywhere, still the whole of that which is in him is not everywhere ... Therefore, since the whole Christ is everywhere, our Mediator is ever present with his own people, and in the supper reveals himself in a special way, yet in such a way that the whole Christ is present, but not in his wholeness (IV.17.30).

The second person of the Godhead is everywhere, but Jesus in his flesh is not everywhere. The incarnate Son of God is not confined to the location of his body. As God he continues to fill all things. Christ's incarnation was an 'addition rather than subtraction', writes Derek Thomas (*A Theological Guide to Calvin's Institutes*, 214).

The Heidelberg Catechism expresses Calvin's teaching in questions 46 through 48.

Q. 46. How do you understand the words: 'He ascended into heaven'?

A. That Christ was taken up from the earth into heaven before the eyes of his disciples and remains there on our behalf until he comes again to judge the living and the dead.

Q. 47. Then, is not Christ with us unto the end of the world, as he promised us?

A. Christ is true man and true God. As a man he is no longer on earth, but in his divinity, majesty, grace, and Spirit, he is never absent from us.

Q. 48. But are not the two natures in Christ separated from each other in this way, if the humanity is not wherever the divinity is?

A. Not at all; for since divinity is incomprehensible and everywhere present, it must follow that the divinity is indeed beyond the bounds of the humanity which it has assumed, and is nonetheless ever in that humanity as well, and remains personally united to it.

Lutherans argued that Calvin's teaching on this point was novel, but in fact it is supported throughout church history. Athanasius eloquently wrote that 'the Word was not hedged in by his body, nor did his presence in the body prevent his being present elsewhere as well. When he moved his body he did not cease also to direct the universe by his mind and might. The marvellous truth is, that being the Word, so far from being himself contained by anything, he actually contained all things himself' (*On the Incarnation of the Word* 3:17).

> A great and mighty wonder.
> A full and holy cure:
> The virgin bears the infant
> With virgin honour pure.
>
> The Word becomes incarnate
> And yet remains on high,
> And cherubim sing anthems
> To shepherds from the sky.
>
> St Germanus

The eternal Son of God became 'flesh of our flesh' and so as man was limited to one place—in the land of Israel during his earthly life, and in heaven at the Father's right hand after his ascension. At the same time he continues to be the omnipresent God. The Son of God did not surrender anything proper to himself as God, but rather 'allowed his divinity to be hidden by "a veil of flesh"' (II.13.2). Bruce McCormack writes: 'Karl Barth's interpretation of the *kenosis* in terms of a laying aside of "recognizability" and an entrance into a kind of "incognito" is wholly apt for describing Calvin's view. God "manifest in the flesh"; that is the heartbeat of Calvin's thought' (*For Us And Our Salvation*, 7).

Christ is one person in two natures.

Christ 'who was the Son of God became the Son of Man not by confusion of substance, but by unity of person' (II.14.1). In Christ the divinity and the humanity 'each retains its distinctive nature unimpaired' (II.14.1). The eternal God took on human nature, but the human nature and the divine nature remained separate. He is both God and man in one person. He is not a 'God-man' in the sense of a third thing—neither God nor man. He is both fully God and fully human. And yet he is one person.

Lutherans hold that there is an exchange of the divine and human attributes in Christ—especially a sharing by the human nature of the attributes of the divine nature, including the divine attribute of omnipresence. (This is an important part, as we will see, of the Lutheran doctrine of the Lord's supper.) For Calvin the 'communication of the attributes' is a hermeneutical device for interpreting what the Bible says about Christ.

- Scripture sometimes attributes to Christ what must be referred solely to his humanity; for example, he 'increased in age and wisdom' (Luke 2:52). Such human attributes are properly applied to Christ because he is true man.

- Scripture sometimes attributes to Christ what must be referred solely to his divinity, for example, his statement that 'before Abraham was I am' (John 8:58). Divine qualities are properly applied to Christ because he is true God.

- Sometimes Scripture describes what embraces both natures but fits neither alone, for example 'those things which apply to the office of the mediator', such as the fact that Christ is the light of the world and that he forgives sin. These passages, says Calvin, 'set forth his true substance most clearly of all' (II.14.3). Divine and human characteristics are properly assigned to Christ because he is both God and man.

- Scripture sometimes attributes to Christ's divinity what more properly belongs to his humanity and vice versa, for example, 'God purchased the church with his own blood' (Acts 20:28). By this 'communicating of characteristics', as it is called, 'the things that [Christ] carried out in his human nature are transferred improperly, although not without reason, to his divinity' (II.14.2). The attribute of one nature ('blood') is affirmed of the person (the man Jesus Christ) who is named by his other nature (God). For Calvin this is a verbal matter, not an actual ontological transfer of attributes. Divine attributes do not cross over and become human or vice versa in the person of Christ. There is no 'confusion of substance'.

The Son of God became the Son of man 'by unity of person' (II.14.1). The two natures remain distinct but do not constitute two persons. The 'two natures constitute one Christ' (II.14.1). Calvin offers several illustrations, something he refuses to do with the doctrine of the Trinity. Human beings possess a body and a soul. Each retains its own distinctive nature, yet there is one man (II.14.1). Calvin compares the two natures of Christ to the two eyes of a person. 'Each eye can have its vision separately; but when we are looking at anything … our vision, which in itself is divided, joins up and unites in order to give itself as a whole to the object that is put before it' (Comm. 1 Tim. 3:16).

Knowing God and ourselves

The hymn 'I greet thee, who my sure Redeemer art' has long been connected with John Calvin. It appeared in the 1545 Strasbourg Psalter and again in the Genevan Psalter of 1551. While it is by no means certain that Calvin wrote the hymn, it beautifully expresses his theology and spirit. Read it, and meditate on it in the light of chapters 12-14 of Book II of the *Institutes*.

I greet thee, who my sure Redeemer art,
   My only trust and Saviour of my heart,
Who pain didst undergo for my poor sake:
   I pray thee from our hearts all cares to take.

Thou art the King of mercy and of grace,
   Reigning omnipotent in every place:
So come, O King, and our whole being sway;
   Shine on us with the light of thy pure day.

Thou art the Life, by which alone we live,
   And all our substance and our strength receive;
O comfort us in death's approaching hour,
   Strong-hearted then to face it by thy power.

Thou hast the true and perfect gentleness,
   No harshness hast thou, and no bitterness;
O grant to us the grace we find in thee,
   That we may dwell in perfect unity.

Our hope is in no other save in thee;
   Our faith is built upon thy promise free;
Come, give us peace, make us so strong and sure,
   That we may conquerors be, and ills endure.

Strasbourg Psalter, 1545:
tr. by Elizabeth Lee Smith, altd.

11. The Work of Christ— 'Prophet, King, Priest'

'In order that faith may find a firm basis for salvation in Christ, and thus rest in him, this principle must be laid down: the office enjoined upon Christ by the Father consists of three parts. For he was given to be *prophet, king, and priest*' (II.15.1).

'We cannot talk about atonement, God's law, righteousness, election, God's mercy, or the out-pouring of the Spirit without in the same breath mentioning Christ, for all of these are enacted, manifest, and understood in and through his threefold office' (Edmondson, *Calvin's Christology*, 174).

Read: *Institutes* II.15-17. [*1541* ch.4, pp.233-257.]

Scripture Text: 'And there is salvation in no one else, for there is no other name under heaven given among men by which we must be saved' (Acts 4:12).

Notable Quote: 'Thus you see how the promises, the sacraments, and all that we ever have must be ratified by Jesus Christ. In short, (if I may make a human comparison and speak in a homely manner) he is the true sauce to give flavour to all things belonging to our salvation' (Sermon on Eph. 2:11-13).

Prayer

O Lord, you are our Creator, and we are the work of your hands. You are our Shepherd, we are your flock. You are our Redeemer, we are the people you have bought back. You are our God, we are your inheritance.

Therefore, be not angry against us, to correct us in your wrath. Recall not our iniquity to punish it, but chastise us gently in your kindliness. Be mindful that your name is called upon among us and that we bear your mark and badge.

Undertake rather the work you have already begun in us by your grace, in order that the whole earth may recognize that you are our God and our Saviour. Amen.

(*Piety of John Calvin*, 126.)

A look back and a look ahead

In Book II.12-17 John Calvin treats the person of Christ—who he is—and then moves to the work of Christ—what he has done. In his commentary on John 1:49, Calvin writes, 'And indeed, faith ought not to be fixed on the essence of Christ alone (so to speak), but ought to attend to his power and office, for it would be of little advantage to know who Christ is, if this second point were not added, what he wishes to be toward us, and for what purpose the Father sent him.' Calvin now treats the work of Christ under his threefold office of prophet, king, and priest. In the Old Testament, prophets, kings, and priests were inducted into office by anointing with holy oil, foreshadowing Christ the Messiah, the anointed one.

Prophet

Christ as prophet was anointed by the Spirit 'to be herald and witness of the Father's grace' (II.15.2). He was God's 'ambassador and interpreter' (Comm. John 3:32). He was the 'faithful expounder' of the Old Testament law so 'that we may know what is the nature of the law, what is its object, and what is its extent' (Comm. Matt. 5:21). 'The perfect doctrine [Christ] has brought has made an end to all prophecies' (II.15.2). After Christ no more revelation is needed.

Christ continues to teach through his servants, for he received the anointing as prophet 'not only for himself that he might carry out the office of teaching, but for his whole body that the power of the Spirit might be present in the continuing preaching of the gospel' (II.15.2). Calvin explains in his commentary on Matthew 28:20 that Christ's ministers 'cannot put forward whatever they may think but must themselves depend solely on the mouth of one teacher'.

King

Christ was anointed king that he might be 'the eternal protector and defender of his church' (II.15.3). Christ is ruling as king now, protecting believers and judging the wicked. His judgment is not always evident in history, but points to a fuller and more complete judgment when the 'full proof' of his rule will appear (II.15.5). Divine judgments fall often enough in this world to let us know that God judges, but seldom enough to let us know that there is a final judgment to come.

Christ's protection of believers appears inadequate and at times totally absent, but we must remember, says Calvin, that 'the happiness promised us in Christ does not consist in outward advantages' (II.15.4). Christ is no less our king when we suffer than when we prosper. 'Thus it is that we may patiently pass through this life with its misery, hunger, cold, contempt, reproaches, and other troubles—content with this one thing: that our king will never leave us destitute, but will provide for our needs until, our warfare ended, we are called to triumph' (II.15.4). By faith the dying thief on the cross saw beyond the darkness of the hour and the apparent weakness of the man on the central cross. 'What marks, what tokens adorned Christ as he saw him, that should raise his mind to kingship? Indeed it was to step from the depths of hell to the heights of heaven' (Comm. Luke 23:42).

Priest

Calvin places Christ's priestly office at the end of II.15 so that it might lead directly to his treatment of Christ as our Redeemer in II.16. Christ is the unique priest because, unlike the Old Testament priests who offered sacrifices, he is 'both priest and sacrifice' (II.15.6). Only Christ was worthy 'to make the offering and to be the offering that brings reconciliation' (Partee, *The Theology of John Calvin*, 165). As our priest, by his sacrifice he blots out our guilt and reconciles us to God, and by his intercession we obtain favour in God's sight (II.15.6). In his commentary on Matthew 27:12, Calvin writes that before Pilate Christ 'kept silence, to be our spokesman now, and by his pleading to free us of our guilt'.

Christ is priest, not only to render the Father favourable toward us but 'also to receive us as his companions in his great office' (II.15.6). As Christians we are priests, sharing the good news of what Christ has done for us, and praying for others as Christ continually intercedes for us.

John R. Mackay, an esteemed minister of the Free Church of Scotland, once said that it seemed as he looked into his own heart he could see only darkness, guilt and pride. 'But then', said he, 'I remembered that Christ is a prophet who can dispel my darkness, Christ is a priest who can remove my guilt, Christ is a king who can humble my pride. And I said it were good that Christ and I should meet' (William Childs Robinson, *The Southern Presbyterian Journal*, March 1944, 9).

Redeemer

All that Calvin has written this far in Book II about 'God the Redeemer in Christ'—his presence in the Old and New Testament (II.6-11), his person (II.12-14), and his work (II.15)—anticipates and leads to Christ as Redeemer. 'What we have said so far concerning Christ must be referred to this one objective: condemned, dead, and lost in ourselves, we should seek righteousness, liberation, life, and salvation in him' (II.16.1).

In II.16 Calvin treats the second article of the Apostles' Creed.

'I believe in Jesus Christ, his only Son, our Lord, who was conceived by the Holy Spirit, and born of the Virgin Mary.'

Calvin has already discussed this in II.13.3-4.

'He suffered under Pontius Pilate, was crucified, died, and was buried.'

Calvin notes that the creed moves directly from the birth of Christ to his suffering and death. Although Christ's life is not mentioned in the creed, it is of great importance. 'From the time when he took on the form of a servant, he began to pay the price of liberation in order to redeem us' (II.16.5).

Not one but two verdicts were given at the trial of Jesus. One was 'guilty'. Christ 'allowed himself to be condemned before a mortal man' because he willed to deliver us from the penalty to which we were subject as sinners. 'He took the role of a guilty man and evildoer' (II.16.5). The other verdict was 'innocent'. 'From his shining innocence' it was obvious that Christ 'was burdened with another's sin rather than his own' (II.16.5). When Christ was crucified, he made himself subject to the 'shame' of the cross, and at the same time changed it into a 'triumphal chariot' (II.16.6).

'He descended into hell.'

These words are a late addition to the Apostles' Creed, but, according to Calvin, they state 'a matter of no small moment in bringing about redemption' (II.16.8). Calvin did not accept the traditional interpretation that Christ between his death and resurrection literally descended to the world of the dead, where he preached repentance, rescued prisoners, and triumphed over Satan. Rather Calvin interprets the phrase as a reference to Christ's redemptive agony on the cross. It describes 'that invisible and incomprehensible judgment which he underwent in the sight of God' (II.16.10), 'a harsher and more difficult struggle than with common death' (II.16.12). The traditional view links the death of Christ and the descent into hell chronologically. Having won the victory on the cross, Christ then went on a journey of triumph through the underworld. Calvin sees the 'descent into hell' as the spiritual victory over sin that Christ won on the cross. His view is stated succinctly in the Geneva Catechism.

> Q. As for what immediately follows, that he descended into hell, what does this mean?
>
> A. That he endured not only common death, which is the separation of the soul from the body; but also the pains of death, as Peter calls them (Acts 2:24). By this word I understand the fearful agonies with which his soul was tormented.
>
> Q. Tell me the cause and manner of this.
>
> A. Because, in order to make satisfaction for sinners, he arraigned himself before the tribunal of God, it was requisite that his conscience be tormented by such agony as if he were forsaken by God, even as if he had God hostile to him.

> Many hands were raised to wound him,
> None would interpose to save;
> But the deepest stroke that pierced him
> Was the stroke that Justice gave.
>
> Thomas Kelly

'The Father never stopped loving his beloved Son, but for a time abandoned him who stood in our place as a criminal and condemned man' (Peterson, *A Theological Guide to Calvin's Institutes*, 235).

'The third day he rose again from the dead.'

The redemptive work of Christ did not end with his death on the cross. Our restoration to life is completed by his resurrection. In his resurrection, Christ 'displayed his heavenly power, which is both the clear mirror of his divinity and the firm support of our faith'. We are 'reborn into righteousness through his power', and are 'assured of our own resurrection' (II.16.13).

'He ascended into heaven and is seated at the right hand of God the Father Almighty. From there he will come to judge the living and the dead.'

'Christ did not ascend to heaven in a private capacity' (Comm. John 14:2). He 'has entered into heaven and he bears us there' (Sermon on Acts 1:6-8). The believer is united to Christ and so experiences ahead of time the joys of heaven. In his ascension Christ did not abandon us but 'he left us in such a way that his presence might be more useful to us' (II.16.14). Just as the incarnation did not remove Christ from heaven, so the ascension did not remove him from earth. He 'is not here … yet he is here' (II.16.14).

At the Father's right hand, Christ is 'invested with lordship over heaven and earth' (II.16.15). Someday he will 'appear to all with the ineffable majesty of his kingdom' (II.16.17). And then as king he shall judge all people. Christians do not fear this judgment because they know that their judge is their Redeemer.

In II.17, John Calvin deals with the question: How can we talk about merit, even the merit of Christ, and grace at the same time? Does not one cancel the other? Calvin's simple answer to this question is that 'it is absurd to set Christ's merit against God's mercy. For it is a common rule that a thing subordinate to another is not in conflict with it' (II.17.1). The Son 'ungrudgingly … took our nature' (II.12.2) but it was the Father's mercy that made Christ's action possible (II.16.2-4). As the Son gladly came, so the Father freely sent. The incarnation reflects the mercy and love of both the Father and the Son. In no other way could God express so wonderfully and powerfully his great love for lost humanity than by the incarnation of the Son and his atoning death in our place.

Salvation is because of God's mercy alone, but 'by his obedience … Christ truly acquired and merited grace for us with his Father' (II.17.3). God chose to save us by grace on the basis of Christ's merit. The motivation, one might say, was grace; the means was merit, but Christ's merit, not ours. Christ merited our salvation, only because God willed it. 'Jesus Christ was unable to merit anything but by God's good pleasure' (II.17.1). The merit of Christ's death depended on the value God chose to assign to it. Without God's grace, there would have been no Redeemer. Without the Redeemer's merit, there would have been no redemption. Salvation is by grace alone through the merit of Christ alone and received by faith alone. The grace and mercy of God are the effective ground of the atonement, not the effect of the atonement. 'Indeed, "because he first loved us", he afterward reconciles us to himself' (II.16.3). B. A. Gerrish writes that for Calvin 'the incarnation was not the first manifestation of his fatherly love, but the pledge of it' (*Grace and Gratitude*, 60). God does not love us because Christ died for us; Christ died for us because God loves us. We place Christ before our eyes and behold 'in him the heart of God poured out in love' (Comm. John 3:16).

The question of God's anger at sinners was addressed briefly at the beginning of Book II, 'How could God, who is pleased by the least of his works, have been hostile to the noblest of all his creatures? But he is hostile toward the corruption of his work rather than toward the work itself' (II.1.11). Calvin returns to this matter in II.15 and II.16. We are estranged from God, and under a curse, so that 'God in his capacity as judge is angry toward us' (II.15.6). In all our sin, however, we 'remain [God's] creatures', whom he has created 'unto life' (II.16.3). Calvin quotes Augustine that God 'loved us even when he hated us. For he hated us for what we were that he had not made; yet because our wickedness had not entirely consumed his handiwork, he knew how, at the same time, to hate in each one of us what we had made, and to love what he had made' (II.16.4).

Biblical expressions about God's wrath 'have been accommodated to our capacity', Calvin says, 'that we may better understand how miserable and ruinous our condition is apart from Christ' (II.16.2). The Bible speaks of God's wrath in order that we might comprehend 'both the full despair of sin and the wonder of Christ's grace' (Stroup, *Calvin*, 40).

Calvin writes that Paul sets forth two ways in which we are loved by God:

> First, because the Father chose us in [Christ] before the creation of the world (Eph. 1:4), and, secondly, because in Christ God hath reconciled us to himself, and hath showed that he is gracious to us (Rom. 5:10). Thus we are at the same time the enemies and friends of God, until, atonement having been made for our sins, we are restored to favour with God. But, when we are justified by faith, it is then, properly, that we begin to be loved by God, as children by a father (Comm. John 17:23).

Calvin presents a 'penal substitutionary' view of the atonement, that is, Christ died to pay the penalty for our sins. He 'bore in his soul the tortures of condemned and ruined man' (II.16.10). 'The chief thing to consider in his death is his expiation, by which he appeased the wrath and curse of God. But he could not have done that without transferring to himself our guilt' (Comm. John 12:23). Edmondson writes: 'When Christ takes our punishment, we are moved both by what he has taken on himself and by what he has taken from us'—God's wrath and our fear—'and thereby we are brought to entrust our lives to him ... We, then, are doubly affected by Christ's substitution for us, relieved of a burden and touched by his love, and this moves us to faith through an awakening to grace ... It is from the objective efficacy of Christ's atoning death that its subjective power to move believers arises' (*Calvin's Christology*, 105, 107).

> Alas! and did my Saviour bleed,
>   And did my Sovereign die!
> Would he devote that sacred head
>   For such a worm as I!
>
> Was it for crimes that I had done
>   He groaned upon the tree!
> Amazing pity! Grace unknown!
>   And love beyond degree!
>
>   Isaac Watts

Robert Peterson finds six pictures of the atonement in Calvin: Christ—the obedient second Adam, the victor, our legal substitute, our sacrifice, our merit, and our example (*A Theological Guide to Calvin's Institutes*, 245). Whatever we needed as sinners, the death of the Redeemer provided. 'If the death of Christ be our redemption, then we were captives; if it be satisfaction, we were debtors; if it be atonement, we were guilty; if it be cleansing, we were unclean' (Comm. Gal. 2:21). 'It was his task to swallow up death. Who but life could do this? It was his task to conquer sin. Who but very righteousness could do this? It was his task to rout the powers of world and air. Who but a power higher than world and air could do this?' (II.12.2) 'For in the cross of Christ, as in a splendid theatre, the incomparable goodness of God is set before the whole world. The glory of God shines, indeed, in all creatures on high and below, but never more brightly than in the cross, in which there is a wonderful change of things—the condemnation of all men was manifested, sin blotted out, salvation restored to men; in short, the whole world was renewed and all things restored to order' (Comm. John. 13:31).

Knowing God and ourselves

'Christ was offered to the Father in death as an expiatory sacrifice, that when he discharged all satisfaction through his sacrifice, we might cease to be afraid of God's wrath.' The transference of guilt from us to Christ constitutes our acquittal and the impact of that forgiveness changes our lives forever. 'We must, above all, remember this substitution, lest we tremble and remain anxious throughout life—as if God's righteous vengeance, which the Son of God has taken upon himself, still hung over us' (II.16.5). Every day of our lives, including and especially the day of judgment, we can rest in the assurance that Jesus paid it all. Samuel Rutherford wrote to a friend, 'Oh, that you and I might meet with joy up in the rainbow, when we shall stand before our Judge.' The rainbow, symbolizing God's mercy and grace, will be around his throne, when we stand before our Judge in heaven (Rev. 4:3).

12. The Holy Spirit—
'The Bond'

'The Holy Spirit is *the bond* by which Christ effectually unites us to himself' (III.1.1).

'The doctrine of the work of the Holy Spirit is a gift from John Calvin to the church of Christ. He did not, of course, invent it ... but it was Calvin who first gave [it] anything like systematic or adequate expression' (Warfield, *Selected Shorter Writings* 1:212-13).

Read: *Institutes* III.1 [*1541* ch.4, pp.257-258.]

Scripture Text: 'For all who are led by the Spirit of God are sons of God' (Rom. 8:14).

Notable Quote: 'It is God's Holy Spirit who puts us in possession of the gospel and of all the benefits it contains, and who supports us in them to the end' (Sermon on Eph. 1:13-14).

Prayer

We call upon our heavenly Father, Father of all goodness and mercy, asking him to cast the eye of his mercy on us his poor servants, not imputing to us the many faults and offenses we have committed, by which we have provoked his wrath against us, but [instead] seeing us in the face of his Son, Jesus Christ our Lord, as he has established him as mediator between him and us.

Let us pray that, as the whole plenitude of wisdom and light is in him, he may guide us by his Holy Spirit to the true understanding of his holy teaching, and may make it bear in us all the fruits of righteousness, to the glory and honour of his name, and the instruction and edification of his church. Amen.

(John Calvin: Writings on Pastoral Piety, 112.)

❧

A look back and a look ahead

- Book I—Knowledge of God the Creator and ourselves as created

- Book II—Knowledge of ourselves as fallen and Christ the Redeemer

- Book III—Knowledge of the Holy Spirit and ourselves as redeemed

In Books I and II God is *for us* as Creator and Redeemer. Book II is about the person and work of Christ, the Redeemer, but Book II is 'useless', Calvin writes, without Book III. 'As long as Christ remains outside of us, and we are separated from him, all that he has suffered and done for the salvation of the human race remains useless and of no value for us' (III.1.1). The Holy Spirit is not mentioned in the title of Book III, but he is 'the way' we receive the 'grace of Christ'.

Book III contains chapters on the Holy Spirit, faith, sanctification, justification, prayer, election, and eschatology. T. H. L. Parker comments that 'a hasty reading' might conclude that these topics were 'a mixed bag thrown in here because they had to go somewhere. But if we pay careful attention to the "stage-directions" we shall see that there is good reason for the ordering. We might even say that the *Institutio* reaches its climax here' (*Calvin: An Introduction to His Thought*, 107). Elsie McKee suggests that Book 3 is the 'devotional center' of Calvin's thought (*John Calvin: Writings on Pastoral Piety*, 23).

Descriptions of the Holy Spirit

The person and deity of the Holy Spirit have already been presented in I.13. In III.1.3, Calvin, who loves the metaphors and images of the Bible, as did Hildegard of Bingen and other medieval mystics, collects the titles and functions of the Holy Spirit in Scripture.

> Holy Spirit,
> Giving life to all life,
> Moving all creatures,
> Root of all things,
> Washing them clean,
> Wiping out their mistakes,
> Healing their wounds,
> Our true life,
> Luminous, wonderful,
> Awakening the heart
> From its ancient sleep.
>
> Hildegard of Bingen

The Holy Spirit is called *the Spirit of adoption* 'because he is the witness to us of the free benevolence of God with which God the Father has embraced us in his beloved only-begotten Son to become a Father to us'.

The Holy Spirit is *the guarantee and seal* of our inheritance. Preaching on Ephesians 4:29-30, Calvin said that God's 'promises are always of no avail until he prints them in our hearts; this he does by his Holy Spirit. For as a letter is rendered authentic by the affixing of the seal, so God authenticates his promises of our salvation in our hearts, by signing them and sealing them there by his Holy Spirit. That then is the reason why it is so often said that God's Spirit seals the inheritance of our salvation in our hearts.'

The Holy Spirit is called *life* in Romans 8:10. 'Paul calls this Spirit of regeneration life, not only because he lives and flourishes in us, but also because he quickens us by his power.'

The Holy Spirit is called *water*, because his 'secret irrigation ... makes us bud forth and produce the fruits of righteousness'. 'We find that the prophet Isaiah says that God's Spirit is comparable to water and milk and wine, and that we are invited to come to God to take our repast' (Sermon on Eph. 5:18-21).

The Holy Spirit is called *oil* and *anointing* (in 1 John 2:20, 27), because 'he restores and nourishes unto vigour of life those on whom he has poured the stream of his grace'.

The Holy Spirit is called *fire*, because 'he enflames our hearts with the love of God and with zealous devotion'. In Luke 3:16 John the Baptist foretells that Christ 'will baptize you with the Holy Spirit and with fire'. 'The term fire is added as an epithet: it goes with the Spirit, for it can only scour off our dirt as gold is refined with fire.'

The Holy Spirit is called the *spring*, from which 'all the heavenly riches flow forth to us'. In his commentary on John 4:14 Calvin wrote that 'the Holy Spirit is a constantly flowing well … a perennial fountain that will never fail us'.

The Holy Spirit is called the *hand of God* by which 'he exercises his might'. Commenting on Acts 11:21, 'And the hand of the Lord was with them, and a great number who believed turned to the Lord', Calvin wrote: 'God was active through his ministers, and made the teaching effectual by his hand, that is, by the secret inspiration of the Spirit.'

Work of the Holy Spirit

In his commentary on Romans 8:14, Calvin describes the work of the Holy Spirit as threefold:

> The action of the Holy Spirit is varied. There is its universal action by which all creatures are sustained and moved. There are also the actions of the Spirit that are peculiar to human beings, and these too are varying in their character. But by 'Spirit' Paul, in Romans 8:14, means sanctification, with which the Lord favours none but his elect, while he sets them apart for himself as his sons.

In the first chapter of Book III, Calvin comes to the primary work of the Holy Spirit in uniting believers to Christ by faith.

'Life comes not to us from God but from God-Man. The Son of God is
the eternal source of life. But the difficulty is for that life to reach fallen
man. There is a legal difficulty which justification removes. But does
there not remain a difficulty as to the vital connexion? Must there not be
some natural tie of life between the Redeemer and his people? ... Now,
the way in which this comes about is that he takes our nature on him
and then gives us his nature, and so we become indeed one' (John B.
Adger, *The Southern Presbyterian Review*, October 1885, 787).

Union with Christ, Calvin says, is 'the sum of the gospel' (III.3.1).
J. Todd Billings writes, 'Union with Christ is theological shorthand for
the gospel itself—a key image that pulls together numerous motifs in the
biblical witness' (*Union with Christ*, 1).

Christ was not a 'private person', Calvin wrote. All that Christ is,
both God and man, and all that he did, as prophet, king, priest, was for
his people. 'As God, he is the destination to which we move; as man, the
path by which we go. Both are found in Christ alone' (III.2.1). Every
event in Jesus' life—his death, his resurrection, and his ascension—
happened so that women and men could draw from it and be made new
by it. For this to happen, Christ 'had to become ours and to dwell within
us' (III.1.1). 'That Christ should be formed in us is the same as our being
formed in Christ' (Comm. Gal. 4:19). 'That joining together of head
and members, that indwelling of Christ in our hearts—in short, that
mystical union—are accorded by us the highest degree of importance,
so that Christ, having been made ours, makes us sharers with him in the
gifts with which he has been endowed' (III.11.9).

How does Christ become ours? 'The way in which we receive the
grace of Christ' is through the Holy Spirit (III.1) working faith (III.2) in
us, and thereby uniting us with Christ our Redeemer, and indeed with
the whole Trinity. 'The Father and Spirit are in Christ, and even as the
fullness of deity dwells in him, so in him we possess the whole of deity'
(III.11.5). Christ's union with believers is a 'mystical union' (III.11.10) and
beyond our understanding (IV.17.1). In a sermon on Ephesians 3:14-19,

Calvin explains that Christ is our head and 'we live of his own substance, as a tree draws its sap from its root, and ... as the head of a man sheds forth its power through all the body, so we have a secret union, and such a one as is wonderful and far above the order of nature, because although Jesus Christ is in heaven, yet he does not cease to dwell in us.'

Knowing God and ourselves

In his commentary on Ephesians 5:32, Calvin confesses, 'I am overwhelmed by the depth of this mystery, and with Paul am not ashamed to acknowledge in wonder my ignorance. Let us therefore labour more to feel Christ living in us than to discover the nature of that communion.' Union with Christ is the priceless possession of the Christian. Let us strive to experience (feel) it continually in all our thoughts and express it by our words and actions.

> For your gift of God the Spirit,
>   Pow'r to make our lives anew,
> Pledge of life and hope of glory,
>   Saviour, we would worship you.
> Crowning gift of resurrection
>   Sent from your ascended throne,
> Fullness of the very Godhead,
>   Come to make your life our own.
>   Margaret Clarkson

13. Faith—
'A Palm Tree'

'Faith sustains the hearts of the godly and truly in its effect resembles *a palm tree*: for it strives against every burden and raises itself upward' (III.2.17).

'The first three chapters of Book III of Calvin's *Institutes* present us with the basic means [of receiving salvation]: the Holy Spirit, faith and assurance, and repentance—all working by and through the word. Calvin's exposition of how these means work in the lives of believers is Christ-centred and God-honouring as well as biblically and experimentally nuanced, clear, and profound … If these three chapters were carefully read, studied, and prayed over by Christians today, the Christian church would be freed from many errors' (Beeke, *A Theological Guide to Calvin's Institutes*, 300).

Read: *Institutes* III.2. [*1541* ch.4, pp.183-208.]

Scripture Text: 'Therefore, since we have been justified by faith, we have peace with God through our Lord Jesus Christ' (Rom. 5:1).

Notable Quote: 'Faith is a singular gift of God, both in that the mind of man is purged so as to be able to taste the truth of God, and in that his heart is established therein. For the Spirit is not only the initiator of faith, but increases it by degrees, until by it he leads us to the kingdom of heaven' (III.2.33).

Prayer

Grant, Almighty God, that since it is the principal part of our happiness that in our pilgrimage through this world there is open to us a familiar access to you by faith, O grant that we may be able to come with a pure heart into your presence. And when our lips are polluted, O purify us by your Spirit, so that we may not only pray to you with the mouth but also prove that we do this sincerely, without any dissimulation, and that we earnestly seek to spend our whole life in glorifying your name; until being at length gathered into your celestial kingdom, we may be truly and really united to you, and be made partakers of that glory, which has been brought forth for us by the blood of your only begotten Son. Amen.

(John Calvin: Writings on Pastoral Piety, 244.)

A look back and a look ahead

John Calvin begins Book III with a brief but important chapter on the Holy Spirit, added for the 1559 edition of the *Institutes*. All of Book III, not just the first chapter, is about the work of the Holy Spirit. For Calvin, salvation accomplished (Book II) and salvation applied (Book III) are both the work of God. Faith, by which we are united to Christ, is, Calvin asserts, 'the principal work of the Holy Spirit' (III.1.4).

Definition of faith

Faith is 'a firm and certain knowledge of God's benevolence toward us, founded upon the truth of the freely given promise in Christ, both revealed to our minds and sealed upon our hearts through the Holy Spirit' (III.2.7). Notice that Calvin's definition includes the Father, Son, and Holy Spirit. Calvin describes faith in four ways.

1. Faith is 'knowledge'

Faith does not rest on 'ignorance' nor in 'reverence for the church', that is, it is not what the scholastic theologians called 'implicit faith'—a pious submission to the judgment of the church. Faith, says Calvin, includes knowledge, 'the knowledge of God and Christ'. This knowledge is an 'explicit recognition of the divine goodness', although Calvin recognizes that 'most things are now implicit for us' (III.2.2). 'In these matters we can do nothing better than suspend judgment, and hearten ourselves to hold unity with the church' (III.2.3). Saving faith, however, is knowledge, 'a firm and certain knowledge', not a total knowledge, nor a common or comprehensive knowledge, but a true knowledge. 'When we call faith "knowledge" we do not mean comprehension of the sort that is commonly concerned with those things which fall under human sense perception ... Even where the mind has attained, it does not comprehend what it feels' (III.2.14). T. F. Torrance illustrates Calvin's point: 'There are acts of conception in which, as it were, we can get our fingers round something and enclose it in our grasp, but there are other acts of conception in which what we are grasping at is too big to get our fingers round, for as we grasp or conceive it, it transcends us, so that even in genuine apprehension there can not be full comprehension' (*Theological Science*, 15).

2. Faith is knowledge of 'God's benevolence toward us'

Calvin moves 'by degrees from general to particular' in his description of what faith knows (III.2.6). He begins with the word of God. 'Take away the word', he writes, 'and no faith will remain' (III.2.6). Believers embrace the word of God in its totality. 'Faith is certain that God is true in all things' (III.2.29). But faith goes on to seek a word within the word, because 'man's heart is not aroused to faith at every word of God' (III.2.7). We find that word within the word in the knowledge of 'God's benevolence toward us' (III.2.7). 'The proper goal of faith' is 'the promise of mercy' (III.2.29). 'The single goal of faith is the mercy of God—to which it ought, so to speak, to look with both eyes' (III.2.43). While faith hearkens to the different parts of God's word—and believes it all—it rests on the promise of God's mercy.

3. Faith is 'a firm and certain knowledge of God's benevolence toward us'

'There is no right faith except when we dare with tranquil hearts to stand in God's sight' (III.2.15). Calvin is describing faith as it ought to be, but he knew that the Christian's faith often falls far below full and firm faith. He knew from his own experience and from the Bible (especially the book of Psalms where we find 'griefs, sorrows, fears, doubts, hopes, cares, anxieties') that 'believers are in perpetual conflict with their own unbelief ... We cannot imagine any certainty that is not tinged with doubt, or any assurance that is not assailed by some anxiety' (III.2.17). 'The godly heart feels in itself a division because it is partly imbued with sweetness from its recognition of the divine goodness, partly grieves in bitterness from an awareness of its [own] calamity; partly rests upon the promise of the gospel, partly trembles at the evidence of its own iniquity; partly rejoices at the expectation of life, partly shudders at death' (III.2.18).

The outcome of the struggle in the Christian between faith and unbelief, however, is not itself doubtful. Calvin explains: 'Thus the godly mind, however strange the ways in which it is vexed and troubled, finally surmounts all difficulties, and never allows itself to be deprived of assurance of divine mercy.' He illustrates: 'When, therefore, faith is shaken it is like a strong soldier forced by the violent blow of a spear to move his foot and give ground a little. When faith itself is wounded it is as if the soldier's shield were broken at some point from the thrust of the spear, but not in such a manner as to be pierced' (III.2.21). In a sermon, Calvin asked, 'How could [St Paul] have such victory against so many temptations and assaults?' He answered, 'It was by knowing that God was the keeper of his soul … He knew that God so worked in him that he would never fall except upon his feet (as men say)' (Sermon on Eph. 3:20-4:2). Calvin's understanding of faith as it exists in our Christian experience is a sure knowledge of God's love for us in Christ, a knowledge which is invariably attacked by doubts and fears, and over which it finally emerges victorious.

Does faith then include assurance? Yes, says Calvin, true faith is 'a firm and certain knowledge of God's benevolence toward us'. This assurance applies not only to the present but also to a 'future immortality' (III.2.40). We know that God loves us now, and that he will love us always. What is the basis of this assurance? It does not rest on 'moral conjecture' (III.2.38), that is, on our good works as Christians. Good works do have a kind of secondary role to play in assurance. They are 'an accessory or inferior aid' (III.14.9) and 'a prop of the second order' (III.14.16). The foundation of assurance is not our works but God's love for us in Christ. Our works have a secondary role of confirmation; but assurance, like salvation itself, is based on grace, not on works. Calvin will let us glance at our works, but he will not allow us to gaze at them. He quickly turns our eyes to Christ. Our self-examination, according to Calvin, is not to be so much 'Am I *trusting* in Christ?' but 'Am I trusting in *Christ*?'

'As John Welch, John Knox's son-in-law, taught, it is not the measure of faith that saves us, but the blood of Christ it holds to that saves—the grasp of faith is itself held in the mighty grasp of Christ. "It is not the measure of faith that saves us, but the strength of Christ's hold upon us" as is revealed in the covenant of grace which is "all of condescension and all of love", a covenant which is sealed and extended to us in baptism. Here Welch likens faith to the weak fingers of little children who are unable to "grip and fathom" the purse of gold which their father holds out to them. It is Christ the object of faith who holds on to us and saves us even when our faith is so weak. The Christ in whom we believe far exceeds the small measure of our faith, and so the believer finds his security not in his poor believing grasp of Christ but in the gift of grace that exceeds his expectations and his capacity to grasp it' (Torrance, *Scottish Theology*, 58).

Do scriptural passages about 'transitory faith' undermine our assurance? If it is possible to have a kind of faith that approaches real faith but which will not last, how can anyone know that his or her faith is real? Calvin states that there is a self-deluding 'faith', which is similar to, but not the same as, the faith of the elect. Calvin describes the transitory faith of Simon as 'some middle position between faith and mere pretence'. 'Mere pretence' is 'gross hypocrisy', in which people profess to believe but because they don't they are 'laughing inwardly'. The middle position describes those who really think that they believe. Theirs is an 'inward', but not 'gross', hypocrisy (Comm. Acts 8:13). People come to this place, according to Calvin, through a process of self-deception. Self-deception is a real possibility, and so self-examination is essential. 'The faithful are taught to examine themselves with solicitude and humility, lest carnal security insinuate itself, instead of the assurance of faith' (III.2.7). Descriptions of transitory faith are in the Bible, Calvin maintains, as a warning and therefore a means God uses in perseverance of the elect.

There are two ways in which transitory faith differs from saving faith: in its strength ('only in the elect does that confidence flourish … that they loudly proclaim, Abba, Father') and in its duration ('the seed of life sown in their hearts may never perish') (III.2.11). Calvin provides a wonderful illustration. In the midst of great assaults against faith, it 'sustains the hearts of the godly and truly in its effect resembles a palm tree: for it strives against every burden and raises itself upward' (III.2.17).

> Chapter 2 of Book III of the *Institutes* 'is one of the greatest chapters ever written on the relationship of faith and assurance, and perhaps one of the greatest in the entire field of soteriology' (Beeke, *A Theological Guide to Calvin's Institutes*, 300).

4. Faith is 'a firm and certain knowledge of God's benevolence toward us revealed to our minds and sealed upon our hearts through the Holy Spirit'

Faith is knowing that God loves us whatever comes. But this knowledge 'is more of the heart than of the brain. It is more of the disposition than of the understanding' (III.2.8). It is best described as 'assurance' (III.2.8), or 'recognition' (III.2.14), or 'persuasion' (III.2.14). Here we come to Calvin's principal point in his definition of faith. Faith is 'the principal work of the Holy Spirit' (III.1.4). It is 'a singular gift of God' (III.2.33). It is not a meritorious condition of salvation, although it can be spoken of as 'the instrumental cause of salvation' (III.11.7). Salvation is not *because of* faith, but it is *by* faith. Faith is our response to the gift of God. Calvin quotes Augustine, who said that 'our Saviour, to teach us that belief comes as a gift and not from merit, says: "No one comes to me, unless my Father … draw him"' (III.2.35). Faith then is receiving, not doing. It is God's work before it is our response.

'More strongly than the other reformers Calvin stresses the purely other-sided basis and content of faith. Faith does not come from us, not even as the recognition of our need. Even when we believe, and precisely when we believe, we have nothing good in us; our treasure is in Christ in heaven. It is the nature of faith to pierce the ears, close the eyes, wait upon the promise, and turn aside from all thoughts of human worth or merit' (Barth, *The Theology of John Calvin*, 168).

Knowing God and ourselves

Calvin writes that John 10:28, 'I give [my sheep] eternal life, and they will never perish, and no one will snatch them out of my hand', 'is a remarkable passage, teaching us that the salvation of all the elect is as certain as God's power is invincible'.

> Blessed assurance, Jesus is mine!
> O what a foretaste of glory divine!
> Heir of salvation, purchase of God,
> Born of his Spirit, washed in his blood.
>
> Fanny J. Crosby

What a tribute to the excellence of faith that by it the Son of God is made ours and makes his home in us! By faith we do not only acknowledge that Christ suffered for us and was raised from death for us; we also receive him as he offers himself to us, to be possessed and enjoyed. This should be noted carefully. Most people regard partaking of Christ and believing in Christ as the same thing. But our partaking of Christ is rather the effect of believing. In short, Christ is not to be looked at by faith from a distance, but so received by the embrace of our souls as to dwell in us (Comm. Eph. 3:17).

Are you looking at Christ 'from a distance'? Come closer and enjoy what is yours.

14. Repentance—
'A Race'

'The closer any man comes to the likeness of God, the more the image of God shines in him. In order that believers may reach this goal, God assigns to them *a race* of repentance, which they are to run throughout their lives' (III.3.9).

Calvin, like Luther, 'taught repentance as the basic form of every Christian's life and not just as occasional emergency measure for the sinner. The first of Luther's Ninety-Five Theses of 1517 reads: "When our Lord and Master Jesus Christ said, Repent [Matt. 4:17], he willed the entire life of the faithful to be one of repentance"' (Oberman, *Luther*, 164).

Read: *Institutes* III.3-5. [*1541* ch.5, pp.295-349.]

Scripture Text: 'God exalted him at his right hand as Leader and Saviour, to give repentance to Israel and forgiveness of sins' (Acts 5:31).

Notable Quote: 'Since it is the Lord who forgives, forgets, and wipes out, sins, let us confess our sins to him in order to obtain pardon. He is the physician; therefore, let us lay bare our wounds to him. It is he who is hurt and offended; from him let us seek peace. He is the discerner of hearts, the one cognizant of all thoughts; let us hasten to pour out our hearts before him. He it is, finally, who calls sinners: let us not delay to come to God himself' (III.4.9).

Prayer

We bow ourselves before the majesty of our good God, in recognition of our faults, praying that he may make us so to feel them that it may draw us to true repentance, so that we may not seek anything except to serve and honour him in his Son our Lord Jesus Christ. May he be pleased to bear with our weaknesses and pardon us for the many vices which still remain, until he has completely purged us of them. May he continue this grace until at last he may receive us to himself and bring us fully to that [heavenly] place. Amen.

(*John Calvin: Writings on Pastoral Piety*, 126.)

A look back and a look ahead

We are united to Christ by the work of the Holy Spirit's creating faith in us. We now come to the blessings that are ours as a result of God's work for us and in us. Calvin treats these blessings in the rest of Book III. This is 'not a list or a sequence, but the full panorama of a landscape. It is a portrait, a description of what the Spirit's transforming grace in Jesus Christ looks like' (Stroup, *Calvin*, 44).

The two-fold grace

'The whole of the gospel is contained under these two headings, repentance and forgiveness of sins' (III.3.19) or, as Calvin describes them later, 'salvation and eternal blessedness' (IV.1.1). By forgiveness of sins and salvation Calvin means justification. By repentance and eternal blessedness Calvin means sanctification. Michael Horton aptly sums up Calvin's teaching: 'United to Christ by faith, we receive the imputation of Christ's righteousness for justification and the impartation of Christ's righteousness for sanctification' (*Calvin on the Christian Life*, 102).

It is surprising that Calvin treats sanctification (repentance) before justification (forgiveness of sins). He explains why: 'Now, both repentance and forgiveness of sins—that is, newness of life and free reconciliation—are conferred on us by Christ, and both are attained by us through faith. As a consequence, reason and the order of teaching demand that I begin to discuss both at this point. However, our immediate transition will be from faith to repentance' (III.3.1). This is not a logical or a theological order, but rather a 'teaching' order. In this way Calvin emphasizes against the Catholics that salvation by faith alone does not lead to a denial of a holy life. Also he warns fellow Protestants that they cannot accept justification by faith alone without embracing at the same time and with equal eagerness the necessity of good works. When he comes to justification in III.11, Calvin explains that justification has been 'more lightly touched upon' in III.3-10, 'because it was more to the point to understand first how little devoid of good works is the faith, through which alone we obtain free righteousness by the mercy of God; and what is the nature of the good works of the saints' (III.11.1).

> 'We might regard it as established beyond any doubt that, as distinct from Luther, Calvin must be called the theologian of sanctification. Sometimes it is said that Lutherans shout "Justification!" and whisper "Sanctification!" If so, Calvin is distinct from Luther in his strong doctrinal emphasis in living the holy life to the glory of God' (Partee, *The Theology of John Calvin*, 213).

Definition of repentance

Repentance is Calvin's favourite word for the whole process by which a sinner turns to God and progresses in holiness. For Calvin, it is not merely the start of the Christian life; it is the Christian life. Sanctification, while it is a progressive life-long work in us and by us, also has a definitive aspect. Our ongoing death to sin and resurrection to life results from our once-for-all union with Christ. Calvin states that even though faith and repentance 'cannot be separated, they ought to be distinguished' (III.3.5). Repentance follows faith: it is 'born of faith' (III.3.1); it cannot stand 'apart from faith' (III.3.5).

According to Calvin, repentance is 'the true turning of our life to God, a turning that arises from a pure and earnest fear of him, and it consists in the mortification of our flesh and of the old man, and in the vivification of the Spirit' (III.3.5).

1. Repentance is a true turning

Repentance 'arises from a pure and earnest fear of [God]'. There is a 'repentance of the law' that comes from a fear and dread of God's judgment, but this is not a 'true turning'. It describes the 'repentance' of Cain, Saul, and Judas, which was 'nothing but a sort of entryway of hell'. The 'repentance of the gospel'—the repentance of Hezekiah, the people of Nineveh, David, Peter, and the people at Pentecost—is a 'true turning' (III.3.4). It does include fear of judgment, which awakens us to repentance. 'It would be vain', Calvin writes, 'for [God] gently to allure those who are asleep' (III.3.7). But it includes much more than fear of judgment. True repentance, or 'the sorrow according to God' (2 Cor. 7:10), comes 'when we not only abhor punishment but hate and abominate sin itself, because we know that it displeases God' (III.3.7).

Repentance is a turning 'not only in outward works, but in the soul itself' (III.3.6). We 'must cleanse away secret filth in order that an altar may be erected to God in the heart itself' (III.3.16). Repentance is intensive, it reaches deep, and it is also extensive, it reaches far. Calvin says that Isaiah speaks of those 'who were actively striving after outward repentance in ceremonies while they made no effort to undo the burden of injustice with which they bound the poor' (III.3.6).

Repentance extends outwardly to one's conduct and inwardly to one's inmost soul, and it continues throughout one's entire life. God assigns to believers 'a race of repentance, which they are to run throughout their lives' (III.3.9). Calvin criticized both the Anabaptists and the Jesuits for limiting 'to a paltry few days a repentance that for the Christian ... ought to extend throughout his life' (III.3.2). Preaching on Ephesians 1:13-14, Calvin said, 'We must endure patiently, because God will not have us come to his kingdom with, so to speak, one leap, but will have us negotiate this world through thorns and briars.'

> 'The Christian life is, as John Bunyan later described it in *Pilgrim's Progress*, a series of episodes of falling down and being lifted up, or of getting off the track and getting back on track' (Charry, *By the Renewing of Your Minds*, 218).

2. Repentance consists of two parts: 'the mortification of our flesh' and 'the vivification of the Spirit'

Mortification is expressed clearly, although 'simply and rudely' in keeping with our human capacity, in the words of Scripture: 'Cease to do evil' (III.3.8). By Christ's death, our 'old man' is crucified. Our dying to sin and self is not something we do of ourselves. It is the work of God in us, whereby he makes effective in our lives the chief fact of our existence—namely, that we were put to death with Christ upon the cross of Calvary.

Therefore, we must 'deny our own nature' (III.3.8). This is not a denial of our true humanity but of our sinful corruption. Calvin speaks of 'a two-fold mortification: the former relates to those things around us … the other is inward' (Comm. Col. 3:5). Inwardly, we die to self through the direct work of the Holy Spirit in our lives. Outwardly, we are conformed to Christ by affliction, suffering, and other providential pressures.

The Bible tells us to 'cease to do evil'; it also tells us to 'do good'. We not only die to sin, we 'live in a holy and devoted manner' (III.3.3). By Christ's resurrection, we are raised up into newness of life, and therefore put on 'the new man' (III.3.9).

What repentance is not

Having described what repentance or sanctification is, Calvin now explains what it is not.

1. Repentance is not perfectionism

'Certain Anabaptists', according to Calvin, held that 'the sway of sin is abolished' in believers (III.3.11). Calvin answers that when we become Christians, sin no longer reigns over us, but it does remain in us. In the regenerate person there is 'a smoldering cinder of evil', or 'a fountain of evil, continually producing desires which allure and stimulate' us to sin (III.3.10). Calvin does not mean 'those inclinations which God so engraved upon the character of man at his first creation', but 'only those bold and unbridled impulses which contend against God's control' in redeemed people (III.3.12). Calvin called these impulses sin. It is sin 'when a man is tickled by any desire at all against the law of God'. In fact, according to Calvin, sin is 'that very depravity which begets in us desires of this sort' (III.3.10). These 'vestiges' of sin remain in us to humble us 'by the consciousness of our own weakness' (III.3.11).

Although sin remains in believers 'until they are divested of mortal bodies' (III.3.10), there is also gradual growth in righteousness. 'This restoration does not take place in one moment or one day or one year; but through continual and sometimes even slow advances, God wipes out in his elect the corruptions of the flesh' (III.3.9). Sanctification is real, but it is not complete in this life. 'Every believer fights against insurgents within and without, the remnants of a defeated foe', writes Michael Horton (*Calvin on the Christian Life*, 106). Although there is much weakness and failure on our part, 'when today outstrips yesterday the effort is not lost' (III.6.5).

2. *Repentance is not sacramentalism*

Despite his intention to deal with this topic 'in as few words as possible', Calvin spends two chapters and many pages in sharply refuting the teaching of 'the scholastic sophists' (the medieval Catholic theologians). His main objection to the sacramental system is that Catholics insist that many things are 'necessary to attain forgiveness of sins'. 'If forgiveness of sins depends upon these conditions which they attach to it, nothing is more miserable or deplorable for us' (III.4.2).

Calvin objected to the Roman Catholic requirement of confession to a priest followed by acts of penance, such as fasting, prayer, and almsgiving. To Calvin this was mere outward repentance, emphasizing 'bodily discipline', and obscured 'what ought to have been of far greater importance' (III.3.16). Calvin also criticizes the Catholic practice of penance for imposing punishments more rigid 'than the gentleness of the church would call for' (III.3.16). Penance torments the conscience because a person can never know when it has been successfully accomplished. Furthermore, it is futile, because Christ alone provides forgiveness for sins. 'There is no other satisfaction whereby offended God can be propitiated or appeased' (III.4.26).

Calvin rejects the Roman Catholic practice of indulgences, which supply what is lacking in penance, and the Roman Catholic teaching about purgatory, which cleanses the sin that is left over at death. He insists that 'the blood of Christ is the sole satisfaction for the sins of believers, the sole expiation, the sole purgation' (III.5.6). It is by faith that 'we gain forgiveness; and by love we give thanks and testify to the Lord's kindness' (III.4.37).

Included in Calvin's lengthy polemic against the Roman Catholic sacramental system are many true and helpful observations, such as the following.

- The unpardonable sin occurs when 'knowledge is linked with unbelief' (III.3.22).

- True scriptural confession is bringing our infirmities to one another 'to receive among ourselves mutual counsel, mutual compassion, and mutual consolation' (III.4.6).

- Confession is to be made before God and then among people 'as often as either divine glory or our humiliation demands it' (III.4.10).

- Private confession, whenever we feel the need of it, may be made to anyone of the church 'who seems most suitable', especially to pastors (III.4.12).

- The minister on every Lord's day should frame 'the formula of confession in his own and the people's name' and seek 'pardon from the Lord' (III.4.11).

- Ministers 'promise forgiveness of sins to all in Christ; they can proclaim damnation against all and upon all who do not embrace Christ' (III.4.21). This is what Christ means by the power of the keys (Matt. 16:19); it is not 'some power separate from the preaching of the gospel' (III.4.14). Because he cannot know everything, the 'minister of the word' absolves 'only conditionally' (III.4.18).

Knowing God and ourselves

Christ has provided full satisfaction for our sins. Therefore, 'Christ's honour [is] kept whole and undiminished' and 'consciences assured of pardon for sin may have peace with God' (III.4.27). We know God as a merciful God who loves to forgive and restore and bless. We know ourselves as redeemed but weak Christians who need to believe and repent and learn more and more to walk in newness of life. Michael Horton writes, 'We never move on from the gospel, but grow more deeply into its nourishing soil, thereby bearing the fruit of love and good works' (*Calvin on the Christian Life*, 94).

> Fountain of never-ceasing grace,
>   Thy saints' exhaustless theme,
> Great object of immortal praise,
>   Essentially supreme;
> We bless thee for the glorious fruits
>   Thine incarnation gives,
> Thy righteousness which grace imputes,
>   And faith alone receives.
>   Augustus M. Toplady

15. *The Life of the Christian— 'Example and Pattern'*

'Christ, through whom we return into favour with God, has been set before us as an *example*, whose *pattern* we ought to express in our life' (III.6.3).

'These chapters (III.6-10) form a kind of little treatise of biblical counsel that is frank about the pain of life and yet offers a moving testimony to how the devout person can appreciate God's good gifts on earth, yet especially see through the veils of the present life and be sustained with joy in the hope of the resurrection. All of it is piety in daily practice' (McKee, *John Calvin: Writings on Pastoral Piety*, 249).

Read: *Institutes* III.6-10. [*1541* ch.17, pp.785-822.]

Scripture Text: 'Then Jesus told his disciples, "If anyone would come after me, let him deny himself and take up his cross and follow me"' (Matt. 16:24).

Notable Quote: 'The knowledge of Christ … is a doctrine not of the tongue but of life. It is not apprehended by the understanding and memory alone … but it is received only when it possesses the whole soul, and finds a seat and resting place in the inmost affection of the heart' (III.6.4).

Prayer

Heavenly Father, we offer you eternal praise and thanks that you have granted so great a benefit to us poor sinners, having drawn us into the communion of your Son, Jesus Christ our Lord, whom you delivered to death for us, and whom you give us as the meat and drink of life eternal. Now grant us this other benefit: that you will never allow us to forget these things, but having them imprinted on our hearts may we grow and increase daily in our faith, which is at work in every good deed. Thus may we order and pursue all our life to the exaltation of your glory and the edification of our neighbours, through the same Jesus Christ, your Son, who in the unity of the Holy Spirit lives and reigns with you, O God, forever. Amen.

(*John Calvin: Writings on Pastoral Piety*, 134.)

A look back and a look ahead

In III.3-5 Calvin set forth the doctrine of sanctification. In III.6-10 he further develops that doctrine in practical and pastoral ways. These chapters became a classic of devotional literature and have been frequently published as a separate little book, sometimes under the title 'The Golden Booklet of the Christian Life.'

Calvin gives a brief description of the Christian life (III.6), followed by four chapters on how we can live that life—through self-denial (III.7), through cross-bearing (III.8), by meditating on the future life (III.9), and by properly using this present life (III.10). According to John T. McNeill, Calvin's treatment is 'balanced, penetrating, and practical' (*Institutes* 1:lx).

The life of the Christian

The first sentence of III.6 reads: 'The object of regeneration … is to manifest in the life of believers a harmony and agreement between God's righteousness and their obedience, and thus to confirm the adoption that they have received as sons' (III.6.1). God wants to have a family of adopted children, who bear the family likeness. It is within the security of our adoption that we strive to realize and display the identity that is already ours. Since we are God's sons and daughters, we are to behave like God's children.

Scripture provides 'a pattern for the conduct of life', so that we do not wander about 'in our zeal for righteousness' (III.6.1). The 'pattern' is given in the law (as we saw in Book II), but here Calvin puts before us the example of Jesus, who perfectly kept the law. We have been adopted as God's children 'with this one condition: that our life express Christ, the bond of our adoption'. Calvin makes it clear that our union with Christ comes before, and enables, our following Christ. Michael Horton suggests 'by way of analogy, that while a little brother or sister certainly looks up to and even imitates an older sibling, the deeper reality is their familial bond' (*Calvin on the Christian Life*, 104). Christ is the source of our lives as Christians, he is the pattern we are to follow, and he is the goal that we attempt earnestly to reach.

Christian living, John Calvin explains, 'is a doctrine not of the tongue but of life … it is received only when it possesses the whole soul, and finds a seat and resting place in the inmost affection of the heart' (III.6.4). In other words, we learn to live the Christian life not merely by reading and studying about it but by trying to live it day in and day out. Our salvation begins with doctrine, but this doctrine 'must enter our heart and pass into our daily living, and so transform us into itself that it may not be unfruitful for us' (III.6.4).

The sum of the Christian life: the denial of ourselves

It may appear that Calvin's summary of the Christian life as self-denial is negative and pessimistic, but as Joel Beeke explains, 'Self-denial helps us find true happiness because it helps us do what we were created for. We were created to love God above all and our neighbour as ourselves' (*The Cambridge Companion to John Calvin*, 142).

Calvin recognizes how hard it is to practice self-denial in relation to other people. 'Now, in seeking to benefit one's neighbour, how difficult it is to do one's duty!' 'Unless you give up all thought of self and, so to speak, get out of yourselves, you will accomplish nothing here' (III.7.5). Calvin gives us two truths to help us practise self-denial.

1. We must remember that we are stewards, not owners, of what God has given us

Therefore, 'whatever benefits we obtain from the Lord have been entrusted to us on this condition: that they be applied to the common good of the church' (III.7.5). In a sermon on Deuteronomy 15, Calvin says, 'As God bestows his benefits upon us, let us beware that we acknowledge it toward him, by doing good to our neighbours … so as we neither exempt ourselves from their want, nor seclude them from our abundance, but gently make them partakers with us, as people that are linked together in an inseparable bond.' In his commentary on Isaiah 16:4, Calvin, who was himself a refugee in Geneva, writes, 'No duty can be more pleasing or acceptable to God than hospitality, especially to refugees.'

'On the duty of alms-giving, and even on the subtle corruptions of alms-giving, few men have written better than Calvin himself. The limit of giving is to be the limit of our ability to give. We must not consider ourselves free to refuse because those who ask us are undeserving, for Scripture here cometh to our aide with this excellent reason, that we respect not what men merit of themselves but look only upon God's image which they bear. We must guard against that subtle insolence which often poisons the gift. Even a merry countenance and courteous words accompanying it are not enough. A Christian must not give as though he would bind his brother unto him by the benefit. When I use my hands to heal some other part of my body I lay the body under no obligation to the hands: and since we are all members of one another, we similarly lay no obligation on the poor when we relieve them' (C. S. Lewis, *English Literature in the Sixteenth Century*, 35-36).

2. Human beings are made in the image of God

We see ourselves in our neighbour; but even more we see the image of God. As often as I see a person, Calvin writes, 'I must necessarily see myself, as reflected in a glass' (Comm. Matt. 5:43). A true understanding of another person comes only by seeing God's image in that person. Calvin eloquently enforces this idea in III.7.6—ending with the words: 'It is that we remember not to consider men's evil intention but to look upon the image of God in them, which cancels and effaces their trans-gressions, and with its beauty and dignity allures us to love and embrace them.' In his commentary on Genesis 9:5-6 Calvin writes, 'No one can be injurious to his brother without wounding God himself.' To hurt a fellow human being wounds God; it causes him pain.

Preaching on Galatians 6:9-11, Calvin said, 'We cannot but behold our own face in those who are poor and despised ... even though they are utter strangers to us. Even in dealing with a Moor or a Barbarian, from the very fact of his being a man he carries about with him a looking-glass in which we can see that he is our brother and our neighbour.' We are to view all people as our brothers and sisters and neighbours regardless of social status, culture, race, or religion. R. S. Wallace writes, 'These two basic facts—that man is created in the image of God, and that all share in a common human nature—are the foundation of all Calvin's teaching about human relationships' (*Calvin's Doctrine of the Christian Life*, 150).

> Reverend Boughton 'fell to thinking about the passage in the Institutes where it says the image of the Lord in anyone is much more than reason enough to love him, and that the Lord stands waiting to take our enemies' sins upon himself. So it is a rejection of the reality of grace to hold our enemy at fault' (Robinson, *Gilead*, 189).

Self-denial reaches out to other people that God brings our way, but it has to do chiefly with God. 'It is with God [the Christian] has to deal throughout his life', Calvin said (III.7.2). He writes about this in some of the most famous words in the *Institutes*:

> We are not our own: let not our reason nor our will, therefore, sway our plans and deeds. We are not our own: let us therefore not set it as our goal to seek for what is expedient for us according to the flesh. We are not our own: in so far as we can, let us therefore forget ourselves and all that is ours.
>
> Conversely, we are God's: let us therefore live for him and die for him. We are God's: let his wisdom and will therefore rule all our actions. We are God's: let all the parts of our life accordingly strive toward him as our only lawful goal (III.7.1).

These words, which appeared for the first time in the 1539 *Institutes*, were put into practice in Calvin's own life when, happily settled in Strasbourg, he struggled with the call to return to Geneva where he had been so mistreated. He wrote to his friend William Farel:

> As to my intended course of proceeding, this is my present feeling; had I the choice at my disposal, nothing would be less agreeable to me than to follow your advice [and return to Geneva]. But when

I remember that I am not my own, I offer up my heart, presented as a sacrifice to the Lord … Although I am not very ingenious, I would not lack pretexts by which I might adroitly slip away, so that I should easily excuse myself in the sight of men, and show that it was no fault of mine. I am well aware, however, that it is God with whom I have to do, from whose sight such crafty imaginations cannot be withheld. Therefore I submit my will and my affections, subdued and held fast, to the obedience of God; and whenever I am at a loss for counsel of my own, I submit myself to those by whom I hope that the Lord himself will speak to me (*Letters of John Calvin*).

Bearing the cross is a part of self-denial

Not only do we as Christians practise self-denial inwardly, we are being conformed to Christ outwardly—by our afflictions and troubles. 'Beginning with Christ, his first-born', God 'follows this plan with all his children', Calvin writes (III.8.1). 'Then only do we rightly advance by the discipline of the cross when we learn that this life, judged in itself, is troubled, turbulent, unhappy in countless ways' (III.9.1). Christian discipleship is a challenging pilgrimage, by no means devoid of joy, but always undertaken in the shadow of the cross.

'Communion with Christ, which is so often accentuated by Calvin, implies communion with the crucified Christ. Consequently the cross plays a part not only in justification but also in sanctification. The Christian life is a life of mortification, a life in which God sometimes poses a cross as a burden to train us in faith and patience; a life in which God leads us into darkness in order to bring us into the light; where God's hand strikes us down in order to teach us that his hand alone can lift us up and raise us again' (Selderhuis, *Calvin's Theology of the Psalms*, 39).

All people experience life's afflictions, but only Christians can be said to 'bear the cross'. 'Although God burdens with the cross both [unbelievers and believers], yet only they are said to bear the cross who freely take it on their shoulders ... The patience of believers therefore consists in willingly bearing the cross laid on them' (Comm. Matt. 16:24). A burden becomes a cross when we willingly accept it and carry it, with trust, patience, and obedience. This does not always happen when trials come. Our natural response is to become hardened and bitter and even to blame God. We expect God's power to remove our trials rather than enable us to receive them. But when we accept God's providential dealings with us, we are blessed. When we are stricken outwardly; we are strengthened inwardly.

When we willingly, and even thankfully, bear the crosses that God sends into our lives, we experience blessing and learn these important lessons.

- Trust in God—'We learn to call upon his power, which alone makes us stand fast under the weight of afflictions' (III.8.2).

- Patience and obedience—'The Lord also has another purpose for afflicting his people: to test their patience and to instruct them to obedience' (III.8.4).

- Thankful and quiet mind—'But if it be clear that our afflictions are for our benefit, why should we not undergo them with a thankful and quiet mind?' (III.8.11)

'I was reading Calvin's *Sermons on the Beatitudes* when, on Good Friday, April 6, 2007, I received a call from a doctor that a recent biopsy showed that my cancer had returned after three years of remission. I had just read the following words from Calvin—words that I returned to again and again the next few days. Calvin said: "While life for believers may be easy today, they will be ready tomorrow to endure whatever afflictions God may send them. He may, perhaps, take from them the goods he has given. They are prepared to surrender them, since they know they received them on one condition—that they should hand them back whenever God should choose. The believer reasons this way: 'Rich today, poor tomorrow.' If God should change my circumstances so that ease gives way to suffering and laughter to tears, it is enough to know that I am still his child. He has promised to acknowledge me always as his, and in that I rest content"' (Sermons on the Beatitudes, 78), David B. Calhoun.

Meditation on the future life

Christians already possess the heavenly life, but 'in hope', and this explains its concealment (Comm. Psa. 118:17). Cross-bearing gives the believer an eschatological perspective—it serves to create in us a longing for heaven.

Meditation on the future life 'is not only a spiritual exercise, but designates the appropriate mental attitude or frame of mind with which the Christian "sees" and interprets all events in the world and in his own life' (Oberman, *'Initia Calvini'*, 126).

'If heaven is our homeland', Calvin reminds us, 'what else is the earth but our place of exile?' (III.9.4) Preaching on Ephesians 3:13-16,

Calvin said that 'God's children who willingly shut their eyes against all the things which have a fair outward show here below, and who see the heritage of heaven by faith, are not much vexed when they see themselves decayed even in eyesight, and when God makes them fade away little by little.'

> 'If we really think that home is elsewhere and that this life is a "wandering to find home", why should we not look forward to the arrival?' (C. S. Lewis, *Letters to an American Lady*).

Is Calvin 'otherworldly'? Paul Helm answers:

> It may well be. For Calvin's understanding of religion is founded on his understanding of God's saving grace in Jesus Christ. All other things take second place … If Christ, in his warnings about the danger of planning to build bigger barns, and to neglect the soul, or in his urging on us of the need to find the pearl of great price, is an 'otherworldly' Christ, then so was Calvin an otherworldly theologian (*Calvin at the Centre*, 339).

If there is a certain measure of 'contempt for the present life' in Calvin, it is balanced by his warning that we must not hate this life nor be ungrateful to God for it (III.9.3). Calvin said: 'It is necessary to hold to this rule: that is, to know that human life is in itself a gift of God so precious and so noble that it deserves to be highly prized' (Sermon 11 on Job).

How we must use the present life and its helps

After focusing our attention on heaven in chapter 9, Calvin, in chapter 10, turns us back to this world. He discusses the future life before the present life to emphasize 'the theological reality that hope in the future life provides for the present life' (Partee, *The Theology of John Calvin*, 220).

'The apostles themselves ... left their mark on earth precisely because their minds were occupied with heaven. It is since Christians have largely ceased to think of the other world that they have become so ineffective in this. Aim at heaven and you will get earth "thrown in": aim at earth and you will get neither' (C. S. Lewis, *Mere Christianity*).

This world is not only 'our place of exile', it is also 'a sentry post at which the Lord has posted us, which we must hold until he recalls us' (III.9.4). As we think of our life in this world, Calvin warns against a double danger: 'this topic is a slippery one and slopes on both sides into error' (III.10.1). 'Some otherwise good and holy men' are too strict and thus rob 'a man of all his senses'. And 'many' men are too loose, and fall into the opposite extreme of 'the lust of the flesh' (III.10.3). Calvin rejects both disuse and misuse of the things of this world in favour of right use.

Calvin sets forth five principles to help us keep to the centre of the path and avoid the dangers on both sides.

1. Use God's gifts according to the end for which he created them for us: that is—both necessity and delight

We are put into this world 'not only to be spectators in this beautiful theatre but to enjoy the vast bounty and variety of good things which are displayed to us in it' (Comm. Psa. 104:31). Creation 'in all its parts' serves mankind as source and resource of happiness (Comm. Psa. 8:7). Some people are surprised to learn that Calvin believed that God made things attractive and delightful beyond their necessary use. Food is not only for nourishment of our bodies but it brings 'delight and good cheer' (III.10.2). Wine is 'among the benefits of God' (III.10.2).

Commenting on the wedding at Cana, where Christ made an abundance of 'most excellent wine', Calvin said, 'It is permissible to use wine, not only for necessity, but also to make us merry' (Comm. John 2:8). He warns, however, that 'we must keep ourselves from being so overcome and vanquished by wine' (Sermon on Eph. 6:18-21). Clothing provides protection for our bodies, but also 'comeliness and decency' (III.10.2). Sex is for procreation, but also 'allows husband and wife to give each other delight' (Comm. Deut. 24:5). About Jacob's love for Rachel, Calvin writes: 'Therefore he who shall be induced to choose a wife because of the elegance of her shape will not necessarily sin' (Comm. Gen. 29:18).

2. Recognize that God is the author of all things and 'give thanks for his kindness toward us'

Calvin often stresses the importance of gratitude, acknowledging in how many ways we are indebted to God. 'It is the very thing in which we ought to occupy ourselves', he told the people of his church. 'It should be our life's chief study' (Sermon on Eph. 5:15-18). Charles Simeon wrote, 'There are but two lessons for the Christian to learn: the one is, to enjoy God in everything; the other is, to enjoy everything in God' (Hopkins, *Charles Simeon*, 203). And a third lesson, adds Calvin, is, be thankful.

3. Know 'how to go without things patiently'

'Let all those for whom the pursuit of piety is not a pretence strive to learn … how to be filled and to hunger, to abound and to suffer want' (III.10.5).

4. Remember that we must one day 'render account' for all those things which 'were so given to us by the kindness of God'

We must so live our lives that 'this saying may continually resound in our ears: "Render account of your stewardship"' (III.10.5).

We are stewards, not owners, of all that God has given us. Both in the *Institutes* and in his commentary on Genesis, Calvin makes the point that God created the world for the sake of human beings, and that we are to use and enjoy but not waste and destroy it.

We have the responsibility to care for this world and all the creatures in it the way God cares for all that he has made.

> The custody of the garden was given in charge to Adam, to show that we possess the things which God has committed to our hands, on the condition, that being content with a frugal and moderate use of them, we should take care of what shall remain. Let him who

possesses a field so partake of its yearly fruits that he may not suffer the ground to be injured by his negligence; but let him endeavour to hand it down to posterity as he received it, or even better cultivated. Let him so feed on its fruits, that he neither dissipates it by luxury, nor permits it to be marred or ruined by neglect. Moreover, that this economy and this diligence, with respect to those good things which God has given us to enjoy, may flourish among us; let every one regard himself as the steward of God in all things which he possesses. Then he will neither conduct himself dissolutely, nor corrupt by abuse those things which God requires to be preserved (Comm. Gen. 2:15).

In his sermon on Deuteronomy 20:16-20, Calvin exhorted the people to be good stewards.

When we find ourselves driven by wickedness or some evil thoughts to the point of destroying trees, houses and other such things, we have to control ourselves and reflect: Who are we waging war against? Not against creatures, but against the one whose goodness is mirrored here. Not against one man only, but against each and everyone, ourselves included. … If now I seek to despoil the land of what God has given it to sustain human beings, then I am seeking as much as I can to do away with God's goodness.

Calvin cautioned people against 'damaging trees' in particular, since 'our Lord ordained the land to be as it were our nursing mother'. We should remember that since the land sustains us, it is 'just as if God extended his hand to us and handed us proofs of his goodness'.

In his commentary on Deuteronomy 22:6, Calvin says that we should never think of killing a mother bird on her nest.

For if there is one drop of compassion in us, it will never enter our minds to kill an unhappy little bird, which so burns either with the desire of offspring, or with love towards its little ones, as to be heedless of life, and to prefer endangering itself to the destruction of its eggs, or its brood.

Teach me, my God and King
In all things thee to see;
And what I do in anything
To do it as for thee.

A servant with this clause
Makes drudgery divine;
Who sweeps a room, as for thy laws,
Makes that and the action fine.

George Herbert

5. Each one should 'look to his calling'

No lawful task 'will be so sordid and base, provided you obey your calling in it, that it will not shine and be reckoned very precious in God's sight' (III.10.6).

Calvin urges believers to be diligent in work, but he did not see work as an end in itself nor did he promote a selfish economic individualism. It is possible for people to 'torment and weaken themselves in vain when they busy themselves more than their common calling permits or requires' (Comm. Matt. 6: 25-30). Excessive work, however, may have been Calvin's greatest temptation. He could have been thinking of himself when he said in a sermon, 'A great many people are their own executioners through working constantly and without measure' (Sermon 2 on 1 Cor.).

Calvin states that God has appointed 'duties for every man in his particular way of life' (III.10.6). The prevailing view in the Middle Ages was that one should accept his lot in life—a man did what his father did, or became a priest or a monk. Women became wives and mothers. Calvin warns against unrest and rash change, but does not forbid thoughtful decisions to improve one's status in life. Commenting on 1 Corinthians 7: 20, 'Every one should remain in the state in which he was called', Calvin said:

> It would be a hard thing if a tailor were not at liberty to learn
> another trade, or if a merchant were not at liberty to take up

farming. That is not what the apostle intends. What he has in mind is to restrain that reckless eagerness which leads some to change their vocation without any proper reason ... [Paul] does not require anyone to continue in the way of life that was once taken up, but instead he condemns that restlessness which keeps an individual from remaining in a calling with a peaceful mind.

Calvin was both conservative and progressive on human vocation. He was conservative in insisting that we stay by our 'sentry post' and not wander about aimlessly and needlessly. He was progressive in asserting that all types of work are good and acceptable to God and that a person may seek to improve his or her status in life.

Knowing God and ourselves

'Ever since God revealed himself as Father to us ... ever since Christ cleansed us ... ever since he engrafted us into his body ... ever since Christ himself, who is our head, ascended into heaven ... ever since the Holy Spirit dedicated us as temples to God ... ever since both our souls and bodies were destined for heavenly incorruption and an unfading crown ... these I say, are the most auspicious foundations upon which to establish one's life' (III.6.3). Examine your foundations. On what are you building?

16. Justification— 'The Main Hinge'

'Therefore we must now discuss [the doctrine of justification] thoroughly. And we must so discuss [it] as to bear in mind that this is *the main hinge* on which religion turns, so that we devote the greater attention and care to it' (III.11.1).

As we look at Calvin's treatment of justification, 'we see that this is something he has been working up to all through the *Institutes*, and that the argument of Romans 1-3 has been the underlying theme' (Parker, *Calvin: An Introduction to his Thought*).

Read: *Institutes* III.11-19, [*1541* ch.6, pp.351-428; ch.14, pp.707-719.]

Scripture Text: 'May the abyss of thy mercy swallow up this abyss of my sin' (1536 *Institutes of the Christian Religion*, 141). This is Calvin's rendering of the tax collector's prayer in Luke 18:13: 'God, be merciful to me a sinner.'

Notable Quote: If the knowledge of justification by faith 'is taken away, the glory of Christ is extinguished, religion abolished, the church destroyed, and the hope of salvation utterly overthrown' (*Calvin: Theological Treatises*, 234).

Prayer

Grant, Almighty God, since we are all lost in ourselves, that we may desire to obtain life where it is laid up for us and where you do manifest it, namely, in your Son. And grant that we may so embrace the grace that has been exhibited to us in the sacrifice of his death that we may be regenerated by his Spirit.

And thus being born again, may we devote ourselves wholly to you and so glorify your name in this world that we may at length be partakers of that glory that the same, your only begotten Son, has acquired for us. Amen.

(*Lifting Up Our Hearts*, 71.)

❦

A look back and a look ahead

From the vantage point of III.11-18, J. I. Packer takes a long look back and a long look ahead.

> Justification by faith, 'the mainstay for upholding religion' (III.11.1), is central [to the *Institutes*], both spatially and theologically, occupying chapters 11-18 of Book III. What precedes it is what must first be known before we can grasp it—that God is triune, holy, and just, yet good and gracious, Lord of history and disposer of all things (I.10-18); that godliness means humble love, gratitude, reverence, submission, and dependence God-ward (I.2); that we humans are by nature guilty, blind, and helpless in sin (II.1-5); that both Testaments witness to Jesus, the divine-human mediator, whose death gained salvation for us (II.6-17); what the law requires (II.8); what faith is (III.2); how God gives faith (III.1); how faith begets repentance (III.3-5); and Christian living (III.6-10).
>
> What follows justification is, in effect, a programme for our spiritual health as justified sinners. We must know that our freedom from the law is for obedience to it (III.19); that we cannot go on without prayer (III.20); that God's election guarantees our final salvation (III.21-24); that we have a sure hope of resurrection in glory (III.25); that we must wait on the ministry of word and sacrament in the church for our soul's growth (IV.1-19); and that we must be good citizens (IV.20) (*A Theological Guide to Calvin's Institutes*, xii).

Justification and sanctification

In beginning Book III, John Calvin faced two topics that equally demanded his attention—justification and sanctification. He chose to deal with sanctification first. He wrote: 'Our immediate transition will be from faith to repentance. For when this topic is rightly understood it will better appear how man is justified by faith alone' (III.3.1). What is the source of the kind of Christian life that we find in III.2-10? Calvin answers: God alone can do this and he begins by justifying the sinner by faith alone. 'Actual holiness of life', he writes, 'is not separated from free imputation of righteousness' (III.3.1).

Calvin 'views justification not as a single, separate, divine gift, but as one of twin gifts, a point that he repeatedly stresses in the *Institutes* and which forms an axis of his soteriology' (Helm, *Calvin at the Centre*, 197). The other gift is sanctification. Both together are the gift of Christ to his people who were chosen 'in him' from eternity. Calvin wrote in his Commentary on Ephesians 1:4-5:

> The foundation and first cause, both of our calling and of all the benefits which we receive from God, is here declared to be his eternal election … It is not from a perception of anything that we deserve, but because our heavenly Father has introduced us, through the privilege of adoption, into the body of Christ.

Both sanctification and justification come from our union with Christ. Both are received by faith. 'Since … it is solely by expending himself that the Lord gives us these benefits to enjoy, he bestows both of them at the same time, the one never without the other' (III.16.1). Justification and sanctification cannot be separated because Christ 'cannot be divided into pieces' (III.16.1). Not only are they inseparable, they are simultaneous. But justification and sanctification should not be confused or confounded. 'If the brightness of the sun cannot be separated from its heat, shall we therefore say that the earth is warmed by its light, or lighted by its heat?' (III.11.6) The sun is the source of both, and its light and heat are inseparable. At the same time, only light illumines and only heat warms. Both are always present without the one becoming the other.

Calvin does not allow the effects of salvation (sanctification) to become the grounds of salvation (justification). Justification is based on what Christ has done *for* us; sanctification, upon what he does *in* us. Justification is accomplished once for all by Christ's work on the cross; sanctification is accomplished day by day through the work of the Holy Spirit in us. Justification frees us from the obligation to obey the law for salvation; sanctification enables us to obey it for holiness. 'Justification offers imputed purity, and sanctification, actual purity' (Beeke, *The Cambridge Companion to John Calvin*).

Justification is logically (not temporally) prior to sanctification. It makes sanctification possible, and also makes it necessary—and, we might say, inevitable—but it is not the cause of sanctification. The faith that is indispensable to justification is also indispensable to sanctification. True sanctification is unintelligible without justification (III.16.1). 'Justification by sanctification is man's way to heaven … Sanctification by justification is God's [way], and he fills the soul with his own goodness' (Thomas Adam, *Private Thoughts on Religion*, 242).

Justification by faith alone

Calvin first tells us what justification is (III.11.1-2) and gives its scriptural basis (III.11.3-4). He then refutes Osiander's views (III.11.5-12) and the Roman Catholic doctrine (III.11.13-20). In III.11.21-23 he returns to his definition and reviews what he has said. In giving nine chapters of the *Institutes* to the doctrine of justification, Calvin writes: 'The thought repeatedly returns to my mind that there is danger of my being unjust to God's mercy when I labour with such great concern to assert it, as if it were doubtful or obscure' (III.14.6).

Calvin gives several definitions of justification:

- 'The acceptance with which God receives us into his favour as righteous … It consists in the remission of sins and the imputation of Christ's righteousness' (III.11.2).

- 'To justify means nothing else than to acquit of guilt him who was accused, as if his innocence were confirmed' (III.11.3).

- 'We define justification as follows: the sinner, received into communion with Christ, is reconciled to God by his grace, while, cleansed by Christ's blood, he obtains forgiveness of sins, and clothed with Christ's righteousness as if it were his own, he stands confident before the heavenly judgment seat' (III.17.8).

God justifies a person by declaring that person righteous because of the righteousness of Christ imputed to him or her. Like Jacob in his brother's clothing, we 'hide under the precious purity of our first-born brother, Christ, so that we may be attested in God's sight'

(III.11.23). Imputation is not an abstraction but an essential and practical doctrine, for apart from imputation, forgiveness would be unintelligible. Imputation means the price has been paid. The words of the hymn state it well:

> Jesus paid it all,
> All to him I owe;
> Sin had left a crimson stain,
> He washed it white as snow.

God justifies a person 'by faith' alone, which means simply that God alone justifies. We cannot add to it. We can just receive it. The Reformers were accused of adding the word 'alone' since that word is not found in the Bible in connection with justification by faith. Calvin answers: 'But if justification depends not either on the law, or on ourselves, why should it not be ascribed to mercy alone? And if it be from mercy only, it is then by faith only' (Comm. Rom. 3:21).

We are justified the moment we are united to Christ by the Holy Spirit, but justification is not merely something that God did in our past. The title of III.14 is 'The Beginning of Justification and Its Continual Progress.' In his commentary on Romans 8:30 Calvin writes that 'justification might quite well be extended to include the continuation of the divine favour from the time of the calling of the believer to his death'. He adds, 'What is more desirable than to be reconciled to God, so that our miseries should no longer be signs of his curse, or lead to our destruction?'

Calvin's answer to Osiander

Calvin addresses the teaching of Osiander, a Lutheran theologian who rejected the idea of the imputation of Christ's righteousness to the sinner. In its place Osiander put what Calvin called 'some strange monster of essential righteousness'. Osiander held that God cannot regard as righteous those who are not actually and personally righteous. We become righteous, he taught, not by mere imputation but by the actual infusion of Christ's essence. The righteousness that is made ours in justification, therefore, is the righteousness that belonged to Christ as divine, actually imparted to us, not forensically imputed. God sees us as righteous because we indeed are righteous.

Calvin criticizes Osiander's theology because it denies the importance of 'Christ's obedience and sacrificial death', accomplished in his human nature, and bases justification on something done within or transfused into the Christian from Christ's divine nature. It is essentially Roman Catholic doctrine in another form—basing justification on righteousness resident in the believer. Like the Catholics, Osiander confounded justification and sanctification, and taught justification by sanctification rather than justification by faith alone. Answering Osiander Calvin insists that believers are given a 'righteousness outside themselves' (III.11.11), by which we 'who are not righteous in ourselves may be reckoned as such in Christ' (III.11.3). This reckoning is not merely a formal declaration but a transforming union with Christ. Calvin writes: 'We do not regard [Christ] as outside of and distant from us, in such a way that his righteousness is imputed to us in a mechanical fashion, but we put him on and are made members of his body' (III.11.10).

Calvin's answer to Roman Catholics

Roman Catholic theology added works to grace by interpreting 'the grace of God not as the imputation of free righteousness but as the Spirit helping in the pursuit of holiness' (III.11.15). Simply put, Roman Catholics believed that 'righteousness is composed of faith and works' (III.11.13) or grace-assisted works, deemed meritorious. Preaching on Ephesians 1:17-18, Calvin said, 'The papists will grant readily enough that without God's grace we cannot walk as we ought to do; but yet, at the same time, they say that we may well further God's grace by our own free will, and so they mix them together.'

The Roman Catholic system of salvation can be outlined as follows:

- One does 'what is in him' (Roman Catholics debated whether this first effort was purely natural or assisted by God).

- God out of his great generosity views this effort as 'meritorious' in some limited sense ('half-merit' or 'congruent merit') and meets it with grace.

- God's grace makes possible truly worthy deeds ('full-merit' or 'condign merit').

- Worthy deeds lead to more grace and more merit,

- Worthy deeds, assisted by God's grace, lead eventually (after purgatory) to everlasting life in heaven, which is both a gift and a reward.

Calvin's 'order of justification' or 'faith-righteousness' contrasts sharply with Catholic 'works-righteousness'. 'Faith-righteousness so differs from works-righteousness, that when one is established the other has to be overthrown' (III.11.13). In the place of faith plus works Calvin puts faith alone, which is a gift of God. God justifies the sinner and he does so out of sheer mercy. Period. Nothing else is needed. Nothing else is possible. Using the words of the Catholic formula ('one does what is in him'), Calvin states that there is nothing in fallen man 'except his miserable condition' and 'the sheer disgrace of need and emptiness' (III.11.16). Man is dead and 'what can a dead man do to attain life?' Calvin asks (III.14.5).

'Mr Spurgeon says, the Romanists have an extraordinary miracle of their own about St Dennis, of whom they tell the lying legend, that after his head was off he took it up in his hands and walked with it two thousand miles; whereupon said a wit, so far as the two thousand miles go, it is nothing at all, it is only the first step in which there is any difficulty. So we believe about salvation. If the dead sinner could take the first step ... without having first felt the life-giving touch of God's power, we see no reason why he could not take all the other steps involved in his salvation' (Reed, *The Gospel as Taught by Calvin*, 73-74).

Calvin's way of salvation may be outlined as follows:

- God 'seeks in himself the reason to benefit man' (III.11.16).

- 'Then God touches the sinner ... this is the experience of faith' (III.11.16).

Faith is not a work. It is receptive, not contributory. It receives; it does not add. 'We compare faith to a kind of vessel', writes Calvin; 'or unless we come empty and with the mouth of our soul open to seek Christ's grace, we are not capable of receiving Christ' (III.11.7). 'Human response to God's grace is not the cause but the consequence of salvation' (Partee, *The Theology of John Calvin*, 90).

- Good works necessarily follow, but do not contribute to, justification. 'We are justified not without works yet not through works' (III.16.1).

- Everlasting life and heaven's rewards are the result of God's grace alone.

God's holiness

In III.12, 'We must lift up our minds to God's judgment seat that we may be firmly convinced of his free justification', Calvin again reminds his readers that the righteousness of works is beyond the ability of sinners; we cannot 'meet and satisfy God's judgment'. In the light of God's holiness, we lose all confidence in ourselves. 'For if the stars, which seem so very bright at night, lose their brilliance in the sight of the sun, what do we think will happen even to the rarest innocence of man when it is compared with God's purity?' (III.12.4)

Free justification

In III.13, 'Two things to be noted in free justification', Calvin sets forth these important points.

1. God's glory is exalted by the doctrine of 'free justification', that is, justification by faith alone

Calvin says that 'man cannot without sacrilege claim for himself even a crumb of righteousness, for just so much is plucked and taken away from the glory of God's righteousness' (III.13.2). 'Thank you, Lord, for helping me' is not the same as 'Thank you, Lord, for saving me.'

2. Because of the doctrine of free justification, believers have peace of conscience

Calvin insists that it is justification by faith alone, that is, salvation as 'a gift of God', that can 'establish a righteousness so steadfast that it can support our soul in the judgment of God'. If salvation is by works, even partially by works, we would never know whether we had done enough to deserve it. Calvin challenges his readers: 'Just go and present yourself before God with your good works and see what will be left of them!' (3,12,2)

> Jesus, thy blood and righteousness
>   My beauty are, my glorious dress;
> Midst flaming worlds, in these arrayed,
>   With joy shall I lift up my head.
>
> Jesus, be endless praise to thee,
>   Whose boundless mercy hath for me—
> For me a full atonement made,
>   An everlasting ransom paid.
>   Nikolaus Ludwig von Zinzendorf

More about justification

In chapter 14 ('The Beginning of Justification and Its Continual Progress') Calvin explains again that salvation in its entirety is the work of God. 'Paul does not say to the Ephesians that we have the beginning of salvation from grace', Calvin states, 'but that we have been saved through grace, "not by works, lest any man should boast"' (III.14.11). 'There is nothing intermediate between these two things, which are represented in Scripture as opposites—being justified by faith and justified by works' (Comm. Psa. 143:2).

Repentance and forgiveness of sins—sanctification and justification—are both gifts of God. Not only does sanctification continue throughout the Christian's life, but so does justification. During the whole of life the Christian requires the continuing work of justification because though we constantly fall short of perfection God's mercy counters our failings and 'by continual forgiveness of sins repeatedly acquits us' (III.14.10). In III.15.7 Calvin describes justification by faith as 'the sum of all piety'. All who are justified by God are 'reborn' and pass from 'the realm of sin into the realm of righteousness', producing good works by God's continuous grace.

Calvin applies Aristotle's four 'causes' to justification and argues that none of them has anything to do with works: the efficient cause of our salvation is the mercy of God; the material cause is Christ; the formal or instrumental cause is faith; and the final cause is the glory of God (III.14. 17, 21). In the first chapter of Ephesians Paul teaches that 'we are received into grace by God out of sheer mercy, that this comes about by Christ's intercession and is apprehended by faith, and that all things exist to the end that the glory of divine goodness may fully shine forth' (III.14.17).

Justification and good works

In III.15-17 Calvin emphasizes again how destructive human claims to righteousness are in that they impair God's glory and injure our peace of conscience. Works cannot contribute to our salvation because even our good works fall short and need to be forgiven. Our good works, even our best works, must be cleansed by God. Calvin says that we experience a 'double justification'—God accepts us in Christ, and he also accepts our works in him. 'Of his own fatherly generosity and loving-kindness, and without considering their worth', Calvin writes, God raises our works to a 'place of honour' and attributes 'value to them' (III.17.3).

Just as Calvin completes his theological treatment of sanctification with a practical description of the Christian life (III.6-10), so he completes his theological treatment of justification (III.16-19) with a description of the good works of Christian people (III.17-19). William Edgar writes: 'Calvin is so concerned for piety, the holiness of life, the knowledge of God and true sanctification, that he sees justification here as a means as much as an end' (*A Theological Guide to Calvin's Institutes*, 321-22). As we have seen, Calvin treats sanctification and good works before his formal treatment of justification. After his chapters on justification he returns again to good works. Calvin surrounds justification by faith alone with good works. 'For justification is withdrawn from works, not that no good works may be done, or that what is done may be denied to be good, but that we may not rely upon them, glory in them, or ascribe salvation to them' (III.17.1).

Calvin again answers those who argue 'that through the justification of faith, good works are destroyed'. He insists that the Bible teaches neither 'a faith devoid of good works' nor 'a justification that stands without them'. 'We are justified not without works yet not through works' (III.16.1). It is necessary to keep beating back those who say that works are part of the cause of our salvation (III.17.1).

In III.17.4 Calvin presents his doctrine of 'double acceptance'. Once we are accepted by the pure mercy of God, the Holy Spirit begins to produce in us good works which God also accepts. So, in a sense, we are accepted for our good works, although, as Calvin adds, 'only because he is their source' (III.17.5).

Calvin deals with biblical passages that appear to contradict the Protestant view that justification is by faith alone and not at all by works. He insists that these texts teach that 'an empty show of faith does not justify, and a believer, not content with such an image, declares his righteousness by good works' (III.17.12). He argues that the many references, particularly in the Psalms, in which believers appeal to their works as proof of their righteousness before God, do not teach justification by works but present works as a sign of God's justification. Furthermore, says Calvin, believers do not 'claim righteousness for themselves with reference to divine perfection but in comparison with evil and wicked men' (III.17.14).

In III.18 Calvin takes up the matter of rewards. Despite the imperfections of our works, God still rewards us for them. Out of his love, God cleanses our works and rewards them. Our rewards, therefore, are gifts of God who enables us to do good works and in his mercy cleanses and receives them. The rewards of the Bible are given to children, not to hired servants—'not a servant's pay but a child's inheritance' (III.18.2). 'There is no reason why we may not justly be said to perform that which the Spirit of God performs in us, although our own will contributes nothing of itself, independently of his grace' (II.5.15). Preaching on Ephesians

2:10, 'For we are his workmanship, created in Christ Jesus to good works which God has prepared for us to walk in', Calvin compares the action of God to that of a kind and generous host.

> When a man has been well kept and looked after, and his host has lent him money for his need, and he has received it from him (to pay him with it), shall he afterwards boast that he has paid his host? There is the kind of host who is not only pleased to be charitable to a man, but who, carrying further his superabundance, after he has found him both bed and board, will say to him, Take here something with which to pay; in order that it may not seem to you that my charitable dealing has made you contemptible, I will receive payment for it at your hand; but yet it shall come from my own purse.

Calvin argues that the biblical expression 'treasures in heaven' does not refer to the value of our works but to the proper investment of our lives: 'If we believe heaven is our country, it is better to transmit our possessions thither than to keep them here where upon our sudden migration they should be lost to us' (III.18.6).

Christian freedom

'Christian freedom was a clearly enunciated dimension of the Christian life as Calvin understood it … It is the practical, everyday embodiment of the doctrine of justification by grace through faith' (Leith, *John Calvin: The Christian Life*, xii).

'Few people have associated the name of Calvin with the idea of liberty. Let them study this great chapter' (Breen, *John Calvin: A Study in French Humanism*, 163).

In III.19 Calvin treats 'Christian Freedom', which he calls 'an appendage to justification' (III.19.1). A proper understanding of Christian freedom protects us from doubt and legalism and enables us to live freely and joyfully for God. 'Unless this freedom be comprehended, neither Christ nor gospel truth, nor inner peace of soul, can be rightly known' (III.19.1). Michael Horton writes, 'We live in freedom and assurance from a present and perfect justification, not toward it as a goal' (*Calvin on the Christian Life*, 96).

Both sanctification and justification affect how we live. In Calvin's treatment, repentance is followed by practical application in the life of a Christian; his treatment of justification is followed by a practical discussion about Christian freedom. What difference has justification made in our everyday lives? Calvin discusses three 'freedoms' that we have as Christians.

1. We have freedom from the law, in the sense that we are free from salvation by works; therefore, we are not 'disturbed and troubled over forgiveness of sins' (III.19.2)

We can forget the law and look only to the grace of God for our salvation. This does not mean, of course, that the law no longer functions in its 'third use'. It 'does not stop teaching and exhorting and urging [believers] to good, even though before God's judgment seat it has no place in their consciences' (III.19.2). The Christian is freed from the law by the righteousness of Christ, but we are now free for the law, free to embrace it joyously and to live according to it.

> To see the law by Christ fulfilled
> And hear his pardoning voice
> Changes the slave into a child
> And duty into choice.
> William Cowper

2. We are free as God's children to obey him, knowing that our adoption is not based on our obedience, but our obedience flows from our adoption

We are assured that our 'small, rude, and imperfect' works are not measured by the rigor of the law's demands—like a hard father who always finds some fault with his child's conduct—but are accepted by the love of God and for the sake of Christ (III.19.5).

> Make me a captive, Lord,
> And then I shall be free;
> Force me to render up my sword,
> And I shall conqueror be.
> I sink in life's alarms
> When by myself I stand;
> Imprison me within thine arms,
> And strong shall be my hand.
> George Matheson

3. We are free in 'indifferent' things

This is what we usually think of when we hear 'Christian freedom'. In the many things not specifically covered by the law, the Christian is free, guided by two principles: moderation and compassion.

Moderation keeps us from two extremes. There is the extreme of asceticism that entraps the conscience in a 'long and inextricable maze, not easy to get out of' (III.19.7). Asceticism fails to recognize that we should use God's good gifts 'for the purpose for which he gave them to us' (III.19.8). The opposite extreme is indulgence. We should 'live', says Calvin, not 'luxuriate' (III.19.9).

The second principle to guide us in our use of Christian freedom is compassion. We must not abuse our Christian freedom but use it only when it helps 'the edification of our neighbour' (III.19.12). Christian freedom 'consists as much in abstaining as in using' (III.19.10). I am exercising my Christian freedom as much when I don't do something, as when I do it.

Calvin issues two warnings here. First, we must distinguish between 'the ignorance of our weak brothers' and 'the rigor of the Pharisees' (III.19.11). Paul agreed to the circumcision of Timothy but not of Titus. In the case of Timothy, Paul restricted his freedom because it was 'fruitful to do so'. But in the case of Titus, Paul asserted his freedom against 'the unjust demands of false apostles' because it was right to do so. Second, we must not 'offend God' in trying to avoid offending our neighbour. Some said that people should be allowed to continue to attend the Catholic mass since they must first be fed with milk before they can be fed with meat. Calvin disagreed; 'Milk is not poison', he said (III.19.13).

We must remember that nothing is totally indifferent, since everything we do is done before the face of God (III.19.8).

Knowing God and ourselves

'We experience such participation in [Christ] that, although we are still foolish in ourselves, he is our wisdom before God; while we are sinners, he is our righteousness; while we are unclean, he is our purity; while we are weak … yet ours is that power which has been given him in heaven' (III.15.5).

'Therefore let us learn to glorify in God's pure mercy [alone] and not boast of any merits. And at the same time let us not fail to be intensely more encouraged to serve him, seeing that he wants to attract us to himself in this way, mastering us by such gentle kindness' (*John Calvin's Sermons on the Ten Commandments*, 298).

17. Prayer—
'The Chief Exercise of Faith'

'Prayer, which is *the Chief Exercise of Faith*, and by which We Daily Receive God's Benefits' (title of III.20).

> 'There's nothing else like Calvin's treatment of prayer. Very few systematic theologies have followed Calvin by including a major chapter on prayer. Calvin is both theological and practical, and as usual, he is very comprehensive. This is a rarity—deep theology with a spiritually elevated tone and savor that makes the reader want to pray' (Keller, *Prayer: Experiencing Awe and Intimacy with God*, 268).

Read: *Institutes* III.20. [*1541* ch.9, pp.517-559.]

Scripture Text: 'For the eyes of the Lord are on the righteous, and his ears are open to their prayer' (1 Pet. 3:12).

Notable Quote: 'Lord, we do not present our prayers before you [on the basis of] our just behaviour but on [the basis of] your mercies, on your great, indeed, your infinite goodness" (Sermon on Psa. 115:1-3).

Prayer

Grant, Almighty God, since you have reconciled us to yourself by the precious blood of your Son, that we may not be our own, but devoted to you in perfect obedience, may we consecrate ourselves entirely to you. May we offer our bodies and souls in sacrifice, and may we be prepared to suffer a hundred deaths [rather] than to turn from your true and sincere worship. Grant us, especially, to exercise ourselves in prayer, to fly to you every moment and to commit ourselves to your fatherly care, that your Spirit may govern us to the end. Defend and sustain us, until we are collected into that heavenly kingdom your only begotten Son has prepared for us by his blood. Amen.

(*Lifting Up Our Hearts*, 255.)

A look back and a look ahead

In the opening words of III.20, Calvin reviews what has been covered thus far in the *Institutes*.

- 'From those matters so far discussed, we clearly see how destitute and devoid of all good things man is and how he lacks all aids to salvation.'

Book I and especially Book II.1-6.

- 'Therefore, if he seeks resources to succour him in his need, he must go outside himself and get them elsewhere. It was afterward explained to us that the Lord willingly and freely reveals himself in his Christ.'

Book II.7-17.

- 'But after we have been instructed by faith to recognize that whatever we need and whatever we lack is in God, and in our Lord Jesus Christ, in whom the Father willed all the fullness of his bounty to abide so that we may all draw from it as from an overflowing spring …'

Book III.1-19.

- '… it remains for us to seek in him, and in our prayers to ask of him, what we have learned to be in him.'

Book III.20.

The importance of prayer

Chapter 20 of Book III is the longest chapter in Calvin's 1559 *Institutes*—seventy pages in the English translation. As the McNeill-Battles edition of the *Institutes* notes, 'This thoughtful and ample chapter, with its tone of devout warmth, takes its place in the forefront of historically celebrated discussions of prayer' (2:850, fn. 1). It bears the impressive title: 'Prayer, which is the Chief Exercise of Faith, and by which We Daily Receive God's Benefits.' Book III is about faith—'the way in which we receive the grace of Christ'—and prayer is the chief exercise of faith, 'by which we daily receive God's benefits'. God, writes Calvin, 'has laid down this order: just as faith is born from the gospel, so through it our hearts are trained to call upon God's name' (III.20.1).

Recognizing that 'whatever we need and whatever we lack is in God', we draw from him as from 'an overflowing spring' (III.20.1). In another image, Calvin says that it is 'by the benefit of prayer that we reach those riches which are laid up for us with the heavenly Father' (III.20.2). John Calvin's favourite picture of prayer is God's adopted children calling upon him as their heavenly Father (III.20.2). Prayer is 'an emotion of the heart within, which is poured out and laid open before God' (III.20.29). By prayer we cast our 'desires, sighs, anxieties, fears, hopes, and joys into the lap of God' (Comm. Matt. 26:39).

Given the riches and blessing available to us through prayer, for Christians not to pray is as senseless as it would be for 'a man to neglect a treasure, buried and hidden in the earth, after it had been pointed out to him' (III.20.1). Not only is prayerlessness foolish, it is idolatry. By it people defraud God, 'just as much of his due honour as if they made new gods and idols, since in this way they deny God is the author of every good thing' (III.20.14).

Questions about prayer

'Calvin treats prayer as a given rather than a problem' (Beeke, *The Cambridge Companion to John Calvin*, 140). True, but Calvin does deal with some questions we have about prayer.

Why should we pray when God already knows, 'even without being reminded, both in what respect we are troubled and what is expedient for us' (III.20.3)? Calvin's short answer is that God ordained prayer 'not so much for his own sake as for ours' (III.20.3). Prayer redirects and focuses the believer's mind and heart. Prayer does change things—most often the one who is praying. What is important in petitioning God is that our faith is exercised and the desires of our hearts are brought into conformity with the desires of God. Calvin gives four reasons for petitionary prayer.

1. That our hearts may be 'fired with zealous and burning desire ever to seek, love, and serve him' and to flee to him in time of need.

2. That we may learn to lay all our desires before God.

3. That we may receive his benefits 'with true gratitude of heart and thanksgiving', knowing that all good things 'come from his hand'.

4. That we may know that God 'ever extends his hand to help his own'.

Does our prayer in some way affect God and cause him to change his mind, or does God just do what he planned all along? Calvin attempts to give full force to biblical passages that seem to suggest that prayer changes God, while maintaining his view that God's perfect will is just that—perfect, and therefore unchangeable.

Calvin writes in his commentary on Psalm 89:47 that God permits us to urge him 'to make haste' and in the *Institutes* writes that God is 'stirred up by our prayers' (III.20.3). God 'so tempers the outcome of events according to his incomprehensible plan that the prayers of the saints … are not nullified' (III.20.15).

Preaching on Deuteronomy 9:13-14, Calvin says that Moses' prayer appears to set bounds to God's liberty to destroy the people. But, Calvin explained, God, out of his goodness, 'does so bind himself to our praying and supplications, that they be, as it were, restraints of his wrath: so that whereas diverse times he would destroy all, he is, as it were, changed, if we come and humble ourselves before him'.

Commenting on Joshua's prayer that the sun stand still, Calvin gives full force to the effect of that prayer, but cautioned that Joshua 10:14 ('There has been no day like it before or since, when the Lord obeyed the voice of a man, for the Lord fought for Israel') should not be interpreted in such a way as 'to give a subordinate office to God'. The verse rather 'celebrates the kindness and condescension of God in hearing Joshua, as well as his paternal favour towards the people, for whom he is said to have fought'.

In his comments on Elijah's prayer in James 5:17, Calvin writes that 'it was a notable event for God to put heaven, in some sense, under the control of Elijah's prayers, to be obedient to his requests. By his prayers, Elijah kept heaven shut for two years and a half. Then he opened it, and made it suddenly pour with a great rain, from which we may see the miraculous power of prayer.'

Moses' prayer resisting God's desire to destroy the rebellious Israelites, Joshua's prayer for the sun to stand still, and Elijah's prayer for drought and then rain, were all answered by God. These, Calvin maintained, are vivid illustrations of the privilege that is open in prayer to all God's children. Commenting on Psalm 145:19, 'He fulfils the desire of those who fear him', Calvin writes that

> the Holy Spirit, by the mouth of David, tells us that God will accommodate himself to the desires of all who fear him. This is a mode of expression of which it is difficult to say how much it ought to impress our minds. Who is man, that God should show complaisance to his will, when rather it is ours to look up to his exalted greatness, and humbly submit to his authority? Yet he voluntarily condescends to these terms, to obtemper [comply with] our desires.

Calvin was not concerned to give a rational explanation of how the unchangeable God can be changed by our prayers. It is important to believe that the Bible teaches that God is omniscient, good, and sovereign, and that he works all things according to his perfect will. And it is important to know that in the Bible, God repeatedly assures us that he will hear and answer our prayers.

In our praying, we can safely follow Christ's example in Gethsemane when he prayed, 'My father, if it be possible, let this cup pass from me; nevertheless, not as I will, but as you will' (Matt. 26:39). Christ did not 'turn his eyes to the divine plan but rested his desire that burned within him upon his Father's knees'. So we 'in pouring out [our] prayers do not always rise to speculate upon the secret things of God'. 'As various musical sounds, different from each other, make no discord but compose a tuneful and sweet harmony', Calvin illustrates, 'so in Christ there exits a remarkable example of balance between the wills of God and of man;

they differ from each other without conflict or contradiction.' There is room in prayer, however, for tension between the human will and the divine will, Calvin maintains, indeed 'a kind of indirect disagreement'. For example, we pray rightly that the church may flourish and have peace when, indeed, at times it pleases God to make it quite otherwise. 'This is faith's due limit, to allow God to decide differently from what we desire.'

In all of this we must remember two truths: in his divine wisdom God anticipates our prayers, and in his divine love he responds to them. Preaching on Ephesians 3:20-4:2, Calvin said that God is 'much more acute than we, in knowing what we have need of and the means also that are fit to meet it for our profit'.

Six reasons why we should pray

Calvin provides six reasons why we should pray (III.20.3). His six points overlap and reinforce one another, exhorting us to flee to God 'as to a sacred anchor', bringing to him our love and our concerns, with thanksgiving for his kindness, with delight in his goodness, with confidence in his faithfulness, knowing that God 'extends his hand to help his own'. Calvin was content to end his short discussion of why we should pray by quoting 1 Peter 3:12: 'For the eyes of the Lord are upon the righteous, and his ears toward their prayers' (III.20.3).

Four rules of right prayer

Calvin next turns to an extended discussion of four rules of right prayer (III.20.4-14).

1. The first rule is reverence

'Moved by God's majesty', we pray with careful thought and deep devotion (III.20.5). 'Intense earnestness of soul', 'sincerity of heart', and 'pure simplicity' are 'the finest rhetoric' that we can bring to God, Calvin wrote in his commentary on Psalm 17:1. Preaching on Ephesians 6:18-19, Calvin said that our prayers must 'proceed from a well-disposed and earnest mind' and should not only be made with our mouth, but also come from 'the bottom of our heart'. Timothy Keller sums up Calvin's first rule: 'Calvin is simply telling us to drop all pretence, to flee from all phoniness' (*Prayer: Experiencing Awe and Intimacy with God*, 100).

2. The second rule is repentance and a sense of need

'Lawful prayer ... demands our repentance' (III.20.7). In the preface to his commentary on the Psalms, Calvin stated: 'Genuine and earnest prayer proceeds first from a sense of our need.' Prayer is the earnest cry of the human heart for help in the midst of circumstances that cannot be met by merely human resources.

3. The third rule is humility

'To sum up: the beginning, and even the preparation, of proper prayer is the plea for pardon with a humble and sincere confession of guilt' (III.20.9).

4. The fourth rule is confident hope

We are 'encouraged to pray by a sure hope that our prayer will be answered' (III.20.11). Calvin develops at some length the implications of this rule. 'If we would pray fruitfully, we ought therefore to grasp with both hands this assurance of obtaining what we ask ... For only that prayer is acceptable to God which is born, if I may so express it, out of such presumption of faith, and is grounded in unshaken assurance of hope' (III.20.12).

We could sum up Calvin's four rules by saying that we must strive to pray reverently, with a deep sense of need, with humility, and with confident hope.

Our weakness in prayer

Calvin sets a high standard for prayer, but he understands our weakness and failure. God will not 'reject those prayers in which he finds neither perfect faith nor repentance, together with a warmth of zeal and petitions rightly conceived' (III.20.16). In David's prayers, for example, there 'come forth—sometimes, rather boil up—turbulent emotions, quite out of harmony with the first rule that we laid down' (III.20.16). God tolerates 'even our stammering and pardons our ignorance' (III.20.16). He allows us to plead with him in a 'babbling manner' (Comm. Psa. 2:171) and to deal 'familiarly' with him (Comm. Psa. 89:38). 'When God descends to us he, in a certain sense, abases himself and stammers with us, so he allows us to stammer with him'

(Comm. Gen. 35:7). 'To pour out our complaints before him after the manner of little children would certainly be to treat his majesty with very little reverence, were it not that he has been pleased to allow us such freedom' (Comm. Psa. 102:2).

Calvin notes that God granted the petitions of Jotham, Samson, and others—even though their prayers were 'not framed to the rules of the word'. 'The prayers that God grants', Calvin explains, 'are not always pleasing to him'. Psalm 107 clearly teaches 'that prayers which do not reach heaven by faith still are not without effect'. In answering such prayers God bestows 'mercy even upon the unworthy', but their prayers are not 'a valid example for imitation' (III.20.15).

All this can be summarized as Calvin's fifth rule of prayer, *the rule of grace*, writes Timothy Keller: 'Only when we see we cannot keep the rules, and need God's mercy, can we become people who begin to keep the rules' (*Prayer: Experiencing Awe and Intimacy with God*, 104).

More about prayer

In developing his chapter on prayer up to this point, Calvin has touched on several points that he will repeat later. We pray invited by God, stirred up by faith, instructed by the word, guided by the Holy Spirit, and enabled by Christ.

1. We are invited by God to pray

God's many invitations in scripture are 'as so many banners set up before our eyes to inspire us with confidence'. He 'opens a way for us in his own words' and invites and bids us 'not to fear for the sweetness of the melody that he himself dictates'. He is 'easily entreated and readily accessible' (III.20.13). 'How gently God attracts us to himself' (III.20.14).

2. We are stirred up by faith to pray

Prayer is the sure outcome of the presence of faith in our hearts. 'To sum up', Calvin writes, 'it is faith that obtains whatever is granted to prayer' (III.20.11). 'We dig up by prayer the treasures that were pointed out by the Lord's gospel, and which our faith has gazed upon' (III.20.2). 'Faith … breaks into prayer and reaches for the riches of the grace of God which are revealed in the word' (Comm. Matt. 21:21).

3. We are instructed by the word in our prayers, which are simply a summing up of God's promises

Preaching on 2 Samuel 7:25-29, Calvin said that God's opening of our ears to hear his word 'opens our mouths as well. When we have heard God speak, then we respond mutually to him, so that there is harmony and accord between his promises by which he draws us to himself, and these prayers through which we come to him.' It is the word of God, then, that shapes and controls the content of our prayers. Calvin notes how often in the Psalms the 'thread of prayer' is broken by meditations on various aspects of God's character (III.20.13). David 'interlaces his prayers with holy meditations for the comfort of his own soul' (Comm. Psa. 57:3). 'As one must frequently lay on fuel to preserve a fire, so the exercise of prayer requires the aid of such helps' (Comm. Psa. 25:8).

4. We are helped by the Holy Spirit in our praying

It is the Spirit of God who 'stirs up in our hearts the prayers which it is proper for us to address to God' (Comm. Rom. 8:26). 'God teaches us in his word what he wants us to ask, and he also sets over us his Spirit as our leader and ruler to restrain our affections, that we may not let them stray beyond due bounds' (Comm. 1 John 5:14). 'We have a rule [for our prayers] prescribed to us in the word of God', but 'our affections remain oppressed with darkness in spite of this, until the Spirit guides them by his light.' The Holy Spirit not only directs the contents of our prayer, he 'affects our hearts in such a way that these prayers penetrate into heaven itself by their fervency' (Comm. Rom. 8:26). We are not to wait, however, until the Spirit moves us to pray, but 'flee to God and demand' that we be 'inflamed with the fiery darts of his Spirit, so as to be rendered fit for prayer' (*Calvin: Theological Treatises*, 121).

5. We are enabled by Christ to pray

Christ not only teaches us to pray but he enables us, sinful creatures, to come to a righteous and holy God in prayer. He is our 'advocate', 'mediator', 'intercessor', and 'intermediary', who transforms God's 'throne of dreadful glory into the throne of grace' (III.20.17). Christians pray 'in Christ's name', since Christ is both our 'mediator' and our 'mouth' (III.20.17, 21). Christ is the 'only mediator, by whose intercession the Father is for us rendered gracious and easily entreated' (III.20.19). He not only enables us to come to God without fear, he also in his priestly work, cleanses our prayers 'by sprinkled blood' (III.20.18). 'Let us learn to wash our prayers with the blood of our Lord Jesus Christ', Calvin told the people in a sermon on Genesis 26:23-25. 'Having entered the heavenly sanctuary', Christ 'alone bears to God the petitions of the people, who stay far off in the outer court' (III.20.20). 'Jesus Christ is our guide and advocate who makes intercession for us, so that we speak only, as it were, by his mouth' (Sermon on Eph. 3:14-19). T. H. L. Parker sums up Calvin's thought: 'It is, then, not simply a matter of praying through Christ, but rather with Christ, of our prayers being united with his intercession for us.' In an illustration that will appeal especially to Scottish Presbyterians, Parker adds, 'Thus Christ becomes the precentor who leads the prayers of his people' (*Calvin*, 110).

Calvin follows his treatment of the intercession of Christ with a rejection of the practice of praying to the saints (III.20.21-27). In this highly polemical section Calvin accuses the Roman Catholic Church of transferring to the saints 'that office of sole intercession which … belongs to Christ' (III.20.21). The saints are our examples in prayer, Calvin argues, but we do not pray to them or through them.

Types of prayer

Calvin next describes various kinds of prayer: private, public, spoken, sung, and silent (III.20.28-33).

In discussing private prayer, Calvin returns to many of the points that he has already made. Prayer includes petition, thanksgiving, and praise. It embraces both our seeking the extension of God's glory and our asking for our own needs.

For Calvin there are three important elements of public worship: preaching, prayers, and the administration of the sacraments. He writes that 'the chief part' of public worship 'lies in the office of prayer' (III.20.29). Calvin entitled his liturgy *The Form of Prayers*. Public prayers should take place at certain convenient stated times, but also at special times because of 'some major need' (III.20.29). Although there ought to be church buildings in which public prayers can be offered to God, 'we ourselves are God's true temple' (III.20.30). Prayer should be in the common language of the people and avoid ostentatious show and artificial eloquence. Prayer should be characterized by perseverance and constancy but not with 'vain repetition', although the frequent repetition of the same request is not vain, 'for hereby the saints, by little and little, discharge their cares into the bosom of God, and this importunity is a sacrifice of a sweet savour before him' (Comm. Psa. 86:7). 'As for the bodily gestures customarily observed in praying, such as kneeling and uncovering the head, they are exercises whereby we try to rise to a greater reverence for God' (III.20.33). Noting that Paul 'knelt down' when he prayed with the elders at Ephesus, Calvin wrote:

> The inward attitude certainly holds first place in prayer, but outward signs, kneeling, uncovering the head, lifting up the hands, have a twofold use. The first is that we may employ all our members for the glory and worship of God; secondly, that we are, so to speak, jolted out of our laziness by this help. There is also a third use in solemn and public prayer, because in this way the sons of God profess their piety, and they inflame each other with reverence of God. But just as lifting up the hands is a symbol of confidence and longing, so in order to show our humility, we fall down on our knees (Comm. Acts 20:36).

Singing

Singing, which is a form of public prayer, 'both lends dignity and grace to sacred actions and has the greatest value in kindling our hearts to true zeal' (III.20.32). In his commentary on Genesis 4:20 Calvin described music as one of the 'bright sparkling remnants of glory' to endure the fall. He urged those who 'have actually tasted the grace of God' to sing loudly with 'great earnestness … the praises of God' (Comm. Isa. 42:12). By singing, we 'with one common voice, and as it were, with the same mouth … glorify God together' (III.20.31). Our singing must 'spring from deep feeling of heart', giving careful attention to the words and with appropriate music suitable to 'the majesty of the church' (III.20.31, 32). By our singing, we not only express our praise and thanksgiving to God, we also help each other. Commenting on Hebrews 2:12, 'In the midst of the congregation I will sing your praise', Calvin wrote that it is not enough for each Christian individually to be grateful to God for the benefits he has received, without giving public evidence of our gratitude and thus mutually encouraging each other to the same purpose. This teaching is the very strongest encouragement to us to bring yet more fervent zeal to the praise of God, when we hear that Christ heeds our praise, and is the chief conductor of our hymns.

Throughout the Bible we find examples and patterns for our prayers. In the introduction to his commentary on the Psalms, Calvin wrote that 'a better and more unerring rule for guiding us in this exercise [of prayer] cannot be found elsewhere than in the Psalms'. Elsie McKee suggests that those who would like to hear the reformer praying 'with pen in hand' read Calvin's commentary and sermons on the Psalms. The Psalms for Calvin are 'the core of the worship and devotional life of the whole people of God, gathered as a body or living out their vocations from day to day' (*John Calvin: Writings on Pastoral Piety*, 22, 85). 'We shall find no better songs nor more appropriate … than the Psalms of David', wrote Calvin in the preface to the Psalter, 'which the Holy Spirit made and spoke through him. And furthermore, when we sing them, we are certain that God puts the words in our mouths, as if he himself were singing in us to exalt his glory.'

The Lord's Prayer

Meditation upon the promises of Scripture furnishes us with words and expressions for our own prayers. The Lord's Prayer is also a model for our prayers, and in III.20.34-49 Calvin gives a lengthy discussion of its meaning and use. We are not bound to the words of the prayers of the Psalms, the Lord's Prayer, and other biblical prayers, as long as we pray according to the patterns they provide. Our words may be 'utterly different, yet the sense ought not to vary' (III.20.49).

In the prayer which 'the heavenly Father has taught us through his beloved Son', we learn 'what is worthy of him, acceptable to him, necessary for us' (III.20.34, 48).

When we pray to 'our Father' we are moved by 'the great sweetness of this name'. 'He names himself our Father, and this is how he wants to be called by us. He takes away all our mistrust by the utter winsomeness of this name' (III.20.36). Praying to God as our Father shapes our attitude and conduct, because if God is our Father 'there ought not to be anything separate among us that we are not prepared gladly and wholeheartedly to share with one another' (III.20.38). 'Strife shuts the gate to prayers', Paul warns, and Christians should strive to 'offer their petitions in common with one accord' (III.20.39).

Calvin says that we are to be 'stirred up by the Holy Spirit to the duty of prayer in behalf of the common welfare of the church. Whilst each man takes sufficient care of his own individual interests, there is scarcely one in a hundred affected as he ought to be with the calamities of the church' (Comm. Psa. 102:1). Each of us, in suffering our 'private miseries and trials', should extend our 'desires and prayers to the whole church' (Comm. Psa. 25:22). Our prayers should reach beyond the church to everyone everywhere. 'Let the Christian man, then, conform his prayers to this rule in order that they may be in common and embrace all who are his brothers in Christ, not only those whom he at present sees and recognizes as such, but all men who dwell on earth. For what God has determined concerning them is beyond our knowing except that it is no less godly than humane to wish and hope the best for them' (III.20.38). When we pray to our Father who is in heaven, we understand that heaven and earth are ruled by his providence and power, and so remember not to measure God 'by our small measure', being assured that he is able to answer our prayers and provide for those who come to him' (III.20.40).

There are six petitions in the Lord's Prayer, grouped in two parts, each containing three points. The first part is concerned with God's glory and the second with our human needs. Both parts, however, Calvin states, are ultimately concerned with both God's glory and our benefit. The first three petitions are similar (because of our apathy, we need the repetition)— the hallowing of God's name is always attached to his reign, the chief feature of which is to be acknowledged in the doing of his will.

'Hallowed be thy name'

When we pray 'hallowed be thy name' we wish God to have 'the honor he deserves' in our lives and among all people, so that 'God may shine forth more and more in his majesty' (III.20.41).

'Thy kingdom come'

In praying 'thy kingdom come' we ask that God cast down all his enemies and humble 'the whole world', and that 'he shape all our thoughts in obedience to his rule'. God's kingdom comes as God gathers 'churches unto himself from all parts of the earth' and as Christians bear the cross. 'For it is in this way that God wills to spread his kingdom' (III.20.42). In his commentary on Matthew 6:10, Calvin comments: 'So we pray that God will show his power both in word and in Spirit, that the whole world may willingly come over to him', and that he will 'bring our hearts to obey his righteousness by the breathing of his Spirit, and restore to order at his will, all that is lying waste upon the face of the earth'. Calvin was impressed that the 'godliness and the sincerity' of the early Christians in Acts 4:25 is evident in their prayers 'not so much for their personal safety as for the advancement of the kingdom of Christ'.

'Thy will be done'

When we pray 'thy will be done' we ask not only that what is opposed to God's will may not be done, but also that 'we may learn to love the things that please him and to hate those which displease him' (III.20.43). Calvin warns believers not to impose any condition on God but 'leave to his decision to do what he is to do, in what way, at what time, and in what place it seems good to him' (III.20.50). In his commentary on 2 Corinthians 12:8, Calvin wrote that we must be careful not to specify too closely the means that God should use in answering our prayers and the exact manner and time in which his answer should come. We ask for those things that God has promised 'with full confidence and without reserve', Calvin asserted, 'but it is not for us to prescribe the means, and if we do specify them, our prayer always has an unexpressed qualification included in it'.

In praying the first three petitions of the Lord's Prayer we 'keep God's glory alone before our eyes', but in descending 'to our own affairs' in the second three petitions we do not 'bid farewell to God's glory' (III.20.43, 44).

'Give us this day our daily bread'

Calvin understands the prayer 'give us this day our daily bread' as a request for physical bread. To pray to God for everything, including the least things, is the ultimate test of faith, because 'by this we give ourselves over to his care, and entrust ourselves to his providence' (III.20.44). We ask God for our daily bread, even when we think we have enough to see us through. 'Unless God feeds us', Calvin wrote in his commentary on Matthew 6:11, 'no amount of accrued capital will mean anything. Although grain, wine, and everything else be there to overflowing, if they do not have the dew of God's unseen benediction, these all vanish on the spot, or that enjoyment is taken away, or the power they have to nourish us is lost, and we starve in the midst of great supply.'

'Forgive us our debts'

When we pray 'forgive us our debts, as we forgive our debtors', we understand that forgiveness on our part can only be accomplished by the power of the Holy Spirit, whose presence in our hearts is the witness of our adoption. God's children forgive; if we do not, we show ourselves not to be his children. Not only does this prayer require us to forgive others, it also comforts 'the weakness of our faith' by assuring us God 'has granted forgiveness of sins to us just as surely as we are aware of having forgiven others' (III.20.45).

'Lead us not into temptation'

In the prayer 'lead us not into temptation' we 'seek to be equipped with such armour and defended with such protection that we may be able to win the victory' (III.20.46). With the preceding petition, Christ has put 'the objects of our soul's eternal salvation and spiritual life … He offers us free reconciliation, by not imputing our sins to us, and he promises the Spirit, to engrave upon our hearts the righteousness of the law' (Comm. Matt. 6:12).

The conclusion to the Lord's Prayer

Calvin notes that the conclusion of the Lord's Prayer—'which it fits so well'—does not appear in the earliest New Testament manuscripts, but 'was added not only to warm our hearts to press towards the glory of

God, and warn us what should be the goal of all our supplications, but also to tell us that all our prayers ... have no other foundation than God alone' (Comm. Matt. 6:13).

By concluding our prayer with the word 'Amen' our hope is 'strengthened' that God hears and answers our prayers, our confidence stemming 'solely from God's nature' (III.20.47).

Persevering in prayer

Calvin states that not only should we pray 'without ceasing', or with steady 'constancy', as he interprets 1 Thessalonians 5:17, but we should also 'set apart certain hours' for prayer (III.20.50). Just as Israel had fixed times in which to present sacrifices, we should also have specific times for prayer. Noting that Daniel prayed three times a day, Calvin advises that 'unless we fix certain hours in the day for prayer, it easily slips from our memory'. He recommended special times of prayer throughout the day and wrote sample prayers for people to use on those occasions: in the morning, when rising; before school or work; before eating; thanksgiving after eating; and before going to sleep at night.

Calvin closes his long chapter on prayer by encouraging us to 'learn to persevere in prayer ... and patiently wait for the Lord' (III.20.51-52). When we do not experience the benefits we seek we must not fall into despair or become indignant with God, but

> our faith will make us sure of what cannot be perceived by sense, that we have obtained what was expedient. For the Lord so often and so certainly promises to care for us in our troubles, when they have once been laid upon his bosom. And so he will cause us to possess abundance in poverty, and comfort in affliction. For though all things fail us, yet God will never forsake us, who cannot disappoint the expectation and patience of his people (III.20.52).

Even when God does not comply with our wishes, he 'is still attentive and kindly to our prayers' (III.20.52). 'The only legitimate proof of trust is when anyone who is disappointed of his desire does not lose heart', Calvin says (Comm. Luke 18:1-6). We learn from Daniel that 'our prayers may be already heard while God's favour and mercy is concealed from us'. We learn from Christ's experience in Gethsemane that 'God often hears our prayers, even when it is least apparent' (Comm. Heb. 5:7). We learn from Paul's prayer in 2 Corinthians 12:8 that we should 'not to be despondent, when God does not meet or satisfy our requests, as though prayer were wasted effort. For his grace ought to be sufficient for us, that is, it should be enough that he has not forsaken us. This is why he sometimes withholds from the godly in his mercy things that he grants to the ungodly in his wrath, because he himself can foresee better than our minds what is good for us.' Even though we are disappointed in our expectations in our prayers, we can make known to God our perplexities about our very prayers—unburdening even this burden to him (Comm. Psa. 22:2).

In the *Institutes* and in his commentaries and sermons, Calvin endeavoured to uphold God's people in prayer, like Aaron and Hur holding up the hands of Moses in Exodus 17, continually exhorting them not to become discouraged but to strive 'toward a goal not immediately attainable' (III.20.16).

Knowing God and ourselves

'Thus we may say that the purpose of prayer is not to inform God, but rather to reform disciples: to wake them up, alert them to their benefits and so to their benefactor, comfort their nerves, sharpen their senses, strengthen their faith, kindle their hearts—in short to revive and restore them' (Boulton, *Life in God*, 179).

18. Election— 'The Book of Life'

'The holy Scripture calls God's election *the book of life* … Jesus Christ serves as a register. It is in him that we are written down and acknowledged by God as his children. Seeing, then, that God had an eye to us in the person of Jesus Christ, it follows that he did not find anything in us which we might lay before him to cause him to elect us. This, in sum, is what we must always remember' (Sermon on Eph. 1:3-4).

'Derived from Scripture, developed and advanced in relation to other key doctrines such as the doctrines of God, sin, grace, justification, Christ, and the church, the doctrine of predestination is understood by Calvin to teach that God has, in Christ, elected to salvation a certain number from all eternity and reprobated others, or decreed that they remain in the state of sin, and that this decree must be traced finally to the unquestionable and inscrutable will of God. He understood this doctrine to be biblical and theologically necessary, and he understood it as a pastoral doctrine, a source of comfort and assurance' to believers (Clark, *A Theological Guide to Calvin's Institutes*, 122).

Read: *Institutes* III.21-24. [*1541* ch.8, pp.463-498.]

Scripture Text: 'Blessed is the one you choose and bring near, to dwell in your courts' (Psa. 65:4).

Notable Quote: 'We shall never be clearly persuaded as we ought to be, that our salvation flows from the wellspring of God's free mercy until we come to know his eternal election' (III.21.1).

Prayer

Grant, Almighty God, that as you have been pleased to adopt us once for all as your people for this end, that we might be engrafted, as it were, into the body of your Son, and so be made conformable to our head, O grant that through our whole life we may strive to seal in our hearts the faith of our election.

May we be the more stimulated to render you true obedience, that your glory may also be made known through us; and those others also whom you have chosen together with us may we labour to bring with us, that we may with one accord celebrate you as the author of our salvation.

May we so ascribe to you the glory of your goodness, that having cast away and renounced all confidence in our own virtue, we may be led to Christ only as the fountain of your election, in whom also is set before us the certainty of our salvation through your gospel, until we shall at length be gathered with him into that eternal glory which he has procured for us by his own blood. Amen.

(*Devotions and Prayers of John Calvin*, 113.)

A look back and a look ahead

John Calvin became known, even in his lifetime, for his doctrine of election. But, despite what some think, Calvin did not invent the doctrine. '"The elect" and "election" are terms used twenty-three times in the New Testament, seven times by Jesus, and are therefore significant in all classical theology, though folklore attributes the notion to Calvin and blames him for it', writes Marilynne Robinson (*John Calvin: Steward of God's Covenant*, xxvi).

What is most surprising about Calvin's treatment of election in the 1559 edition of the *Institutes* is its location. Calvin does not deal with election in Book I, although he occasionally reminds his readers that it could be explored, as part of the doctrine of providence, for example. It is not treated in Book II, but never seems far from Calvin's mind. In Book 3 the doctrine of election is given ample treatment in four chapters. In the earlier editions of the *Institutes* Calvin treats predestination along with providence as part of the doctrine of God. But in the final edition, although providence remains as part of Book I, Calvin moves predestination to Book 3, where he sets forth the doctrine of salvation. The reason for this new location for specific and detailed treatment of election is 'not deeply theological but pedagogical and strategic', writes Paul Helm (*Calvin at the Centre*, 132). 'If you begin with predestination, it becomes virtually impossible to hear Calvin say anything else', writes B. A. Gerrish (*Grace and Gratitude*, 170). Therefore, Calvin doesn't begin his theology with predestination or election. When he finally comes to it, we are ready to hear what he has to say.

Calvin's chapters on election follow his discussion about prayer. True prayer is the casting away of all thought of our own glory and worth and in humility giving glory completely to God. The doctrine of election—God's great grace and our total emptiness before him—continues the same theme. 'The practice of this doctrine [of election] ought also to flourish in our prayers', Calvin writes. We pray to God who has already chosen to rescue and redeem us as beloved children, for 'it would be preposterous' for them to pray as if their salvation were somehow in doubt, as if to say, 'O Lord, if I have been chosen, hear me' (III.24.5).

Election

'To make it clear that our salvation comes about solely from God's mere generosity, we must be called back to [the doctrine] of election' which ought to be 'gloriously and vociferously proclaimed' (III.21.1).

> 'The old minister was a splendid Calvinist, of heroic type, and as he discoursed of God's sovereignty and election, his face glowed and his voice rang out' (Ralph Connor, *Black Rock: A Tale of the Selkirks*, 285).

Calvin's doctrine of election was basically the same as that of Luther and the other reformers, and greatly influenced by Augustine's writings. Calvin writes, 'If I wanted to weave a whole volume from Augustine, I could readily show my readers that I need no other language than his.' But 'let us imagine that these [church] fathers are silent', adds Calvin. 'Let us pay attention to the matter itself' (III.22.8).

To 'pay attention to the matter itself' means to examine the Scriptures, which is what Calvin does. We must believe and teach the doctrine of election, but we must be careful not go beyond what Scripture says. 'To desire any other knowledge of predestination than that which is expounded by the word of God is no less infatuated [or unreasonable] than to walk where there is no path, or to seek light in darkness' (III.21.2). 'Let us, I say, permit the Christian man to open his mind and ears to every utterance of God directed to him, provided it be with such restraint that when the Lord closes his holy lips, he also shall at once close the way to inquiry' (III.21.3). 'When, therefore, one asks why God has so done, we must reply: because he has willed it. But if you proceed further to ask why he so willed, you are seeking something greater and higher than God's will, which cannot be found' (III.23.2).

Calvin does not treat the doctrine of election in a philosophical or speculative manner but by means of practical questions. Warfield says that it is not to 'cosmical predestination' that Calvin's thought turned 'but rather to that soteriological predestination on which, as a helpless sinner needing salvation from the free grace of God, he must rest' (*Calvin and Augustine*, 483).

Why do some people hear the gospel preached and others do not? And why do some who hear respond and others do not? Calvin answers: 'In actual fact, the covenant of life is not preached equally among all men, and among those to whom it is preached, it does not gain the same acceptance either constantly or in equal degree. In this diversity the wonderful depth of God's judgment is made known' (III.21.1). 'Rare indeed is the mind that is not repeatedly struck with this thought: whence comes your salvation but from God's election' (III.24.4).

The doctrine of election functions in a very specific way in Calvin's theology. As one writer has expressed it, predestination 'is a long way from being the centre of Calvinism; much rather it is the last consequence of faith in the grace of Christ in the presence of the enigmas of experience' (Wendel, *Calvin*, 265). The doctrine of election makes absolutely clear that salvation is completely of God. 'We shall never be clearly persuaded, as we ought to be, that our salvation flows from the well-spring of God's free mercy until we come to know his eternal election', Calvin writes (III.21.1). B. B. Warfield agrees, 'When you teach free grace, absolutely free grace, and mean it, you are a predestinarian' (*Selected Shorter Works* 1:402).).

'One week night, when I was sitting in the house of God, … the thought struck me, How did you come to be a Christian? I sought the Lord. But how did you come to seek the Lord? The truth flashed across my mind in a moment—I should not have sought him unless there had been some previous influence in my mind to make me seek him. I prayed, thought I, but then I asked myself, How came I to pray? I was induced to pray by reading the Scriptures. How came I to read the Scriptures? … Then … I saw that God was at the bottom of it all, and that he was the author of my faith, and so the whole doctrine of grace opened up to me' ('A Defence of Calvinism', *The Early Years: The Autobiography of C. H. Spurgeon*).

The human order is first faith, then election, but the 'divine order', according to Calvin, is first election, then faith. Election precedes faith as to its divine order, but is understood by faith. Faith is the only way into the doctrine of election. 'Take away faith and election is mutilated', wrote Calvin (Comm. John 6:40). At the same time, 'election is the mother of faith' (III.22.10). The doctrine of election answers the question 'Where did my faith come from?' It is an *ex post facto* reflection on how, amid the darkness and death of our sin, God's grace has broken through and saved us. 'When one comes to election, there mercy alone appears on every side' (III.24.1). R. C. Reed wrote, 'Through all the endless future, redeemed sinners will find no explanation of the blessedness which they enjoy other than the love which glowed in the heart of God before the foundations of the world were laid' (*The Gospel as Taught by Calvin*).

> Pause, my soul, adore, and wonder!
> Ask, O why such love to me?
> Grace hath put me in the number
> Of the Saviour's family:
> Hallelujah!
> Thanks, eternal thanks, to thee!
>
> James George Deck;
> quoted by C. H. Spurgeon, 'A Defence of Calvinism',
> *The Early Years: The Autobiography of C. H. Spurgeon.*

Calvin understands the Scriptures to teach that predestination is sovereign, particular, and includes both the elect and the reprobate. 'Experience teaches' what Scripture clearly proclaims—God 'does not indiscriminately adopt all into the hope of salvation but gives to some what he denies to others' (III.21.1).

Sovereign predestination

When Calvin looks reverently into 'the wonderful depth of God's judgment', he finds first of all that God's predestination rests solely on God's will.

- 'God adopts some to hope of life, and sentences others to eternal death' (III.21.5).

- Election is 'God's eternal decree, by which he compacted with himself what he willed to become of each man' (III.21.5).

- God 'not only offers salvation but so assigns it that the certainty of its effect is not in suspense or doubt' (III.21.7).

- God 'is not a watcher but the author of our salvation' (III.22.6).

Particular predestination

There is, Calvin says, a double election by God. First, there is the national election of Israel by which God joined all Israel to his family as 'inferior' members until they cut themselves off. This was 'a kind of middle way between the rejection of mankind and the election of a small number of the godly' (III.21.7). There is 'a second, more limited degree of election', by which God chose individuals (III.21.6).

Calvin asserts that God's election of the human person of Jesus is an illustration of his particular election. 'By what virtues will they say that [Christ] deserved in the womb itself to be made head of the angels, only-begotten Son of God, image and glory of the Father, light, right-eousness, and salvation of the world … But if they wilfully strive to strip God of his free power to choose or reject, let them at the same time also take away what has been given to Christ' (III.22.1).

Double predestination

Calvin did not use the expression 'double predestination', but it is a convenient way to describe Calvin's teaching that predestination includes both salvation and reprobation.

- 'God adopts some to hope of life, and sentences others to eternal death' (III.21.5).

- 'God once established by his eternal and unchangeable plan those whom he long before determined once for all to receive into salvation, and those whom, on the other hand, he would devote to destruction' (III.21.7).

The ultimate cause of both election and reprobation is the will of God, but there is a proximate cause in reprobation—sin, in which resides the reason for damnation—but no proximate cause in election. 'When it is said that God hardens or shows mercy to whom he wills, men are warned by this to seek no other cause outside his will' (III.22.11). The only cause behind the election of the elect is God; 'the real and remote cause behind the reprobate is also God, but the real and proximate cause of reprobation is the self', writes Charles Partee (*The Theology of John Calvin*, 241). People want to know why God chose some and passed by others. Don't ask me, says John Calvin; don't ask any man; but ask God. And God's answer is Deuteronomy 29:29, 'The secret things belong to the Lord our God, but the things revealed belong to us and to our children forever.' God chose some to holiness and sonship because it pleased him to do so. Why it pleased him to do so, it has not pleased him to reveal.

Some have argued that Calvin's doctrine of reprobation is based more on logic than on Scripture. There are a few places where Calvin uses logic in treating this doctrine, especially in III.23.1. 'Election itself could not stand except as set over against reprobation.' 'God is said to set apart those whom he adopts into salvation; it will be highly absurd to say that others acquire by chance or obtain by their own effort what election alone confers on a few.' 'It is utterly inconsistent to transfer the preparation for destruction to anything but God's secret plan.' Calvin occasionally appeals to logic when it furthers his argument, but the foundation of his doctrine of election and reprobation is not logic but Scripture. Writing about Calvin's doctrine of reprobation, Edward Dowey states that it seems 'unlikely that we have here a sudden abandonment of Calvin's whole method for a single experiment in philosophy, especially when he denied it so continuously … We have here, one might say, a reckless consistency in working out of the biblical teaching of the gratuitousness of divine mercy' (*The Knowledge of God in Calvin's Theology*, 218-19). Or rather we have here a persistent consistency in Calvin's setting forth 'the biblical teaching of the gratuitousness of divine mercy'.

Calvin's treatment of this doctrine is saturated with Scripture, especially III.21.5-7. He ends III.21 with a summary survey of the doctrine of election that begins with the words, 'As Scripture, then clearly shows …' (III.21.7) and adds another chapter with the title 'Confirmation of this Doctrine from Scriptural Testimonies'. Calvin rests his doctrine of predestination on Scripture, but declares it is also consonant with observation and experience.

Practically and pastorally, Calvin emphasizes election but not reprobation. We can and must preach election in order to set forth the fullness and freeness of God's grace, but we cannot preach reprobation. 'The distinction [between election and reprobation] was vital to [Calvin], for we find him frequently returning to it even in his sermons, in order to throw into relief the absolutely gratuitous nature of election' (Wendel, *Calvin*, 272). But we must not preach the doctrine of reprobation to condemn those who do not believe. That, Calvin says, would be 'cursing rather than teaching' (III.23.14). When a Calvinist minister described one of the leading persecutors of Protestants in France as reprobate, Calvin wrote that 'we must guard against presumption and temerity, for [there is no one who can know that] but one Judge before whose tribunal we have all to render an account' (*John Calvin: Writings on Pastoral Piety*, 310). In his commentary on Psalm 109:16, Calvin wrote, 'As we cannot distinguish between the elect and the reprobate, it is our duty to pray for all who trouble us; to desire the salvation of all men; and even to be careful for the welfare of every individual.'

We must never use the doctrine of election to obscure or weaken the freeness of the gospel invitation. People must hear from us what will draw them to Christ, not what will discourage them. 'God is undoubtedly ready to pardon whenever the sinner turns' (III.24.15). 'We try to make everyone we meet a sharer in our peace' (III.23.14). Calvin often ended his sermons by a prayer calling on Christians to praise God for his blessing in their lives and asking God 'to grant this grace not only to us but also to all peoples' (see Sermon on Eph. 1:1-3). In his discussion of the Christian life, Calvin says that there is a difference between believers and unbelievers, and adds 'now you must choose in which group you would prefer to be numbered' (III.8.6).

The cause and ground of election and reprobation

God's decree to elect some to salvation cannot rest on their good works, because the decree was made before the foundation of the world and so before the existence of individuals. 'What basis for distinction is there among those who did not yet exist?' Calvin asks (III.22.2). Neither can the decree rest on foreseen good works of individuals, for there were no good works to be foreseen. 'The grace of God does not find, but makes, persons fit to be chosen' (III.22.8). God's decree to elect some to salvation rests solely on God's good pleasure. 'The intrinsic cause of this is in himself', Calvin insists. Note that Calvin includes Christ as the author of election, along with God the Father. Christ claims with the Father 'the right to choose' (III.22.7). 'But, as many as were at last incorporated into the body of Christ were God's sheep, as Christ himself testifies (John 10:16), though formerly wandering sheep and outside the fold. Meantime, though they did not know it, the shepherd knew them, according to that eternal predestination by which he chose his own before the foundation of the world, as Augustine says' (*Concerning the Eternal Predestination of God*, 150).

> 'I believe the doctrine of election because I am quite certain that if God had not chosen me, I should never have chosen him; and I am sure that he chose me before I was born, or else he never would have chosen me afterwards; and he must have elected me for reasons unknown to me, for I never could find any reason in myself why he should have looked upon me with special love' ('A Defence of Calvinism', *The Early Years: The Autobiography of C. H. Spurgeon*).

God's decree of reprobation does not rest on sinful works nor on foreseen sinful works. Pointing to Romans 9:13, 'Just as it is written: Jacob I loved, but Esau I hated', Calvin says that 'Paul does not defend God's righteousness by saying that God recompensed Esau according to his works but insists that the reprobate are raised up in order that the glory of God may be thereby displayed' (III.22.11).

Calvin is awestruck but unrelenting in his insistence that the Bible teaches that God is the author of reprobation. By his 'just and irreprehensible but incomprehensible judgment [God] has barred the door of life to those whom he has given over to damnation' (III.21.7). Calvin recognizes the seriousness of what he is saying and admits that the decree of reprobation is 'dreadful indeed'—in the sense of awesome or mysterious, not, of course, wicked or evil (III.23.7).

Reprobation is grounded in God's judgment, and that judgment is 'incomprehensible'—not in the sense that it is incoherent, but in the sense that it is 'unfathomable' (Helm, *Calvin at the Centre*, 148-49).

According to Marilynne Robinson, Calvin 'believes in eternal repro-bation, but ... never seems to allow himself to imagine it' (*The Death of Adam*, 222).

While God's good pleasure is the ultimate cause of reprobation, there is also a proximate or evident cause—not of reprobation as such, but of condemnation. The evident cause is human sin. In sin resides all the blame and guilt for a person's damnation. 'Man falls according as God's providence ordains, but he falls by his own fault.' 'Accordingly, we should contemplate the evident cause of condemnation in the corrupt nature of humanity—which is closer to us—rather than seek a hidden and utterly incomprehensible cause in God's predestination' (III.23.8). In thinking of their salvation, Christians look to God's election alone, not to anything in themselves. But in thinking of the condemnation of the lost, we look to human sin, which is closer to us, rather than to God's decree, which is beyond us. God stands in a direct relation to the elect, and in both a direct and indirect or accidental relation to the reprobate. 'When ... Christ says that he is come for judgment, when he is called a stone of stumbling, when he is said to be set for the falling of many, it may be regarded as accidental, or so to say, foreign. For those who reject the grace offered in him deserve to find him the judge and avenger' (Comm. John 3: 17).

The ultimate goal of election is the glory of God and the proximate goal is the sanctification of the believer. 'Paul teaches that we have been chosen to this end: that we may lead a holy and blameless life' (III.23. 12). The ultimate goal of reprobation is the glory of God. God is glorified in the setting forth of his justice and righteousness. 'When mention is made of the glory of God', says Calvin, 'let us think also of his right-eousness' (III.23.8).

Uses of the doctrine of election

'Calvin frames his discussion of predestination ... in terms of humility, hope, gratitude, confidence, and doxology' (Boulton, *Life in God*, 147). There are three proper uses of the doctrine of election, which Calvin calls 'its very sweet fruit' (III.21.1).

1. The doctrine of election gives glory to God and humbles us

The knowledge of predestination keeps those who obey from being proud, as though their faith was 'something of their own', and leads them to 'glory in the Lord' (III.23.13). Preaching on Ephesians 1:7-10, Calvin said, 'As soon as we presume to bring anything at all to God, surely it is a putting forward of ourselves to the obscuring of God's grace so that it no longer has its beauty and pre-eminence as it ought.'

In his commentary on Psalm 65:4, 'Blessed is the one you choose and bring near, to dwell in your courts', Calvin wrote: 'We are near him, not as having anticipated his grace and come to him of ourselves, but because in his condescension, [God] has stretched out his hand as far as hell itself to reach us.'

> John Leith: 'Predestination undercuts all confidence in work-righteousness and lays bare the source of human salvation. It is the negation of all merit and places salvation solely in the mercy of God. It means that salvation is rescue and not achievement' (*John Calvin's Doctrine of the Christian Life*, 122).

2. The doctrine of election encourages confidence

Rather than producing fear and uncertainty in the believer about his or her ultimate destiny, predestination encourages confidence. 'Predestination, rightly understood, brings no shaking of faith but rather its best confirmation' (III.24.9). We do not 'find assurance of our election in ourselves'—that is, in our own good works (III.24.5). Good works are not worthless in pointing to our salvation and so to our election. Calvin wrote, 'Purity of life is rightly regarded as the illustration and evidence of election' (Comm. 2 Pet. 1:10). Our good works, however, are so small and unstable that our confidence cannot rest completely upon them. 'Faith totters when it pays attention to works' (III.11.11). Selderhuis comments, 'If one had to contribute even only a pebble to one's own salvation, one would live in lifelong fear that one's pebble was just not big enough' (*John Calvin: A Pilgrim's Life*, 190). God's saints do not place their ultimate confidence in their good works but 'regard them solely as gifts of God from which they may recognize his goodness and as signs of the calling by which they realize their election' (III.14.20). Preaching on Ephesians 1:3-4, Calvin said that 'when our Lord intends to assure us of our salvation, he brings us back to … eternal election'.

Furthermore, we cannot find assurance of our election 'in God the Father, if we conceive him as severed from his Son' (III.24.5). We do not have direct knowledge of the electing decree of God. 'Christ', says Calvin, 'is the mirror wherein we must, and without self-deception may, contemplate our own election.' Calvin bids believers to seek the 'sure establishment' of their election 'from the word of the gospel' (III.24.7). Preaching on Ephesians 1:4-6, Calvin uses the illustration of the mirror in a double way. God looks in the mirror and sees Christ; the believer looks in the mirror and sees Christ. 'Jesus Christ is the mirror in which God beholds us when he wishes to find us acceptable to himself. Likewise, on our side, he is the mirror on which we must cast our eyes and look, when we desire to come to the knowledge of our election.'

'If Pighius [Dutch theologian who wrote against Calvin's views] asks how I know I am elect', writes Calvin, 'I answer that Christ is more than a thousand testimonies to me.' 'God begins with himself, when he sees fit to elect us; but he will have us begin with Christ so that we may know that we are numbered among his peculiar people' (*Eternal Predestination of God*, 127, 130). A person cannot know whether he or she is predestined to life 'by *a priori* reasoning, or by directly divining God's will, but only *a posteriori*, through his relationship to Christ' (Helm, *Calvin at the Centre*, 59). Faith is the only way into the doctrine of election, and all that it sees there is God's mercy in Christ.

In a sermon, Calvin puts this truth in a striking way: 'Whosoever then believes is thereby assured that God has worked in him, and faith is, as it were, the duplicate copy that God gives us of the original of our adoption. God has his eternal counsel, and he always reserves to himself the chief and original record of which he gives us a copy by faith' (Sermon on Eph. 1:4-6). One of the texts, says Calvin, that tells us that we can know God's election is John 3:16—a text that is often used to deny the doctrine of election! The verse 'ascribes the glory for our salvation entirely to [God's] love'.

Calvin warns us not to try to understand predestination outside of Christ.

> Satan has no more grievous or dangerous temptation to dishearten believers than when he unsettles them with doubt about their election, while at the same time he arouses them with a wicked desire to seek it outside the way. I call it 'seeking outside the way' when mere man attempts to break into the inner recesses of divine wisdom and tries to penetrate even to highest eternity, in order to find out what decision has been made concerning himself at God's judgment (III.24.4).

> Is my name written there,
>   On the page white and fair?
> In the book of thy kingdom,
>   Is my name written there?
>
> Lord, my sins they are many,
>   Like the sands of the sea,
> But thy blood, O my Saviour,
>   Is sufficient for me.
>
> For thy promise is written,
>   In bright letters that glow,
> 'Though your sins be as scarlet,
>   I will make them like snow.'
>   W. E. Biederwolf

3. The doctrine of election leads us to reverence and to worship

Calvin delights in quoting Augustine on God's election: 'Thou seekest reason? I tremble at the depth. Reason thou; I will marvel. Dispute thou;

I will believe. I see the depth; I do not reach the bottom. Paul rested, for he found wonder' (III.23.5).

Objections to predestination answered

1. Predestination makes God a tyrant

'The will of God', Calvin says, 'is not only free of all fault but is the highest rule of perfection' (III.23.2). Calvin points to scriptures such as Romans 9:20-21: 'Does the potter have no capacity to make from the same lump one vessel for honour, another for dishonour?' That God so willed to deal with the human race this way is right, but why he so willed to do this 'is not for our reason to inquire, for we cannot comprehend it' (III.23.5).

2. Predestination removes human guilt and responsibility from human beings

Calvin answers that 'man falls as God's providence ordains, but he falls by his own fault' (III.23.8).

'That God predestines, and yet man is responsible, are two facts that few can see clearly. They are believed to be inconsistent and contradictory to each other. If, then, I find taught in one part of the Bible that everything is foreordained, that is true; and if I find, in another Scripture, that man is responsible for all his actions, that is true; and it is only my folly that leads me to imagine that these two truths can ever contradict each other. I do not believe that they can ever be welded into one upon any earthly anvil, but they certainly shall be one in eternity. They are two lines that are so nearly parallel, that the human mind which pursues them farthest will never discover that they converge, but they do converge, and they will meet somewhere in eternity, close to the throne of God, whence all truth doth spring' ('A Defence of Calvinism', *The Early Years: The Autobiography of C. H. Spurgeon*).

3. Predestination leads to the view that God shows partiality toward persons

God does not discriminate on the basis of race or riches or anything else. God chooses those whom he pleases, according to the good pleasure of his will, not according to the characteristics or qualities of persons. Election is not due to partiality but to God's mercy. Acts 10:34 and Galatians 2:6 state that 'God shows no partiality.' Galatians 3:28 asserts that Jews and Greeks, slave and free, male and female are 'all one in Christ Jesus'. First Corinthians 1:26 declares that God does not call many who are wise, powerful, or of noble birth. Predestination doesn't depend on who the person is who is chosen; it depends on God who chooses.

4. Predestination destroys zeal for holiness

There is a great difference, Calvin writes, between these two things: 'to cease well-doing because election is sufficient for salvation', and 'to devote ourselves to the pursuit of good as the appointed goal of election' (III.23.12). Preaching on Ephesians 1:4-6, Calvin said, 'Seeing then that he has chosen us to be holy and to walk in purity of life, our election must be as a root that yields good fruits.'

5. Predestination makes admonitions meaningless

It did not for Paul, that 'outspoken preacher of free election'. Nor for Christ, who said, 'No one can come to me unless it has been granted him by my Father.' Nor for Augustine, who said, 'let preaching then take its course that it may lead men to faith, and hold them fast in perseverance with continuing profit' (III.23.13). Nor for Calvin, who deplored the decline in morality and faithfulness to God that he had observed during his lifetime, but rejoiced in evidence of God's continued outpouring of mercy—'God's grace is preached, forgiveness of sins is announced; God calls those that were lost a hundred thousand times over' (Sermon on Eph. 3:1-6).

Knowing God and ourselves

Let us humble ourselves and give all the glory of God for our salvation. Let us rejoice in confidence that our salvation is in the hands of God, and has been from before the foundation of the world. Let us, like the apostle Paul, find 'wonder' in what God has done.

19. The Final Resurrection— 'Promised Glory'

'Since Scripture everywhere bids us wait in expectation for Christ's coming, and defers until then the crown of glory, let us be content with the limits divinely set for us: namely, that the souls of the pious, having ended the toil of their warfare, enter into blessed rest, where in glad expectation they await the enjoyment of *promised glory*' (III.25.6).

'For Calvin, a fruitful consideration of the eternal glory of the believer in Christ was the logical end and crown of an orderly theological discussion on God's grace' (Andrew Davis, *A New Assessment of John Calvin's Eschatology*, 265).

Read: *Institutes* **III.25.** [*1541* ch.4, pp.287-293.]

Scripture Text: 'For we know that if the tent, which is our earthly home, is destroyed, we have a building from God, a house not made with hands, eternal in the heavens' (2 Cor. 5:1).

Notable Quote: 'We are redeemed by our Lord Jesus Christ … but we do not have the effect and full fruition of it as yet. There is, then, a double redemption—one which was accomplished in the person of our Lord Jesus Christ, and another which we wait for and which shall be shown to us at his coming again' (Sermon on Eph. 1:13-14).

Prayer

Almighty God, we have already entered in hope upon the threshold of our eternal inheritance, and know that there is a mansion for us in heaven since Christ, our head and the first fruits of our salvation, has been received there. Grant that we may proceed more and more in the way of your holy calling until at length we reach the goal and so enjoy the eternal glory of which you have given us a taste in this world, by the same Christ our Lord. Amen.

(This prayer is the last in Calvin's commentary on Ezekiel, which ends with Ezekiel 20:44. A few days after writing these words, Calvin died.)

'When Calvin died in 1564 he instructed his friends to see to it that he was buried in an unmarked grave … The memorial he wanted was the memorial he already had, the living legacy of the men and women whose lives he had influenced, and the sermons, commentaries, treatises, catechetical literature, letters, confessions, and multiple editions of the *Institutes* he bequeathed to the church' (Steinmetz, *The Cambridge Companion to Reformation Theology*, 129).

A look back and a look ahead

Calvin's chapter on 'The final resurrection' is the 'crowning act' of Book III (Wendel, *Calvin*, 284). In the opening section of III.25, Calvin collects thoughts from earlier chapters of the *Institutes*—just as the great west window in the Princeton University Chapel, portraying the second coming of Christ, displays many of the images from the other windows of the chapel, pictures from the Old Testament, the New Testament, and church history. For Calvin, eschatology is not the end of all things, but the majestic summing up of all things. Cornelis P. Venema writes: 'Eschatology, or a consideration of the goal or *telos* of the works of the triune God, constitutes a pervasive thread that is interwoven throughout the entirety of the *Institutes* as well as Calvin's other writings' (*A Theological Guide to Calvin's Institutes*, 442).

In Book III John Calvin has presented at length the redemptive work of Christ, the mediator, and the ministry of the Holy Spirit, who creates and unites believers to Christ. They thereby receive the double benefit of justification and sanctification—acceptance with God and renewal after the image of God. 'In union with Christ, believers are justified, sanctified, and ultimately glorified. Considering the location of chapter 25 in the *Institutes* [at the end of Book III], it might well be titled, "The Believer's Glorification in Union with Christ"' (Venema, *A Theological Guide to Calvin's Institutes*, 445). Preaching on Matthew 28:1-10, Calvin said that we are nourished by Christ daily 'until we are united with him in his glory in another fashion than we are now' (*John Calvin: Writings on Pastoral Piety*, 123).

'For all the many centuries of church history, powerful applications of eschatology like those of John Calvin have been the healthiest theological treatments. These applications have helped prepare God's chosen people for eternity, as each generation has been born, has lived, and has died. The eschatological applications have exhorted us to flee the wrath to come, to live holy and godly lives worthy of the calling we have received, to be ready in season and out of season, to do the work of evangelists. They have encouraged us to stand firm until the end in times of terrible persecutions, to avoid excessive grief at the death of loved ones, to love our enemies, and to live for the joy of rewards which only God can give' (Andrew Davis, *A New Assessment of John Calvin's Eschatology*, 330).

Calvin is aware of the brevity of his treatment of 'the final resurrection' in the *Institutes* and confesses his inability to do justice to the topic, explaining, 'I am only touching upon what could be treated more fully and deserves to be set out more brilliantly' (III.25.3). Two chapters in Book III of the *Institutes* focus on eschatology—chapter 9, 'Meditation on the Future Life' and chapter 25, 'The Final Resurrection'. Calvin's prayers at the end of his sermons almost always end with words about the life to come. In his letters Calvin often wrote about heaven to encourage and strengthen believers in times of suffering and trouble, as he does in the last sentence of III.25: 'Although by his mere glance [God] scatters and brings to nought all mortal men, he urges his own worshippers on, the more because they are timid in this world, that he may inspire them, burdened with the cross, to press forward, until he himself is "all in all".'

Calvin did not write a commentary on the book of Revelation. Thomas Philpot noted that Calvin 'had expounded all the books of Scripture except the Revelation, which his not doing of was an excellent commentary'. Others have regretted Calvin's neglect of Revelation. Andrew Davis wrote, 'While many writers on eschatology have trampled down the boundaries of restraint which Calvin so valued, Calvin himself failed to go right up to the limits of what God had tendered to us, thus leaving some of the field of scripture untilled and unfruitful' (*A New Assessment of John Calvin's Eschatology*, 2). Calvin did write commentaries on Daniel and the first twenty chapters of Ezekiel, books that bear some resemblance to Revelation, and may have intended to write a commentary on Revelation, but died before he could accomplish that task.

In III.25 Calvin repeats his frequent warning about curiosity and speculation. He writes, 'I not only refrain personally from superfluous investigation of useless matters, but I also think I ought to guard against contributing to the levity of others by answering them' (III.25.11). His treatment of eschatology is cautious, restrained, and practical. He urges Christians to be satisfied with what is clearly revealed. 'Let this, then, be our short way out', Calvin writes, 'to be satisfied with the "mirror" and its "dimness" until we see him face to face' (III.25.11).

Calvin begins III.25 by reminding us that we must keep 'our eyes fast fixed on Christ' as 'we wait upon heaven' (III.25.1). Calvin insisted in the previous section on election that our eyes must be fixed on Christ, the mirror of our election, not on God's decree itself or on our good works. Here he instructs us to fix our eyes on Christ, not on heaven itself. Calvin's answer to our concern about the past (our election) is Christ; his answer to our concern about the future (our death) is also Christ.

We will examine Calvin's treatment of some of the major points of eschatology. He does not deal with all of these topics in III.25, so I will supplement what he writes in this chapter by references to other parts of the *Institutes* and to his commentaries.

The last days

The whole New Testament time 'from the point that Christ appeared with us with the preaching of [the] gospel even to the Day of Judgment, is designated by "the last hour", "the last times", "the last days"'. Therefore, we must 'be content with the perfection of Christ's teaching', Calvin explains, and not add anything else to it (IV.8.7). The church lives between the comings of Christ, satisfied with 'the last closing word' of Christ, and in constant expectation of his return (Comm. Heb. 1:1). Christians know that during this time, we are 'grievously exercised under hard military service', and, therefore, we 'must cling' to hope (III.25.1). Calvin develops this thought in his commentary on Acts 3:21:

Christ, by his death, has already restored all things as far as the power to achieve this and the cause of it are concerned; but the effect of it is still not fully visible because that restoration is still in the process of completion and so, too, our redemption, insofar as we still groan under the burden of servitude. For just as the kingdom of Christ has only begun and the perfection of it is still deferred until the last day, so too, the benefits that are joined to it are now seen only in part. Therefore, if, at the present time, we see much confusion in the world, let that faith encourage us and revive us, the faith that Christ shall one day come and restore all things to their former condition.

The worldwide advance of the gospel will mark 'the last days' during which the elect will be gathered and the image of God progressively restored in them. Calvin does not have a separate chapter in the *Institutes* on evangelism and missions, but in his writings there are many statements about the universal spread of Christ's kingdom through the preaching of the gospel.

- The Father has appointed Christ to 'rule from sea to sea, and from the rivers even to the ends of the earth' (Prefatory Address, *Institutes* 1:12).

- The Lord will show, 'not only in one corner, what true religion is … but he will send forth his voice to the extreme limits of the earth' (Comm. Mic. 4:3).

- Jesus did not come to reconcile a few individuals only to God but 'to extend his grace over all the world' (Sermon on 1 Pet. 2:5).

- The Holy Spirit descended to 'reach all the ends and extremities of the world' (Sermon on Acts 2:1-4).

- 'God's grace must be preached abroad everywhere, so that people of all countries and nations may call upon God' (Sermon on Eph. 3:13-16).

The work of extending his kingdom throughout the world is God's work, but he uses us as his 'co-workers' (IV.1.6).

- 'We are called by the Lord on this condition, that everyone should afterwards strive to lead others to the truth, to restore the wandering to the right way, to extend a helping hand to the fallen, to win over those that are without' (Comm. Heb. 10:24).

- We are reconciled to God 'in order that each should endeavour to make his brethren partakers of the same benefit' (Comm. Psa. 32:8).

- To seek first the kingdom of God, 'we must first endeavour, as much as is possible, that God may be honoured and that the world may be gathered unto him' (Sermon on Deut. 33:18,19).

- 'We should remember that the gospel is preached not only by the command of Christ but at his urging and leading' (Comm. Matt. 13:24-30).

- 'It is our duty to proclaim the goodness of God to every nation' (Comm. Isa. 12:5).

In his pastoral prayer, Calvin prayed every Sunday for the worldwide spread of the gospel:

> We pray you, O most gracious God and merciful Father, for all people everywhere. As it is your will to be acknowledged the Saviour of the whole world, through the redemption wrought by your Son Jesus Christ, grant that those who are still estranged from the knowledge of him, being in the darkness and captivity of error and ignorance, may be brought by the illumination of your Holy Spirit and the preaching of your gospel to the straight way of salvation, which is to know you, the only true God, and Jesus Christ whom you have sent (*John Calvin: Writings on Pastoral Piety*, 128).

The Antichrist

During the period between the first and second coming of Christ there will be constant opposition to the advance of the gospel. This opposition the Scripture describes as the spirit of 'antichrist'. 'The name antichrist', Calvin wrote, 'does not designate a single individual, but a single kingdom which extends throughout many generations' (Comm. 2 Thess. 2: 7). 1 John 2:18, 'Children, it is the last hour, and as you have heard that antichrist is coming, so now many antichrists have come', predicts the coming of heretics in the Christian church—persons doing the devil's bidding and not God's will. One form of this spirit, in Calvin's view, was the Roman Catholic perversion of the gospel, and especially the role of the papacy in the corruption of true Christianity. God works to restrain and defeat evil all along, 'until at last he slays antichrist with the Spirit of his mouth, and destroys all ungodliness by the brightness of his coming' (III.20.42).

The millennium

In III.25.5 Calvin comes out strongly against 'the chiliasts', perhaps too strongly. He claimed that those who hold to a literal thousand-year reign of Christ on earth believe a fiction 'too childish either to need or to be worth a refutation' (III.25.5). He argues that Revelation 20:4 does not support 'the chiliasts'. 'For the number "one thousand" does not apply to the eternal blessedness of the church but only to the various disturbances that awaited the church, while still toiling on earth. On the contrary, all Scripture proclaims that there will be no end to the blessedness of the elect or the punishments of the wicked' (III.25.5).

Death

Everyone is naturally afraid of death. Preaching on Job 27, Calvin says: 'We flee from it as much as possible. And why? Because God etched this sense in us that death is a malediction, a corruption of nature, and a change of the order of God from what it was before the fall.' But with a confident and certain hope of heaven, believers are able to 'face death with a joyous courage' (Sermon on Job 42). Commenting on 1 Corinthians 15:26, 'the last enemy to be destroyed is death', Calvin wrote that death 'has been destroyed in such a way as to be no longer fatal for believers, but not in such a way as to cause them no trouble. The sword of death used to be able to pierce right to the heart, but now it is blunt. It wounds still, of course, but without any danger; for we die, but in dying, we pass over into life.'

'Death to a godly man is like a fair gale of wind to convey him to the heavenly country; but to a wicked man it is an east wind, a storm, a tempest, that hurries him away in confusion and amazement, to destruction' (Matthew Henry).

The intermediate state

Following the death of the body, the soul of the Christian awaits the resurrection of the body in a state of conscious joy and peace. For Calvin, there are three stages in the Christian's experience: salvation in Christ; resting after death in the joyous expectation of even greater blessing; and the resurrection of the body and restoration of all things. Of the intermediate state, Calvin writes that Scripture goes no further than to teach 'that Christ is present with [believers], and receives them into paradise', where they enjoy 'blessed rest' (III.25.6). This blessed rest is not 'soul sleep', but a conscious sharing of God's presence and blessing while awaiting 'the enjoyment of promised glory'. Michael Horton writes, 'While we rejoice in the promise of being in God's presence upon death, the ultimate confidence of Christians is "the resurrection of the body and the life everlasting"' (*Calvin on the Christian Life*, 247).

Calvin's first theological work was *Psychopannychia*, a Greek title meaning 'the all-night vigil of the soul'. In this book Calvin refuted certain 'Anabaptists' who held that souls sleep during the time between death of the body and the final resurrection. He argued from the Scriptures that the soul of a believer exists after physical death in a state of conscious blessedness as it awaits union with its resurrection body. 'The souls of the saints, divested of their bodies, still stand in the courts of the Lord, admitted to rest but not yet to glory. Into that most blessed abode they shall neither enter without us, nor without their own bodies.' The souls of the reprobate, on the other hand, 'suffer such torments as they deserve'. They are 'held in chains' until they are given over to the full 'punishment appointed for them' (III.25.6).

Purgatory

Calvin's most thorough refutation of purgatory, the Roman Catholic idea that believers will be 'purged' from their sins by a temporary, though probably lengthy, period of suffering after death, is found in the *Institutes* III.5.6-10. After showing that the doctrine of indulgences has no biblical basis, Calvin says that purgatory also falls, 'because with this ax it has already been broken, hewn down, and overturned from its foundations'. Since 'the blood of Christ is the sole satisfaction for the sins of believers, the sole expiation, the sole purgation, what remains but to say that purgatory is simply a dreadful blasphemy against Christ?' (III.5.6)

The second coming of Christ

Calvin believed in a literal, physical second coming of Christ, but he had no interest in predicting its date or in describing in detail its nature (III.25.11). He is satisfied with saying that Christ's second coming will majestically display his glory and vindicate the humble and downtrodden church. The doctrine of the second coming of Christ should serve as a stimulus to Christian living and service. We must stand in continual expectancy of the coming of Christ, while at the same time being patient and diligent in our relentless warfare against evil.

Commenting on Matthew 24:42, 'Therefore, stay awake, for you do not know on what day your Lord is coming', Calvin writes: 'Note that the uncertainty of the time of Christ's coming … ought to be a stimulus to our attention and watchfulness. God deliberately wished it kept hidden from us, that we should never be so carefree as to neglect our unbroken lookout.' Calvin translates the beginning of 2 Peter 3:12, 'looking for and earnestly desiring the coming of the day of God', and explains it by saying, 'We ought to wait quietly and in haste. This seeming contradiction has not a little neatness in it, as in the proverb "*Festina lente*" [make haste slowly].' Calvin urges us to live quietly and calmly in hope for the coming of the Lord, while we 'labour earnestly in good works and run swiftly the race of our calling'.

The general resurrection

Even non-Christians, in their burial rites, witness to the resurrection of the body, Calvin writes (III.25.5). He describes the burial rites of the

Old Testament patriarchs as 'a rare and precious aid to faith' (III.25.8). In support of the doctrine of the resurrection, Calvin points to the omnipotence of God and to the fact of Christ's resurrection. He briefly reviews evidences for the resurrection of Christ—the empty tomb, the appearances of the risen Christ, and especially the power of the gospel. 'Now truly', he writes, 'it was not by a dead man's power that Paul was thrown prostrate on the road' (III.25.3).

Calvin stresses the fact that 'Christ rose again that he might have us as companions in the life to come.' 'In this mirror [of Christ's resurrection] the living image of the resurrection is visible to us, so is it a firm foundation to support our minds' (III.25.3). When Christ rose from the dead, 'many bodies of the saints ... came out of the tombs', a 'prelude to' and 'pledge of' the 'resurrection for which we hope' (III.25.7). Calvin writes on 1 Thessalonians 1:9-10 that 'Paul intimates that [Christ's] resurrection would be of no effect unless he appears a second time as [our] Redeemer, and extends to the whole body of the church the fruit and effect of that power which he displayed in himself.'

At the resurrection we shall rise again in the 'same flesh we now carry about with us' (Comm. 1 Cor. 15:43). In his commentary on 1 Corinthians 15:50-54, Calvin contrasts the 'spiritual body' of the life to come with the 'natural body' of this life; but the contrast is more a deliverance from 'hard and wretched' conditions of our earthly existence than a different kind of body. It is the same body that God originally created and that he will reclaim and renew. 'God does not call forth new matter from the four elements to fashion men, but summons dead men from the grave' (III.25.7).

Calvin affirms that our resurrection bodies shall be the same, yet different. He explains: 'For just as the substance of human and animal flesh is the same, but not the quality, and all stars are of the same material, but differ in their brilliance, so [Paul] teaches [in 1 Cor. 15] that, although we shall retain the substance of our bodies, there will be a change, that its condition may be far more excellent' (III.25.8). Even though Calvin occasionally seems to denigrate the body—calling it 'the prison house of the flesh' (III.25.1) and 'a hut' (III.25.6)—he also says that 'God has dedicated to himself [our bodies] as temples' (III.25.7).

He notes that in the Old Testament 'we see the Spirit no less attentive to the burial rites than to the chief mysteries of the faith' (III.25.8). In the New Testament Christ commends practices honouring the body as 'no mean office', pointing to the woman who brought an alabaster flask of very expensive ointment to pour upon Jesus' head, doing, as Jesus said, 'a beautiful thing to me' (Comm. Matt. 26:10). 'Both our souls and our bodies [are] destined for heavenly incorruption and an unfading crown' (III.6.3). We are encouraged to raise "our eyes from gazing upon a grave that corrupts and effaces everything, to the vision of renewal' (III.25.8). In his commentary on 1 John 3:2, 'we know that when he appears we shall be like him', Calvin explains that the verse does not mean that 'we shall be equal to [Christ] ... but we shall be like him because he will make our vile body conformable to his glorious body ... the final end of our adoption is that what has in order preceded in Christ shall at length be completed in us'. Richard A. Muller comments about Calvin's view of the resurrection body, 'Rather than passing from corporeality to spirituality the body passes from corruptible corporeality to incorruptible corporeality' (*Harvard Theological Review* 74:1, 36).

At the resurrection, the bodies of both the faithful and the wicked will be raised, but the main emphasis in Scripture is on the resurrection to life of Christians, 'because properly speaking Christ did not come to destroy the world but to save it', and so this is 'the chief emphasis to be found in the word of God' (III.25.9). Saving the world means more than the resurrection of human bodies, it means the restoration of all things. In his commentary on John 12:31, 'Now is the judgment of this world; now will the ruler of this world be cast out', Calvin interprets 'judgment' not as 'condemnation' but as 'reformation', when the world will be 'restored to due order'. He writes, 'The Hebrew word ... means a rightly ordered constitution. Now we know that outside of Christ there is nothing but confusion in the world; and although Christ has already begun to set up the kingdom of God, his death was the true beginning of ... the complete restoration of the world.' On Romans 8:19-25 Calvin writes that 'there is no element and no part of the world which, being touched, as it were, with a sense of its present misery, does not intensely hope for a resurrection'. And there will be in God's time a restoration in which nothing will be 'deformed or fading'. The creation will be purified but not destroyed. God will not abandon what he has made, but he will renovate or restore it. The fires of judgment (2 Pet. 3:10-13) will not destroy creation but will purify it. In a rare comment about the future world, Calvin stated that he would say 'just one thing about the elements of the world, that they will be consumed in order to receive a new quality while their substance remains the same' (Comm. 2 Pet. 3:10).

Herman Selderhuis comments, 'In Calvin's thought there is … no preoccupation with personal salvation to the exclusion of any concern with the restoration of all reality' (*Calvin's Theology of the Psalms*, 173). Susan Schreiner writes, 'Calvin's is a salvation-history theology. Christianity begins with creation and is the story of God's covenant with Israel, a covenant that is renewed in Christ and encompasses all peoples. Throughout this history, God governs his creation both in the cosmos and in human history. So, too, Calvin's God not only secures the salvation of the elect but reclaims all aspects of his creation' (*The Theatre of His Glory*, 121).

Preaching on Ephesians 3:9-12, Calvin points out that both the first and second creation are accomplished by Christ.

> In saying that God created all things by Jesus Christ [in Eph. 3:9], the apostle brings us back again to the creation of the world, where he speaks of the renewal that was made when God repaired the things that were scattered and ruined by Adam's sin … For Adam had perverted and marred all order by his fall, so that there was nothing but confusion both in heaven and earth, until all was mended again by Jesus Christ. Now then, the restitution that was made by our Lord Jesus Christ, may well be referred to this second creation, as though at his coming God had set the world in its former state again, which had been, as it were, put out of order before.

> The whole creation groans,
>   And waits to hear that voice
> That shall restore her comeliness,
>   And make her wastes rejoice.
> Come, Lord, and wipe away,
>   The curse, the sin, the stain
> And make this blighted world of ours,
>   Thine own fair world again.
>   Horatius Bonar

The final judgment

The present temporal judgments of God anticipate the final judgment but God graciously defers the final judgment to give people time for repentance. 'God's patience only proves conclusively that there will most certainly be a final judgment day' (I.5.7). For believers in Christ, the judgment due to them for their sins has already been borne by Christ. The wicked, however, 'will be unwillingly haled before the judgment seat of Christ, whom they now refuse to listen to as their Master and Teacher' (III.25.9).

Calvin says that the judgment 'may ... be considered as the last act of [Christ's] reign' and as the point at which Christ will have 'fully performed the work of the mediator' (II.15.5). He explains this more fully in his commentary on 1 Corinthians 15:24, 'Then comes the end, when he delivers the kingdom to God the Father':

> Christ will then hand back the kingdom which he has received, so that we may cleave completely to God. This does not mean that he will abdicate from the kingdom in this way, but will transfer it in some way or other from his humanity to his glorious divinity, because then there will open up for us a way of approach, from which we are now kept back by our weakness. In this way, therefore, Christ will be subjected to the Father, because, when the veil has been removed, we see God plainly, reigning in his majesty, and no more will Christ's humanity be intermediate, which [now] restrains us from the vision of God lying beyond.

If Christ's mediatorial work in some sense comes to an end, Christ will still mediate and rule, 'as the bond between believers and God and as the eternal head of the church, a position he maintains because of the eternity of his divine-human person', writes Richard A. Muller (*Harvard Theological Review* 74:1, 59).

Heaven

Calvin warns against 'trifling and harmful questions' about the exact nature and details of heaven (III.25.10). Some 'leave no corner of heaven exempt from their search' in trying to find out everything about it (III.25.11). Calvin interprets the physical descriptions of heaven in the Bible as figures of speech. 'The prophets because they could not find words to express that spiritual blessedness in its own nature, merely sketched it in physical terms' (III.25.10). Calvin encourages us to move beyond the pictures of heaven to the reality they point to, that is, our being forever with the Lord and with each other. 'We will feast together in heaven forever', Calvin wrote to his friend Philip Melanchthon (*Melanchthon in Europe*, 22).

Calvin teaches that there will be different degrees of glory in heaven as there are different gifts on earth. In this way God is simply crowning his own gifts. 'As Christ begins the glory of his body [the church] in this world with manifold diversity of gifts, and increases it by degrees, so also he will perfect it in heaven' (III.25.10).

Hell

Calvin believed in an actual hell where the devil, his angels, and the wicked suffer eternally for their rebellion against God and their sin against humanity. The biblical descriptions of hell—fire, darkness, weeping, gnashing of teeth, the worm—are figurative but serve to 'confound all our senses with dread' (III.25.12). If heaven is fellowship with God, hell is the opposite. It is not a location but the condition of living estranged from God. The thought of hell should cause us 'to fix our thought upon this: how wretched it is to be cut off from all fellowship with God' (III.25.12).

> 'One of the ladies, Veda Dyer, got herself into a considerable excitement talking about flames, that is perdition, so I felt obliged to take down the *Institutes* and read them the passage on the lot of the reprobate, about how their torments are "figuratively expressed to us by physical things", unquenchable fire and so on, to express "how wretched it is to be cut off from all fellowship with God". I have the passage in front of me. It is alarming, certainly, but it isn't ridiculous. I told them, If you want to inform yourselves as to the nature of hell, don't hold your hand in a candle flame, just ponder the meanest, most desolate place in your soul' (Robinson, *Gilead*, 208).

In the *Institutes* Calvin does not dwell on hell, giving it only one long paragraph. He did not include hell in his Geneva Catechism, which followed the Apostles' Creed, from which it is also absent.

> *Minister*: Why, then, is there mention only of eternal life and not of hell?
>
> *Child*: Since nothing is held by faith except what contributes to the consolation of the souls of the pious. Hence there are here recalled the rewards which the Lord has prepared for his servants. Therefore it is not added what fate may await the impious whom we know to be outcasts from the kingdom of God (*Calvin: Theological Treatises*, 104).

Knowing God and ourselves

Calvin ends chapter 25 of Book III with a word of encouragement for believers:

> The Ninetieth Psalm has a memorable statement: although by his mere glance he scatters and brings to nought all mortal men, he urges his own worshippers on, the more because they are timid in this world, that he may inspire them, burdened with the cross, to press forward, until he himself is 'all in all'.

Because of what God has done, and will do, let us be encouraged, whatever comes, and press on in our Christian walk until we are taken to heaven where Christ has gone to prepare a place for us.

20. The Church—
'Mother and School'

'For those to whom [God] is Father the church may also be *Mother*' (IV.1.1). 'Our weakness does not allow us to be dismissed from her *school* until we have been pupils all our lives' (IV.1.4).

The church is our mother, 'for there is no other way to enter into life unless this mother conceive us in her womb, give us birth, nourish us at her breasts, and lastly, unless she keeps us under her care and guidance until, putting off mortal flesh, we become like the angels' (IV.1.4).

The church is our school, where we study our great textbook, the Bible, and learn how to live as members of God's family. David Steinmetz writes about Calvin's understanding of the church as school:

Just as the knowledge of God is not a simple matter of cognition but also of trust, obedience, and love, so, too, not all the lessons the church as school teaches are matters of intellectual apprehension. The church moulds the character of its members, reshapes their disordered affections, disciplines their unruly wills, invites them to sacrifice, and even instructs them how to die (*The Cambridge Companion to Reformation Theology*, 123).

In his commentary on Psalm 135:13, Calvin describes the church as the orchestra. 'The whole world is a theatre for the display of the divine goodness, wisdom, justice, and power, but the church is the orchestra, as it were—the most conspicuous part of it.' Calvin doesn't develop this idea, and, as far as I know, doesn't use the image of the church as an orchestra elsewhere. The whole world displays God and his attributes and even more so the church, the orchestra, sounds forth his praises in all the world: 'Your name, O Lord, endures forever, your renown, O Lord, throughout all ages' (Psa. 135:13).

All that dedicated city,
    Dearly loved of God on high,
In exultant jubilation
    Pours perpetual melody;
God the One in Three adoring
    In glad hymns eternally.

                    Latin, 7th century
                    Tr. by John Mason Neale

Read: *Institutes* IV.1-3. [1541 ch.4, pp.259-287; ch.15, pp.727-732.]

Scripture Text: 'So then you are no longer strangers and aliens, but you are fellow-citizens with the saints and members of the household of God, built on the foundation of the apostles and prophets, Christ Jesus himself being the cornerstone' (Eph. 2:19-20).

Notable Quote: 'If the foundation of the church is the teaching of the prophets and apostles, which bids believers entrust their salvation to Christ alone—then take away that teaching, and how will the building continue to stand?' (III.2.1)

Prayer

Grant, Almighty God, that since you have gathered us to your Church, and enclosed us within the boundaries of your word, by which you preserve us in the true and right worship of your majesty, grant that we may continue contented in this obedience to you. Though Satan may, in many ways, attempt to draw us here and there, and we be also ourselves inclined to evil, grant, that being confirmed in faith and united to you by that sacred bond, we may yet constantly abide under the restraint of your word. May we cleave to Christ your only begotten Son, who has joined us forever to himself, that we may never by any means turn aside from you, but be, on the contrary, confirmed in the faith of the gospel, until at length he will receive us all into his kingdom. Amen.

(*Devotions and Prayers of John Calvin*, 15.)

❖

A look back and a look ahead

In the four books of the *Institutes* Calvin's thought unfolds in a great spiral: all that goes before depends upon what is coming next. Book I—Knowledge of God the Creator—would do us no good, Calvin said, without Book II—Knowledge of God our Redeemer in Christ. But knowledge of Christ does not benefit us unless we are united to him by the Holy Spirit, the topic of Book III. And it is by the ministry of the church—the topic of most of Book IV—that God begets and nourishes his children.

In Book III Calvin presented the internal means of our salvation, that is the work of the Holy Spirit producing faith in us, uniting us to Christ, promoting Christian obedience in us, and at last perfecting us in heaven. In Book IV he presents the 'external means' by which the Spirit works 'to beget and increase faith in us' (IV.i.i). In Book III Calvin expounds the great blessings that come to us through union with Christ. In Book IV he writes, 'We must firmly believe that by God's generosity, mediated by Christ's mercy, through the sanctification of the Spirit, sins have been and are daily pardoned to us who have been received and engrafted into the body of the church' (IV.i.21). We are not only united to Christ, we are united to the church. Elsie McKee writes, 'If the heart of piety, "reverence and love of God", is clearly the work of the Holy Spirit, the ordained earthly instrument for building up that piety is the church' (*John Calvin: Writings on Pastoral Piety*, 23).

Calvin begins Book IV with a look back. 'As explained in the previous book, it is by faith in the gospel that Christ becomes ours and we are made partakers of the salvation and eternal blessedness brought by him.' Then Calvin looks ahead. 'Since, however, in our ignorance and sloth … we need outward helps to beget and increase faith within us, and advance it to its goal, God has also added these aids that he may provide for our weakness' (IV.i.i). Calvin began a brief 'Summary of doctrine concerning the ministry of the word and sacraments' with these words: 'The end of the whole gospel ministry is that God, the fountain of all felicity, communicates Christ to us who are disunited by sin and hence ruined, that we may from him enjoy eternal life; that in a word all heavenly treasures be so applied to us that they be no less ours than Christ's himself' (*Calvin: Theological Treatises*, 171).

In Book IV Calvin sets forth 'the external means' God uses to bring us to himself and to preserve us in the faith—'the church, its government, orders, and power; then the sacraments; and lastly, the civil order' (IV.i.i).

Calvin and the church

> Calvin 'was a man of the church, and its unity was his deepest passion. Luther had brilliantly expressed what it meant to be saved by God. That discovery had changed Europe. Calvin's genius was to discover the church, and teach what it was to be part of that body if one lived in a besieged city, under a capricious Tudor monarch or as a refugee facing persecution and exile' (Gordon, *Calvin*, viii).

The length and thoroughness of John Calvin's treatment of the doctrine of the church in Book IV—a third of the 1559 *Institutes*—indicates the growing importance he gave to this subject. T. H. L. Parker states that Calvin more and more took on 'the character and stature of a doctor of the Catholic Church'—not the Roman Catholic but the universal catholic church (*Calvin*, vi). Calvin's early reluctance to become personally and directly involved with the church is well known. William Farel's threats in August 1536 turned the startled young man from scholarly ambitions to pastoral work. He spent two years in Geneva with Farel, and three years in Strasbourg with Martin Bucer. In 1541 he was convinced that God was calling him back to Geneva. Calvin gave the rest of his life to the work of the church in that city—and, by his writings and letters, to churches throughout Europe.

All of Calvin's accomplishments—his *Institutes* and commentaries, his correspondence and counselling, his preaching and teaching—flowed out of and supported his pastoral calling. John Leith writes, 'Calvin's work in Geneva was that of a preacher who was concerned that Christian faith should be embodied not simply in books, not simply in institutions, but primarily in Christian people living in the Christian community and in society' (*John Calvin: The Christian Life*, x).

In his commentary on Daniel 9:25 Calvin reflects on the challenges facing the church in his time (and ours as well).

> Although God's loving kindness to us was wonderful when the pure Gospel emerged out of that dreadful darkness in which it had been buried for so many ages, our affairs are still troubled. The impious still ceaselessly and furiously oppose the unhappy church, both by the sword and the virulence of their tongues. Internal enemies use covert arts in their schemes to subvert our edifice; wicked men destroy all order and interpose many obstacles to impede our progress. But God still wishes in these days to build his spiritual temple amidst the anxieties of the times. The faithful must still hold the trowel in one hand and the sword in the other, because the building of the church must still be combined with many struggles.

Even when the outward condition of the church seems hopeless, especially when it seems hopeless, Calvin urges us to follow the example of David, who 'not only persevered in prayer, but [found] ground for hope even from the ... apparent hopelessness of his outward condition' (Comm. Psa. 5:9). The hopeless condition of the suffering church is itself a source of hope.

External means

It is through external means that God 'invites us into the society of Christ and holds us therein'. We need 'external means' because we have not yet attained 'angelic rank' but are still shut 'in the prison house of our flesh'. Therefore, 'in his wonderful providence', God accommodates himself 'to our capacity' by giving us 'outward helps' so that we can 'draw near to him' (IV.i.1).

The church and the sacraments are not means by which we get grace but means by which God gives grace to us. The preaching of the gospel is the ordinary means by which God 'invites us' into 'the society of Christ'. Preaching, the sacraments, and church discipline are the means by which God 'holds us therein'. God does not raise us to perfection in a moment but makes us grow 'little by little under the nurture of the church' (IV.1.5). The place of our Christian growth is not in our isolated individual lives but among the congregation of believers, where 'all the blessings which God bestows upon them are mutually communicated to each other' (IV.1.3). Paul's words in Ephesians 3:21, 'Let glory be rendered to God in the church', Calvin said, show 'that it is not enough that every one of us should privately acknowledge the benefits that God has bestowed upon him, but that we must all join together in that mind. For if the body is comfortably at ease, surely no member will be so addicted to itself that it will have no regard to all the rest' (Sermon on Eph. 3:20-4:2). In another sermon, Calvin said that 'there should be such a union among us as might show that we are in very deed the body of our Lord Jesus Christ. For it is not enough for us to be piled up together like a heap of stones, but we must be joined together with cordial affection' (Sermon on Eph. 4:1-5).

Calvin makes it clear that 'although God's power is not bound to outward means, he has nonetheless bound us to this ordinary manner of teaching' (IV.1.5). In other words, God could do without the church, but we cannot. 'Whoever refuses to be a child of the church vainly desires to have God as Father', Calvin writes; 'for it is only by the ministry of the church that God begets and nourishes children' (IV.1.4).

Invisible and visible church

In IV.1.2-3, Calvin returns to the Apostles' Creed, discussing 'I believe in the holy, catholic church' and 'the communion of saints', which brings us, 'a wealth of comfort'. One does not believe in the church in the same way that one believes in the triune God. However, it is in the church that our faith in God is born and nurtured. 'It is more appropriate, therefore, not to say "I believe in the church", but to say "in the church I believe"' (Stroup, *Calvin*, 56).

It is important, of course, to know what the church is. Calvin describes the church as both visible and invisible. These are not two different churches, but neither are they identical. The invisible church is 'all the elect from the beginning of the world' (IV.1.7). This is the church as God sees it. For us the invisible church is a matter of faith. We believe that it exists but we cannot see it. The visible church is 'the whole multitude of men spread out over the earth who profess to worship one God and Christ' (IV.1.7). This is the church as we know it. Calvin acknowledged that sometimes and in some places it is difficult to see the visible church, but 'God always preserves a hidden seed, that the church should not be utterly extinguished: for there must always be a church in the world' (Comm. Ezek. 16:53).

In *Concerning Scandals*, Calvin wrote:

> Let us remember that the outward aspect of the church is so contemptible that its beauty may shine within; that it is so tossed about on earth that it may have a permanent dwelling-place in heaven; that it lies so wounded and broken in the eyes of the world that it may stand, vigorous and whole, in the presence of God and his angels; that it is so wretched in the flesh that its happiness may nevertheless be restored for it in the spirit.

God alone knows who are the elect, for 'to know who are his is a prerogative belonging solely to God' (IV.1.8). Therefore, we cannot identify the visible church with the elect. In the visible church chaff is mixed with the wheat. Calvin quotes Augustine that there are 'many sheep without and many wolves within' (IV.1.8). 'The church ... has had no enemies more inveterate than the members of the church' (Comm. John 13:18). Calvin warned that 'more danger threatens us from our own victory than from that of our enemies, and ... no disasters are to be so feared so much as what I call a highly triumphal gospel' (*Concerning Scandals*).

Just as there are some members of the visible church who are not true Christians, there are some of the elect who are outside the visible community of the church. Calvin did not believe that baptism—or church membership—was essential to salvation. He recognized that there are some situations in which it was not possible for a true Christian to be baptized or to identify with a church, for example, in those places where because of opposition and persecution no Christian church exists.

Calvin urges Christians to 'recognize as members of the church those who, by confession of faith, by example of life, and by partaking of the sacraments, profess the same God and Christ with us' (IV.1.8).

Marks of the church

Calvin accepts the traditional Nicene description of the church—one holy, catholic, apostolic church—but adds marks not merely descriptive but dynamic 'in which the face of the church comes forth and becomes visible to our eyes' (IV.1.9). Paul affirmed, Calvin writes, that despite the many sins of the Corinthians, 'the church abides among them because the ministry of the word and sacraments remains unrepudiated there' (IV.1.14).

The first mark of the church is 'the word of God purely preached and heard' (IV.1.10)

When the word is purely preached, says Calvin, it is 'just as if [God] himself spoke' (IV.1.5). That word must not only be preached in the church but also heard—indeed 'reverently heard' (IV.1.10).

> 'There cannot be a Presbyterian church, there cannot be a Protestant church, without knowledge of the Bible in depth so that the language of scripture is the "native" tongue of the Christian' (Leith, *Crisis in the Church*, 49).

The second mark of the church is the 'sacraments administered according to Christ's institution' (IV.1.10)

For Calvin there were two sacraments: baptism and the Lord's supper. Just as the word must be purely preached, so the sacraments must be purely or rightly administered. What this means we will see in Calvin's treatment of the sacraments in IV.14-19.

Discipline

Church discipline is not a third mark of the church, but it is necessary if the church is to preserve its character as a true church. In a memorable image, Calvin describes discipline as 'the sinews' which holds the church together. 'As the saving doctrine of Christ is the soul of the church, so does discipline serve as sinews, through which the members of the body hold together' (IV.12.1). Calvin warns that 'all who desire to remove discipline or to hinder its restoration … are surely contributing to the ultimate dissolution of the church' (IV.12.1). Word and sacraments are gifts of God; our Christian obedience is urgently important, even essential, but it belongs to the organization of the church, not to its foundation, which is the sheer objectivity of God's grace given in the preaching of the word and the administration of the sacraments.

'Discipline depends for the most part upon the power of the keys and upon spiritual jurisdiction' (IV.12.1). This means, says Calvin, that 'any right of binding or loosing which Christ conferred upon his church is bound to the word' (III.11.4). The church may exercise the power of the keys ['Whatever you bind on earth shall be bound in heaven, and whatever you loose on earth shall be loosed in heaven'] in discipline in accordance with the word and under the guidance of the Holy Spirit. Believers 'have the word of God with which to condemn the perverse; they have the word with which to receive the repentant into grace' (IV.11.2).

Calvin uses several images to describe the function and purpose of church discipline: it is like a bridle to restrain the unruly, like a spur to arouse the careless, and like 'a father's rod to chastise mildly and with the gentleness of Christ's Spirit' the lapsed (IV.12.1).

Dealing with concealed sins (those against an individual) Calvin advises private conversation; open sins (those that have caused a public scandal) should be dealt with more openly. He distinguishes between light and grave sins. For lighter sins verbal correction is enough—'and that mild and fatherly—which should not harden or confuse the sinner, but bring him back to himself, that he may rejoice rather than be sad that he has been corrected' (IV.12.6). Graver sins must be corrected by the fuller process of church discipline.

Calvin set forth three aims of church discipline. *First,* discipline preserves the honour of God by correcting heresy and scandal in the church, and protects the Lord's Supper from misuse. *Second,* discipline protects the righteous from the wicked, since we are so easily led astray by bad examples. *Third,* discipline leads the offender to repentance. Calvin notes that not only the contemporary Roman Catholic Church but also the ancient church exercised 'excessive severity' in discipline. He stresses the importance of moderation, so that the 'remedy' will bring recovery and not destruction (IV.12.8). In a sermon on Galatians 6:1-2, Calvin says, 'Let us not be so sharp in rebuking others for their faults that we forget to mix oil with the vinegar, or to act in a spirit of gentleness.' Commenting on 1 Thessalonians 2:7, 'But we were gentle among you, like a nursing mother taking care of her own children', Calvin warns against all show of pomp in the exercise of authority in the church, 'for a mother in nursing her infant shows nothing of power'. Pastors must be patient with their people. If they 'cannot cleanse all that needs correction according to their heart's desire, [they] should not for that reason resign their ministry or disturb the entire church with unaccustomed rigor' (IV.12.11). Herman Selderhuis comments that for Calvin, church discipline 'was not meant as a military drill but as a means to help keep the people close to God and to each other' (*John Calvin: A Pilgrim's Life,* 249). The church is both school and mother. It is the place where we are shaped, taught, and corrected. It is also the place where we are accepted, loved, and nourished.

Calvin outlines three steps in church discipline—private warning, public admonition, and exclusion from communion. The matter of excommunication was a point of long contention between Calvin and the Geneva magistrates. It was not until 1555 that the church consistory attained the right to exercise the sentence of excommunication without the approval of the magistrates. Most excommunications in Geneva were of brief duration, requiring the guilty party to miss one or more of the four annual communions. Calvin did not consider excommunication to be final. He insists that it is 'not our task to erase from the number of the elect those who have been expelled from the church, or to despair as if they were already lost' (IV.12.9).

True and false churches

Calvin held that as long as the church retains the two marks of pure preaching and proper sacraments, we must not reject it 'even if it otherwise swarms with many faults' (IV.1.12). He went so far as to admit that there may even be 'some fault' in teaching or doctrine. These faults, however, only touched 'non-essential matters' and not necessary doctrines, such as, there is only one God, Christ is God, our salvation rests in God's mercy, 'and the like'. Calvin doesn't give a complete list of the essential doctrines but indicates in a general way those major doctrines that cannot be rejected or weakened if the church is to remain a true church. If we find ourselves in a church that has 'some fault' in 'non-essential matters' we should not leave the church, Calvin says, but 'try to correct what displeases us' (IV.1.12).

Furthermore, a church may have 'imperfections of life', and still be a true church (IV.1.13). We cannot form an ideal church composed only of perfect people, as the Anabaptists and other 'airy spirits desired'. 'It is a dangerous temptation to think there is no church where perfect purity is lacking.' Calvin notes that the Corinthians had many problems, 'yet the church abides among them' (Comm. 1 Cor. 1:2). The Galatians were 'foolish', but Paul still recognized churches among them (IV.1.14). The Jerusalem or Old Testament church was far from perfect, 'still the prophets ... did not establish new churches for themselves' (IV.1.18). Calvin points out that in the Apostles' Creed the 'forgiveness of sins' follows 'the holy catholic church'. The people of the church are not perfect; they need to be forgiven of many sins.

We must, therefore, practise 'kindness' and not 'immoderate severity' when we examine the faults of a church (IV.1.13). 'The Lord esteems the communion of his church so highly that he counts as a traitor and apostate from Christianity anyone who arrogantly leaves any Christian society, provided it cherishes the true ministry of word and sacraments' (IV.1.10).

In IV.1.16 Calvin lists five reasons why we must avoid rejecting a church.

- There may be present many 'truly holy and innocent' people.

- Many of those who 'seem diseased' are genuinely sorry and 'aspire to a more upright life'.

- 'A man is not to be judged for one deed, inasmuch as the holiest sometimes undergo a most grievous fall.'

- The ministry of the word and participation in the sacraments are more important than the presence of some wicked people.

- 'In estimating the true church, divine judgment is of more weight than human.'

In chapter 1 of Book IV Calvin seems to come close to saying that there is never a time when Christians should leave a church; in chapter 2 he makes clear that in some circumstances Christians may be constrained to depart from a church—that is, when 'falsehood breaks into the citadel of religion and the sum of necessary doctrine is overturned and the use of the sacraments is destroyed' (IV.2.1). He distinguishes, as did Augustine, between 'schismatics' who wrongly 'break the bond of fellowship' with a church, and 'heretics' who 'corrupt the sincerity of the faith with false dogmas' (IV.2.5).

Calvin believed that the Catholic Church of his time lacked 'the lawful form of the church' (IV.2.12). The marks of a true church were missing. 'As soon as falsehood breaks into the citadel of religion and the sum of necessary doctrine is overturned and the use of the sacraments is destroyed, surely the death of the church follows—just as a man's life is ended when his throat is pierced or his heart mortally wounded' (IV.2.1). The Catholic Church had replaced the sacrifice of Calvary with the mass, which was, in Calvin's view, not a true sacrament but a form of idolatry. In the Catholic Church, 'Christ lies hidden, half buried, the gospel overthrown, piety scattered, the worship of God nearly wiped out. In them, briefly, everything is so confused that there we see the face of Babylon rather than the Holy City of God' (IV.2.12).

The situation was so serious that the Roman Catholic Church could no longer be considered a true church, and Calvin felt constrained to 'withdraw from them that we might come to Christ' (IV.2.6). The unity of the universal church is preserved not by allegiance to Rome, for 'apart from the Lord's word there is not an agreement of believers but a faction of wicked men' (IV.2.5). Protestants were not guilty of schism because what they were leaving was no longer the church. Calvin wrote: 'Indeed it is certain that we ought to disregard the whole world, and to embrace only the truth of God; for it is a hundred times better to renounce the society of all mortals and union with them, than to withdraw ourselves from God' (Comm. Zech. 8:23).

Calvin believed, however, that 'traces' of the church are still present as long as the Roman Catholics maintain baptism and 'other vestiges' (IV.2.11). There are still churches among them 'to the extent that the Lord wonderfully preserves in them a remnant of his people … but every one of their congregations and their whole society lack the lawful form of the church' (IV.2.12). Even when the universal apostasy that Paul refers to in 2 Thessalonians 2:3 seizes the church, 'many scattered members' will 'persevere in the true unity of faith' (IV.7.25). In his commentary on Psalm 102:14, 'For your servants hold her stones dear and have pity on her dust', Calvin applies the words about the ruined temple in Jerusalem to the Catholic Church of his day, where God's word is trampled under foot and his worship defiled, but adds that 'no desolation ought to prevent us from loving the very stones and dust of the church'. Even when the church lies in ruins, we still love that heap of ruins.

Calvin worked hard to promote the unity of the Protestant churches. He wrote in his commentary on 1 Corinthians 1:10 that 'the most important principle of our religion is this, that we should be in concord among ourselves'. He wrote to Archbishop Cranmer in April 1552 that he was so concerned for the unity of the Protestant churches that he 'would not grudge to cross even ten seas, if need be, on account of it'.

Bruce Gordon writes, 'Having witnessed at first hand the divisions among the Protestants, Calvin offered a distinctive perspective as a basis for unity … There was room for differences of theology and method as long as it was among those whose primary commitment was to the word of God' (*Calvin*, 105). In his commentary on 1 Corinthians 14:36, 'Or was it from you that the word of God came? Or are you the only ones it has reached?' Calvin wrote:

No church can be taken up with itself exclusively to the neglect of others; but on the contrary, they ought all ... to hold out the right hand to each other, in the way of cherishing mutual fellowship and accommodating themselves to each other ... Let there be nothing of pride and contempt for other churches—let there be on the other hand a desire to edify—let there be moderation and prudence; and in that case, amid a diversity of observances, there will be nothing that is worthy of reproof.

Knowing God and ourselves

In a sermon on Psalm 115:1-3, Calvin asked, 'Are we the church?' He answers:

We must have a spiritual connection with all the faithful. As there is only a single God, a single Redeemer, a single true teaching, a single faith, one baptism, so we ought to be one body. So we should have a union each with the others. If one member suffers, we all ought to have compassion. Now we see that this [situation] is not a question of one member; all the church is scattered: here a handful, there another. We all have the same gospel, we are surrounded by enemies. Should we separate [from each other]? Should we say: 'Those [people in Germany] are far from us?' Not at all. They are of the church, and we are its members; because we have the same Father in heaven, let us have a brotherhood together which is indeed more than fraternal! (*John Calvin, Pastoral Piety*, 166-67)

Pray that we will indeed experience in our churches 'a brotherhood' that is more than 'fraternal'!

21. The Church—
'The Body of Christ'

'Election did not subvert the church for Calvin, but rather under-scored its central importance ... God elected to save in and through the church. The church was included in the decree and provided the means of grace—scripture, baptism, eucharist, preaching, catechesis—without which faith would have been impossible' (Steinmetz, *Cambridge Companion to Reformed Theology*, 122).

Read: *Institutes* IV.3-4. [*1541* ch.13, pp.689-692, 701-703.]

Scripture Text: 'And he gave the apostles, the prophets, the evangelists, the pastors and teachers, to equip the saints for the work of ministry, for building up the body of Christ' (Eph. 4:11-12).

Notable Quote: 'If anyone is desirous of a clearer and more familiar illustration, I would say, that rule in the church, the pastoral office, and all other matters of order, resemble the body, whereas the doctrine which regulates the due worship of God, and points out the ground on which the consciences of men must rest their hope of salvation, is the soul which animates the body, renders it lively and active, and, in short, makes it not to be a dead and useless carcase' (*Tracts and Treatises* 1:126-27).

Prayer

We pray, O Father and Saviour, for all those whom you have ordained pastors of your faithful people, to whom you have entrusted the care of souls and the ministry of your holy gospel. Guide them by your Holy Spirit, that they may be found faithful and loyal ministers of your glory, having but one goal: that all the poor, wandering sheep be gathered and restored to the Lord Jesus Christ, the chief Shepherd and Prince of bishops, so that they may grow and increase in him daily unto all righteousness and holiness. Amen.

(John Calvin: Writings on Pastoral Piety, 127-28.)

❖

A look back and a look ahead

Calvin introduced the topic of the church by presenting the necessity of the church for Christians, its definition, its marks, and our attitude toward its imperfections. Now he turns to a detailed examination of its organization and ministers.

Form and freedom

John Calvin maintains that scripture reveals an order for church government of permanent validity 'handed down to us from God's pure word' (IV.4.1). At the same time, he insists on a sensible freedom in secondary matters. God 'did not will in outward discipline and ceremonies to prescribe in detail what we ought to do' because 'he foreknew that this depended upon the state of the times, and he did not deem one form suitable for all ages'. Church practices and ceremonies, therefore, 'ought to be variously accommodated to the customs of each nation and age' (IV.10.30). Church practices and ceremonies may be changed, but we must remember that God has restricted our freedom in these matters 'in such a way that it is only from his word that we can make up our minds about what is right' (Comm. 1 Cor. 14:10).

Since God has not prescribed in detail what we should do in all aspects of the church's organization, we follow 'those general rules which he has given, that whatever the necessity of the church will require for order and decorum should be tested against these' (IV.10.30). In 1 Corinthians 14:40, 'Let all things be done decently and in order', Paul sums up everything he has set forth concerning the 'external organization' of the church with the statement that 'seemliness should be preserved, and disorder should be avoided' (Comm. 1 Cor. 11:4). In the *Institutes* Calvin writes, 'If we let love be our guide, all will be safe' (IV.10.30).

Perhaps we can call Calvin's approach to these matters 'directional' rather than 'regulative'. He embraced the possibility of change, even the desirability and necessity of change at times, and diversity of practice in church organization and worship guided by the application of scriptural principles. Michael Horton writes, 'While wanting to obey everything that Christ commanded, [Calvin] realized that not everything was equally clear or equally important' (*Calvin on the Christian Life*, 199).

Church offices

The head of the church is Christ, who 'alone should rule and reign in the church'. Christ chooses to work through the ministry of men 'just as a workman uses a tool to do his work' (IV.3.1). Calvin writes that God connects himself with his servants but 'he never resigns to them his own office' (Comm. Mal. 4:6). 'The Holy Spirit uses an external minister as instrument ... both in the preaching of the word and in the use of the sacraments.' The external minister preaches and administers the sacraments; 'the internal minister, who is the Holy Spirit ... effects in the hearts of whomsoever he will their union with Christ' (*Calvin: Theological Treatises*, 173).

Why does God use human instruments? Calvin gives three reasons. *First*, because of 'his regard for us'. It shows the significance of human beings that God 'takes some to serve him as his ambassadors in the world, and to be interpreters of his secret will and ... to represent his person'. *Second*, it is for us an 'exercise in humility'. We receive God's word from a preacher, even if 'he excels us in nothing'. *Third*, it 'fosters mutual love'. The human ministry is 'the chief sinew by which sinners are held together in one body' (IV.3.1, 2). 'That we have ministers of the gospel is [Christ's] gift', Calvin wrote; 'that they excel in necessary gifts is his gift; that they execute the trust committed to them is likewise his gift' (Comm. Eph. 4:11).

Calvin surveys church offices under two categories: temporary or extraordinary, and permanent or ordinary. Under the first category he places apostles, evangelists who were next to the apostles in office and functioned in their place, and prophets. These are offices that God raised up 'at the beginning of his kingdom, and now and again revives ... as the need of the times demands' (IV.3.4). Calvin thinks that God 'has sometimes at a later period raised up apostles, or at least evangelists in their place, as has happened in our own day' with Luther, 'a distinguished apostle of Christ' (IV.3.4).

Calvin describes apostles and evangelists as those who were sent by God to 'lead the world back from rebellion to true obedience to God, and to establish his kingdom everywhere by the preaching of the gospel' (IV.3.4). By defining the apostle/evangelist in this way, and by viewing the office as normally temporary, Calvin has no category for the missionary. Perhaps Calvin would have seen pioneer missionaries as fulfilling in some ways the office of apostle/evangelist.

Prophets are 'those who excelled in a particular revelation'. Calvin thinks that 'this class either does not exist today or is less commonly seen' (IV.3.4). In his remarks on 1 Corinthians 12:10, Calvin writes, 'I take the term prophecy to mean that unique and outstanding gift of revealing what is the secret will of God, so that the prophet is, so to speak, God's messenger to men.' 'Prophets are outstanding interpreters of Scripture, and men endowed with extraordinary wisdom and aptitude for grasping what the immediate need of the church is, and speaking the right word to meet it. That is why they are, so to speak, messengers who bring news of what God wants' (Comm. 1 Cor. 12:28). The main thrust of Calvin's view of the work of the prophets seems to be what we sometimes call 'prophetic preaching'—forceful and timely application of the word of God to particular situations. Why then does Calvin say that prophets do not exist today or are 'less commonly seen'? Perhaps it is because of the connection with revelation and prediction that he mentions in his commentary on Ephesians 4:11, where he describes prophets as 'outstanding interpreters of prophecies, who, by a unique gift of revelation, applied them to the subjects on hand; but I do not exclude the gift of foretelling, so far as it was connected with teaching'.

Under the category of permanent or ordinary, Calvin lists four offices: pastors, teachers, elders, and deacons.

Pastors correspond to apostles/evangelists in that they are 'sent by the Lord and are his messengers' (IV.3.5). In Calvin's view, New Testament apostles/evangelists had no set limits, whereas a pastor is called to a particular church. 'What the apostles performed for the whole world, each pastor ought to perform for his own flock, to which he is assigned' (IV.3.6). At the same time the pastor of one church 'can aid other churches' (IV.3.7).

Pastors are responsible for the administration of the sacraments, church discipline, and especially preaching (IV.3.6). In a beautiful illustration, Calvin describes preachers as those who carve and divide the word, 'like a father dividing the bread into small pieces to feed his children' (Comm. 2 Tim. 2:15).

Calvin believed that the office of pastor or elder and bishop are one and the same. He emphasized the parity of ministers lest anyone should arrogate to himself the 'sole bishopric' of Christ (IV.2.6). He wrote in the commentary on 1 Corinthians 5:4 that 'there is nothing in greater opposition to the discipline of Christ than tyranny; and the door is wide open to it, if all the power is surrendered to one man'. Calvin admitted that there were bishops in the early church, but thought that 'the ancient bishops did not intend to fashion any other form of church rule than that which God has laid down in his word' (IV.4.4). Calvin was willing to accept bishops and even archbishops who conformed to the bishops of the early church.

In Calvin's view, teachers may have a separate office from pastors. 'Teaching is the duty of all pastors; but there is a particular gift of interpreting Scripture so that sound doctrine may be kept' (Comm. Eph. 4:11). As noted above, the teacher in some way corresponds to the prophet. His ministry is scriptural interpretation and teaching (IV.3.4). In his sermons on Ephesians Calvin described the ministry of pastors and teachers. All 'who are ordained to teach are called [in 1 Cor. 3:10] the masons and carpenters of God's house' (Sermon on Eph. 2:19-22).

Calvin exhorts preachers and teachers to depend on God and to humility. 'Let such as are called to the office of teaching God's church understand their own weakness, and put themselves wholly into God's hand so that they may be able to perform the work, well knowing that they will never accomplish it, no, nor one hundredth part of it, unless it is given them from above' (Sermon on Eph. 6:19-24). 'Although Jesus Christ has appointed certain men to be leaders and guides to show other men the way, yet it does not follow that they are so wise that they must not be learners as well as the rest. For he that speaks must take instruction by it himself, and a man will never be fit to declare God's will to other men, unless he himself learns daily' (Sermon on Eph. 4:11-14).

Calvin wished that pastors were not called 'clergy'. 'I would have preferred them to be given a more proper name, for this appellation arose from error or at least from a wrong attitude, since Peter calls the whole church "the clergy", that is, the inheritance of the Lord' (Comm. 1 Pet. 5:3). Calvin emphasized that all Christians must carry the teaching of Christ 'always in our hearts to put it into practice', and 'must also be like trumpeters to waken such as are asleep, and like guides to direct such as go astray, and to bring those into the right way who had wandered away' (Sermon on Eph. 5:11-14).

Elders, or what we sometimes call ruling elders as distinct from teaching elders or pastors, are 'chosen from the people', and are responsible with the pastor for the spiritual welfare of the people and discipline (IV.3.8).

The office of deacon, Calvin says, is 'highly honourable' (Comm. 1 Tim. 3:9). In the Roman Catholic Church this office had degenerated into a kind of liturgical assistant to the priest. In Geneva it was restored to its original function of supervising the church's benevolences and caring for the sick and the poor. Elsie McKee calls it 'the love office' and writes, 'in the Reformed tradition, the diaconate is the formal, structured office charged with seeing that the church as a body is active in loving its neighbours' (*The Reformed Journal*, November 1989, 7).

In Calvin's Geneva there were two kinds of deacons: the financial officers who administered the benevolences of the church and the welfare workers who cared for the poor and needy. Bruce Gordon writes, 'The deacons of the Genevan church did just about anything and everything. They purchased clothing and firewood, provided medical care, and not infrequently were present at births. They arranged guardians for the children of the sick. Essentially, they attempted to meet any need' (*Calvin*, 201). They also supported the missionary work emanating from Geneva by providing catechisms, psalters, and Bibles for use in France and giving aid to ministers and their families and to the families of those martyred in France.

The second office of deacon was the only church position that, in Calvin's view, could be filled by women. He based this on the description of the work of widows in 1 Timothy 5:9-10 (IV.3.9) and the example of Phoebe, who 'exercised a very honourable and holy ministry in the church' (Comm. Rom. 16:1). Calvin often praises the faithful women of the Bible. He wrote that at his resurrection, Christ 'made a start with the women, and not only let them see him but gave them the message of the gospel for the apostles, making them their teachers ... Though the intention to anoint Christ was not free of censure (they were reckoning him still to be dead), he pardons their weakness and honours them with exceptional distinction, taking the apostolic office away from the men for the moment and committing it to them' (Comm. Mark 16:1). Calvin recognized and praised the witness and valour of Christian women throughout history. To Christian women facing martyrdom in Paris Calvin wrote:

> How many thousands of women have there been who have spared neither blood nor their lives to maintain the name of Jesus Christ, and announce his reign! Has not God caused their martyrdom to fructify? ... Have we not still before our eyes examples of how God works daily by their testimony, and confounds his enemies, in such a manner that there is no preaching of such efficacy as the fortitude and perseverance they possess in confessing the name of Christ? (*Letters of John Calvin* 3:365-66)

Calvin stresses that caring for the poor and needy was the responsibility of all Christians. The deacons are the church's officers in overseeing this ministry of love to which all are called. They were charged with seeking out the needy as well as caring for them. In his commentaries and sermons, Calvin's concerns for those who are suffering and in need are 'woven like golden threads of kindness throughout the fabric of exegesis' (McKee, *John Calvin on the Diaconate and Liturgical Almsgiving*, 298).

The early church

In IV.4 Calvin gathers evidence that the church remained basically healthy for about five hundred years, both in teaching and practice. The early church mainly followed scriptural principles in its church government. Calvin is willing to tolerate the extra-biblical refinements and innovations of that period. He accepts bishops, archbishops, and patriarchs as long as these ministers did not 'have lordship' over their brethren; archdeacons as 'a new and more exact kind of administration'; and even doorkeepers, acolytes, and subdeacons, which were offices in preparation for the ministry. He approves of the practice of the early church of training young men for the ministry—'that they might leave a seedbed [a seminary] for the church' (IV.4.9). He notes that in the early church no one was promoted to the office of presbyter or bishop 'without actually undergoing for many years examination under the eyes of the people' (IV.4.10). The people were allowed to choose their own bishops or pastors. 'No one was to be thrust into office who was not acceptable to all' (IV.4.11).

Calvin draws some lessons about the collection and use of money in the early church. Bishops are to be sure that they distribute goods 'to whom they are owed, with the greatest awe and reverence, as if in God's presence, without partiality' (IV.4.6). Those who work for the church should be adequately but not extravagantly supported, and the poor, at home and elsewhere, must not be neglected. Church buildings must be maintained but without 'excessive splendour' (IV.4.8).

Calvin says that post-apostolic customs in celebrating the Lord's supper 'are not to be disapproved' (IV.10.9), and he admits that there were good traditions of the apostles that were 'not committed to writing' (IV.10.31). It is useful 'to recognize in those characteristics of the ancient church the form which will represent to our eyes some image of the divine institution' (IV.4.1). The early church maintained basic purity for about five hundred years, Calvin believed, but the Roman Catholic or Papal Church was another matter. He held that Gregory was 'the last bishop of Rome' during its time of relative purity (IV.17.49).

Knowing God and ourselves

In his book on the canons and decrees of the Council of Trent, Calvin gives good advice to us today as well as to people of his time:

> In regard to the whole body of the church, we commend it to the care of its Lord! Meanwhile, let us not be either slothful or secure. Let each do his best. Let us contribute whatever is in us of counsel, learning, and abilities, to build up the ruins of the church (*Calvin's Tracts* 3:188).

22. *The Roman Catholic Church—*
'A Half-Demolished Building'

'And just as often happens when buildings are pulled down [and] the foundations and ruins remain, so [God] did not allow his church either to be destroyed to the very foundations by Antichrist or to be levelled to the ground, even though to punish the ungratefulness of men who had despised his word he let it undergo frightful shaking and shattering, but even after this very destruction willed that *a half-demolished building* remain' (IV.2.11).

Notre Dame University professor Randall C. Zachman wrote an article with the title, 'Called to Rebuild a Church in Ruins: The Life and Work of John Calvin', for *The Expository Times* 2014.

> 'Calvin wrote to the Catholic Cardinal Sadoleto, "Place before your eyes the ancient form of the church, and then look upon the ruins that remain. The foundation of the church is in the doctrine, discipline, and sacraments, and in the light of these the church must constantly be judged" … Calvin's reply to Sadoleto became his life's program' (Berkouwer, 'Calvin and Rome', in *John Calvin: Contemporary Prophet*, 185).

Read: *Institutes* IV.5-13, 19. [*1541* ch. 13, pp.669-706.]

This section of the *Institutes* may be omitted without losing the theological flow of Calvin's thought. It is mainly a historical and polemical attack on the Roman Catholic Church of his day. There are, however, embedded in his criticism of Roman Catholic practices many positive and enlightening nuggets of truth.

Scripture Text: 'But you have turned aside from the way. You have caused many to stumble by your instruction. You have corrupted the covenant of Levi, says the Lord of hosts' (Mal. 2:8).

Notable Quote: 'I have chosen to mention these few instances from many, partly that my readers may see how gravely the church had wasted away, partly that they may also recognize into what great sorrow and anguish all the godly were cast by this calamity' (IV.7.18).

Prayer

Grant, Almighty God, as your church at this day is oppressed with many evils, that we may learn to raise up not only our eyes and our hands to you, but also our hearts, and that we may so fix our attention on you as to look for salvation from you alone; and that though despair may overwhelm us on earth, yet the hope of your goodness may ever shine on us from heaven, and that, relying on the mediator whom you have given us, we may not hesitate to cry continually to you, until we really find by experience that our prayers have not been in vain, when you, pitying your church, have extended your hand and given us cause to rejoice and have turned our mourning into joy, through Christ our Lord. Amen.

(Lifting Up Our Hearts, 267.)

✦

A look back and a look ahead

John Calvin's treatment of the requirements for a true church in IV.1-3 ('the order of church government as it has been handed down to us from God's pure word') is followed by IV.4, in which Calvin examines the history of the early church before the rise of the papacy, and IV.5-13, and argues that because of its deviation from biblical teaching, the later Roman Catholic Church can no longer be a true church of Christ. In IV.14-17, Calvin treats the two sacraments of baptism and the Lord's supper, and in IV.18 considers the papal mass 'by which Christ's supper was not only profaned but annihilated'. In IV.19 Calvin discusses 'the five other ceremonies' or sacraments of the Roman Catholic Church. In these chapters Calvin demonstrates a considerable knowledge of church history. He makes use of the writings of the early church fathers to support his positions on questions of doctrine and to challenge the teaching and practice of the Catholic Church of his day.

We must remember that in these chapters Calvin is discussing the Roman Catholic Church of his time, not the early church nor, of course, the modern Roman Catholic Church. He sums up his view of the medieval papacy, 'Here there is no preaching, no care for discipline, no zeal toward the churches, no spiritual activity—in short, nothing but the world' (IV.7.22). There was nothing novel or extreme in Calvin's denunciation of the vices and abuses of the medieval popes. Dante, Wycliffe, Hus, Savonarola, Erasmus, and others made the same charge, as does the modern historian Barbara W. Tuchman, who wrote about 'the Renaissance Six'—the popes from Sixtus IV to Clement VII (from 1471 to 1534)—concluding that they 'possessed no sense of spiritual mission, provided no meaningful religious guidance, performed no moral service for the Christian world' (*The March of Folly*, 126).

Calvin marshals biblical, historical, theological, and moral arguments to show that the Roman Catholic Church was not a true church of Christ. He does this, he says, that his readers may judge 'what sort of church the Romanists have, for the sake of which they make us guilty of schism, since we have separated from it' (IV.6.1).

'The ancient form of government was completely overthrown by the tyranny of the papacy' (IV.5)

Calvin describes how the ancient form of church government was completely overthrown by papal practices in the medieval church—such as the appointment of unworthy bishops without the consent of the people; simony and pluralism; and absenteeism. 'Boys scarcely ten years old' have been made bishops 'by the pope's dispensation' (IV.5.1). The people's voice in the election of bishops was taken away. Ordination became 'nothing but pure mockery' (IV.5.3). Presbyters abandoned teaching and preaching and became 'priests to perform sacrifices' (IV.5.4). Deacons abandoned the poor and became liturgical assistants to the priests. 'But the proper ordination of a presbyter is a call to govern the church; of a deacon, to gather alms' (IV.5.5). Priestly livings, called 'benefices', were conferred to benefit the men who received them, not the churches they were supposed to serve. Those who had never seen 'a sheep of his flock', Calvin writes, cannot be the shepherd of it (IV.5.11).

'The primacy of the Roman see' (IV.6)

In IV.6 Calvin comes to 'the capstone of the whole structure, that is, the primacy of the Roman see' (IV.6.1). He refutes the papal claims that scriptures such as Matthew 16:18 and John 20:23 support the papacy. Calvin admits that Peter was given 'honour of rank', but that this is 'greatly different from power' (IV.6.5). 'The preaching of the same gospel was entrusted to all the apostles, with a common power to bind and loose' (IV.6.4). The keys of the kingdom refer to the preaching of the gospel, and 'with regard to men it is not so much power as service. For Christ has not given this power actually to men, but to his word, of which he has made men ministers' (IV.11.1).

Christ, not the pope, is 'the sole head of the church, under whose sway all of us cleave to one another' (IV.6.9). Calvin admitted that Peter may have died in Rome, but Calvin was not persuaded that he was bishop there, 'especially for a long time' (IV.6.15). Calvin contrasts the proud titles of the later Roman bishops with a proper view of pastoral leadership. He admits that the bishop of Rome was one of the chief bishops of the church, but refuses to accept that 'he had dominion over all' the church (IV.7.8).

'The origin and growth of the Roman papacy until it raised itself to such a height that the freedom of the church was oppressed, and all restraint overthrown' (IV.7)

In IV.7 Calvin continues his history of the popes—whose conduct is 'utterly abhorrent not only to a sense of piety but also of humanity' (IV.7.21). He mentions a few examples from many so that his readers 'may see how gravely the church had wasted away' and 'may recognize into what great sorrow and anguish all the godly were cast by this calamity' (IV.7.18). The apostle Paul wrote of a 'universal apostasy' that will seize the church, even though 'many scattered members of the church persevere in the true unity of faith' (IV.7.25). Calvin sums up what he has said before: 'The first task of the bishop's office is to teach the people from God's word. The second and next is to administer the sacraments. The third is to admonish and exhort, also to correct those who sin and to keep the people under holy discipline' (IV.7.23). At one time Rome was 'indeed the mother of all churches; but after it began to become the see of Antichrist, it ceased to be what it once was' (IV.7.24). 'Today it is not worthy of being regarded among the smallest toes of the church's feet' (IV.7.29).

'The power of the church with respect to articles of faith; and how in the papacy, with unbridled license, the church has been led to corrupt all purity of doctrine' (IV.8)

In IV.8 Calvin sums up the corruption of doctrine under the papacy. He insists that Christ alone is 'the schoolmaster of the church', of whom alone it is written, 'hear him' (Comm. Matt. 17:5). 'The power of the church, therefore, is not infinite, but subject to the Lord's word and, as it were, enclosed within it' (IV.8.4). Calvin returns to a brief exposition of the authority and validity of God's word for the church. Despite footnotes 7 and 9 on pages 1155-57 of the McNeill-Battles edition of the *Institutes*, Calvin does not deny verbal inspiration of the Bible. He insists that the apostles were 'sure and genuine scribes of the Holy Spirit, and their writings are therefore to be considered oracles of God' (IV.8.9). There is no reason to believe that here, or anywhere else, Calvin sought to hear the voice of God apart from the words of the Bible.

'Councils and their authority' (IV.9)

Calvin accepts the first four councils of the ancient church. In fact, he says, 'I venerate them from my heart, and desire that they be honoured by all' (IV.9.1). But he insists that Scripture stands out 'in the higher place, with everything subject to its standard' (IV.9.7). Of some of the later councils Calvin writes that 'we see shining forth the true zeal for piety, and clear tokens of insight, doctrine, and prudence', but notes that things gradually get worse. He agrees that 'the best and surest remedy' in establishing doctrine and interpreting scripture is 'for a synod of true bishops to be convened', and, 'invoking Christ's Spirit', to agree and 'bring forth a definition derived from Scripture' (IV.9.13). Despite the problems with many of the later councils, Calvin is convinced that 'truth does not die in the church, even though it be oppressed by one council, but is wonderfully preserved by the Lord so that it may rise up and triumph again in its own time' (IV.9.13).

'The power of making laws, in which the pope, with his supporters, has exercised upon souls the most savage tyranny and butchery' (IV.10)

In IV.10 Calvin deals with papal laws and their effects, and especially the question of 'whether the church may lawfully bind consciences by its laws'. He says that 'holy and useful' rules provide for 'the preservation of discipline or honesty or peace' (IV.10.1). He then shows how papal rules 'benumb the people rather than … teach them' and 'overturn rather than preserve discipline' (IV.10.12).

Calvin agrees that some rules and ceremonies are helpful, with the provision that 'the means used ought to show Christ, not to hide him' (IV.10.14). He supports Augustine's contention that Christian observances and practices, established by the apostles or by councils, are 'most healthful in the church'. These include, Augustine writes, 'the celebration with annual rites of the Lord's passion and resurrection, his ascent into heaven, and the coming of the Holy Spirit, and any similar event that has occurred which is celebrated by the whole church' (IV.10.19).

Furthermore, 'some form of organization is necessary in all human society to foster common peace and maintain concord'. These practices must not be 'considered necessary for salvation', but for the proper organization of the church, that 'all things be done decently and in order' (IV.10.27). Calvin lists some examples of true decorum in worship (IV.10.29) but notes that the Lord 'did not will in outward discipline and ceremonies to prescribe in detail what we ought to do (because he foresaw that this depended upon the state of the times, and he did not deem one form suitable for all ages)'. Practices can and ought to be 'variously accommodated to the customs of each nation and age'. It is, therefore, fitting 'to change and abrogate traditional practices and to establish new ones' (IV.10.30).

Calvin sums up his critique of Catholic rules by insisting that church observances and practices be few, useful, and accompanied by the teaching of a faithful pastor. Christian freedom should give way to love, that we not be too fastidious in our judgment of others, and that all that we do should be for 'the upbuilding of the church' (IV.10.32).

'The jurisdiction of the church and its abuse as seen in the papacy' (IV.11)

In IV.11 Calvin discusses Matthew 16:19, 'I will give you the keys of the kingdom of heaven, and whatever you bind on earth shall be bound in heaven, and whatever you loose on earth shall be loosed in heaven.' He explains that 'the power of the keys is simply the preaching of the gospel, and that with regard to men it is not so much power as ministry. For Christ has not given this power actually to men, but to his word, of which he has made men ministers' (IV.11.1).

Ecclesiastical power must be completely separate from the power of the state and must 'be administered not by the decision of one man but by a lawful assembly' (IV.11.5). He criticizes the Catholic bishops for seizing, 'with blind zeal', worldly power, by which 'they have destroyed themselves, their successors, and the church' (IV.11.10). He quotes Bernard saying that 'a ministry has been laid upon us, not a lordship given. Learn that you need a hoe, not a sceptre, to do the prophet's work' (IV.11.11).

'The discipline of the church: its chief use in censures and excommunication' (IV.12)

In IV.12.1-13 Calvin discusses church discipline (which we have already looked at in connection with his treatment of the marks of the church in chapter 1 of Book IV). He then deals with the topic of fasting. He says that pastors, as the need arises, should 'urge the people to public fasting and extraordinary prayers' (IV.12.14). 'When the heart is affected as it ought to be, it can hardly help breaking into outward ceremony' (IV.12.15). He warns, however, against misconceptions and misuses of fasting—fasting as an outward show without inner meaning, fasting as a work of merit, and extreme forms of fasting.

'Vows; and how everyone rashly taking them has miserably entangled himself' (IV.13)

The practice of clerical celibacy is a harmful innovation, refuted by Scripture, Calvin argues. Catholics extol the superiority of celibacy and denigrate marriage, 'despite the fact that God deemed it not alien to his majesty to institute marriage; that he declared it honourable among all men; and that Christ, our Lord, sanctified it by his presence, deigning to honour it with his first miracle' (IV.13.2). The vow of celibacy is 'wrongly considered as service of God and is rashly made by those to whom the power of continence has not been given'. Calvin acknowledges that celibacy is sometimes necessary, as in the case of the widows in 1 Timothy 5:10, who could not carry on their work 'without being their own masters and free of the marriage yoke' (IV.13.18). In his commentary on 1 Timothy 3:4, Calvin writes: 'However much we may admire celibacy and a philosophical life remote from ordinary living, wise and thoughtful men have learned from their own experience that those who know ordinary life and are well practiced in the duties that human relations impose are far better trained and fitted to rule our church.'

Calvin discusses other 'vows which are made apart from God's express word' (IV.13.1). A vow or promise to God is to be made carefully and sanely, with proper purpose and intention. Vows are lawful, says Calvin, 'provided they are supported by God's approval, agree with our calling, and are limited to the endowment of grace given us by God' (IV.13.5).

Calvin critiques monasticism in IV.13.8-21. He looks briefly at its history and judges the monasticism of his time in the light of the better practices of the earlier monks. Calvin praises the early monasteries that served as 'monastic colleges' or 'seminaries of the ecclesiastical order' in which 'pious men customarily prepared themselves by monastic discipline to govern the church, that thus they might be fitter and better trained to undertake so great an office'. These monasteries constituted communities 'in aid of piety, whose rule was tempered by their goal of brotherly love' (IV.13.8-9). But Calvin concludes that monasticism lacks biblical support, creates 'a conventicle of schismatics … cut off from the lawful society of believers', and has resulted in many evils. He does not deny that there are some good monks, 'but these few lie hidden, scattered in that huge multitude of evil and depraved men' (IV.13.15).

'The five other ceremonies, falsely termed sacraments; although commonly considered sacraments hitherto, they are proved not to be such, and their real nature is shown' (IV.19)

In IV.14-18 Calvin presents the Reformed view of the sacraments of baptism and the Lord's supper (which we will treat in our next three chapters). In IV.19 he critiques the five other Catholic sacraments. The medieval Catholic Church finally settled on seven sacraments, defined as 'visible forms of an invisible grace', 'instruments for conferring righteousness', and 'means of obtaining grace' (IV.19.1). Calvin believed that these five Catholic practices had neither a scriptural command nor promise necessary to make them sacraments. He argues that the early church did not hold to seven sacraments, quoting Augustine to support his position.

Confirmation

The early church examined those baptized as infants 'at the end of their childhood' and blessed them by the laying on of the hands of a bishop. Calvin warmly approved this practice, but was critical of later Catholic elaborations, including anointing with oil. He also argues that Catholic confirmation devalued baptism, since Catholics taught that 'the Holy Spirit is given in baptism for innocence; in confirmation, for the increase of grace' (IV.19.8). It was necessary, therefore, according to Catholic teaching, that all believers be anointed with oil by episcopal confirmation in order to become 'complete Christians' (IV.19.9).

Calvin approved a true confirmation in which 'children or those near adolescence' ('a child of ten' years of age) would be examined before the church as to their understanding of Christian doctrine (IV.19.13). This was a good practice, he believed, but not a sacrament.

Penance

Calvin approved of the early church practice by which a repentant sinner was, by the laying on of hands, assured of God's pardon and of the church's receiving him 'kindly into favour'—called by Cyprian 'giving peace' (IV.19.14). Even so Calvin judges that the laying on of hands in penance 'is a ceremony ordained by men, not by God, one that ought to be classed among things indifferent and outward exercises'. These things ought not to be despised, but must occupy a lower place than those practices commended to us by the Lord's word (IV.19.14). Calvin rejects, however, the Catholic understanding of penance as a sacrament, 'the second plank after baptism', by which a baptized person who has sinned is restored. He prefers to call baptism 'the sacrament of penance', since it is given 'as a confirmation of grace and a seal of assurance' (IV.19.17).

In rejecting the Catholic doctrine of penance, Calvin did not dismiss the need for confession and repentance. Herman Selderhuis comments, 'The confessional was not thrown out [by Calvin] but was relocated to the living room. The shepherds became mobile and visited the sheep rather than waiting for the sheep to come to them' (*John Calvin: A Pilgrim's Life*, 88).

Extreme unction

Anointing the sick and especially the dying with oil is not a sacrament, Calvin says. He shows how the Catholic practice failed to follow the instructions of James 5:14-15. Although the gift of healing was sometimes given to the apostles, 'the Lord is indeed present with his people in every age; and he heals their weaknesses as often as necessary, no less than of old; still he does not put forth these manifest powers, nor dispense miracles through the apostles' hands' (IV.19.19).

Holy orders

Catholics held that there were seven (some said nine) ecclesiastical orders or grades. Ordination into these offices constituted a sacrament. Calvin teaches the priesthood of all Christians and the calling of some to the office of presbyter or elder. For those called to be pastors there is a scriptural ceremony of ordination that is 'a faithful token of spiritual grace', according to 1 Timothy 4:14. Calvin does not make ordination a third sacrament, along with baptism and the Lord's Supper, because it is 'not ordinary or common with all believers, but is a special rite for a particular office' (IV.19.28).

Marriage

Marriage was instituted by God but was not seen as a sacrament until the time of Gregory VII (pope from 1073 until 1085). Calvin argues that Catholics misunderstand Ephesians 5:28-32 by seeing marriage as 'a great sacrament'. The correct reading, 'this is a great mystery', describes the relationship between Christ and the church. Calvin did not believe that marriage was a sacrament, but he said Scripture describes marriage as 'a holy covenant, and therefore it calls it divine' (Sermon on Eph. 5:22-26).

Knowing God and ourselves

Calvin's treatment of the Roman Catholic Church of his time is sharply critical, but not without sorrow and not without hope. Calvin concluded his reply to Cardinal Sadoleto with a fervent plea: 'The Lord grant, Sadolet, that you and all your party may at length perceive that the only true bond of ecclesiastical unity consists in this, that Christ the Lord, who has reconciled us to God the Father, gather us out of our present dispersion into the fellowship of his body, that so, through his one word and Spirit, we may join together with one heart and one soul' (*Calvin: Theological Treatises*, 256).

While attacking the Catholic Church for its departure from the truth, Calvin does not cast a blind eye on the failures of Protestants. Preaching on Ephesians 4:23-26, he said to his Geneva congregation,

As for us, although we have the light of the gospel, and can say that the superstitions of papistry are but trifles, yet we are nevertheless far off from God's teaching. And if someone should sift our lives, where would this true holiness be? Where this righteousness?

23. The Sacraments—
'Ladders'

'Because we are unable to fly high enough to draw near to God, he has ordained sacraments for us like *ladders*' (4,14,8). 'The [Lord's] Supper ought to serve as *a ladder* in the search for our Lord Jesus Christ' (Sermon on Eph. 5:25-27).

'In his interpretation of Psalm 51:9 ["Hide your face from my sins, and blot out all my iniquities"] Calvin does look extensively into the meaning of the sacrament. When David asks whether God wants to purify him with hyssop, the psalmist is aware that this has to do with purification of the heart. Nevertheless man also needs the external sign of purification. Here Calvin turns to consider the Lord's supper. Only by the blood of Christ is there reconciliation, Calvin says. Yet, because we humans want to see tangible evidence of this grace and even hold it in our hands, our conscience comes to rest only when we have used the outward signs. It is notable here how strongly Calvin connects the visible signs with grace, even speaking of wanting to hold that grace in one's hand. The sinner who wishes to receive grace must direct his eye at the sacrifice of Christ and, for the confirmation of his faith, at the Lord's supper and baptism' (Selderhuis, *Calvin's Theology of the Psalms*, 125).

Read: *Institutes* **IV.14.** [*1541* ch. 10, pp.561-577.]

Scripture Text: 'Purge me with hyssop, and I shall be clean; wash me, and I shall be whiter than snow' (Psa. 51:7).

Calvin comments on this verse: 'It is no doubt to the blood of Christ alone that we must look for the atonement of our sins; but we are creatures of sense, who must see with our eyes, and handle with our hands; and it is only by improving the outward symbols of propitiation that we can arrive at a full and assured persuasion of it.'

Notable Quote: 'Our sacraments figure Christ absent as to sight and place, but testify that he has been once manifested. But they now also present him to be enjoyed. They are not, therefore, bare shadows, but rather symbols of Christ's presence, for they contain that Yea and Amen of all the promises of God, which has been once manifested in Christ' (Comm. Col. 2:17).

Prayer

Almighty God, you have been pleased to prescribe a rule for us by which we may truly and purely worship you. Grant that we may follow this plain rule, and never indulge our own imaginations nor trifle with you through our own fancies or through the foolish wisdom of our flesh. May we continue in your law and in the doctrine your only begotten Son, our Lord, has delivered to us, so that we may advance more and more in the knowledge of that glory, the foretaste of which you give us now, until we shall at length fully and perfectly enjoy it, when we shall be gathered into that celestial kingdom your Son has procured for us by his own blood. Amen.

(*Lifting Up Our Hearts*, 287.)

❧

Definition of sacrament

John Calvin begins with Augustine's famous definition of a sacrament—'a visible form of an invisible grace'—and expands it as follows: 'an outward sign by which the Lord seals on our consciences the promises of his good will toward us in order to sustain the weakness of our faith; and we in turn attest our piety toward him in the presence of the Lord and of his angels and before men' (IV.14.1).

Outward signs

The sacraments are outward signs, given to us 'to sustain the weakness of our faith'. Because 'we have souls engrafted into bodies, [God] imparts spiritual things under visible ones' (IV.14.3). The 'surest rule of the sacraments' is 'that we should see spiritual things in physical as if set before our very eyes' (IV.15.14). By these outward and visible signs, God 'condescends to lead us to himself'. In this way he 'provides first for our ignorance and dullness, then for our weakness' (IV.14.3). It is not that the word is weak so that it needs the support of the sacraments, but that we are weak so that we need the sacraments as 'another aid to our faith' (IV.14.1).

Sacraments of the Old and New Testaments

Commenting on Genesis 3:23, Calvin calls 'the sanctuary, the ark of the covenant, the table, and its furniture' the 'ladders and vehicles' by which the people of the Old Testament 'might themselves rise to heaven'. The Old Testament sacraments prefigured Christ; the New Testament sacraments attest him 'as already given and revealed' (IV.14.20). The Old Testament sacraments were multiplied and elaborate, because the gospel of God's grace present from the fall of Adam in the garden was not yet known in its fuller and brighter New Testament form. At the end of his discussion of baptism and the Lord's supper, Calvin states that by the various sacraments in the Old Testament the Jews 'were warned not to halt with such figures, whose condition was impermanent, but to await from God something better' (IV.18.20). The New Testament sacraments, Calvin says, are 'fewer in number, more majestic in signification, more excellent in power' (IV.14.26).

In IV.14.18 Calvin says that 'the term "sacrament" … embraces generally all those signs which God has ever enjoined upon men to render them more certain and confident of the truth of his promises. He sometimes willed to present these in natural things, at other times set them forth in miracles', for example, the tree of life for Adam and Eve, the rainbow for Noah, the smoking fire pot for Abraham, the wet and dry fleece for Gideon, and the setting back of the sun dial in 2 Kings 20. These 'sacraments' are not efficacious in themselves but because 'they had a mark engraved upon them by God's word, so that they were proofs and seals of his covenants'. 'Since these things were done to support and confirm their feeble faith, they were also sacraments.' 'If [God] had imprinted such reminders upon the sun, stars, earth, stones, they would all be sacraments for us' (IV.14.18).

Testimonies of God's grace

The sacraments are testimonies of God's good will or 'divine grace toward us' (IV.14.1). They are testimonies that repeat and seal the word in which we hear about the grace of God. Through the sacraments, we see, feel, and, in the Lord's supper, even taste the goodness of God that we read about in the word and hear about in sermons. 'The sacraments bring the clearest promises; and they have this characteristic over and above the word because they represent them for us as painted in a picture from life' (IV.14.6). The sacraments picture what the word declares: the promises in Jesus Christ, or simply Christ himself, who is the substance of the sacraments.

> **At the Communion**
>
> Here, O my Lord, I see thee face to face;
>   Here would I touch and handle things unseen;
> Here, grasp with firmer hand eternal grace,
>   And all my weariness upon thee lean.
>
> Here would I feed upon the bread of God,
>   Here drink with thee the royal wine of heav'n,
> Here would I lay aside each earthly load,
>   Here taste afresh the calm of sin forgiv'n.
>
>   Horatius Bonar

Confirming and sealing

The sacraments are joined to the promise 'as a sort of appendix, with the purpose of confirming and sealing the promise itself'. The word has precedence over the sacrament, since the word sets forth the promise that the sacraments confirm. Augustine had written: 'Let the word be added to the element and it will become a sacrament' (IV.14.4). The sacraments are 'visible words'; they represent the promise 'as painted in a picture from life' (IV.14.5). In the Baptismal Liturgy Calvin said, 'As [Christ] communicates his riches and blessings by his word, so he distributes them to us by his sacraments' (*John Calvin: Writings on Pastoral Piety*, 154).

The sacraments add nothing to the promise as such, but confirm and seal the promise, so they 'have the same office as the word of God—to offer and set forth Christ to us' (IV.14.17). Joel Beeke writes, 'The sacraments hold forth the same Christ as the preached word but communicate him through a different mode. We don't get a better Christ in the sacraments, but sometimes we get Christ better' (*The Cambridge Companion to John Calvin*, 134)—or, perhaps we should say, we get Christ again. Baptism and the Lord's supper repeat, confirm, reinforce, illustrate, and dramatize the preached word. The sacraments, Calvin repeats again and again, 'have the same office as the word of God: to offer and set forth Christ to us, and in him the treasures of heavenly grace' (IV.14.17). Karl Barth writes, 'We should not trust in the sacraments but in God alone, the ministry of the sacraments being to help us to do this' (*The Theology of John Calvin*, 176).

Means of grace

The sacraments are a means of grace. They are more than signs; they 'sustain, nourish, confirm, and increase our faith' (IV.14.7). They are not only a representation but also a presentation, not only a showing but a giving. In the sacrament the Lord 'does not feed our eyes with a mere appearance only, but leads us to the present reality and effectively performs what it symbolizes' (IV.15.14). But the sacraments do not by themselves confer grace. To become a means of grace the sacraments need:

- The word. 'Let the word be added to the element and it will become a sacrament' (IV.14.3).

- The Holy Spirit. 'The sacraments properly fulfil their office only when the Spirit, that inward teacher, comes to them … If the Spirit be lacking, the sacraments can accomplish nothing more in our minds than the splendor of the sun shining upon blind eyes, or a voice sounding in deaf ears' (IV.14.9). Through the sacraments God truly fulfils what he promises, but without resigning to them the primary operation, which remains his.

- Faith. The sacraments 'confer no advantage or profit without being received by faith' (IV.14.17).

Note Calvin's illustration of wine poured over a vessel that does not have a mouth open to receive it (IV.14.17). The sacraments do not accomplish their purpose when there is no open mouth—no faith—to receive them. Receiving the sacraments is not a work, however; we bring nothing to it but 'begging' (IV.14.26).

Confession of faith

The sacraments are a confession of our faith. Calvin says that the 'first point' is that the sacraments 'serve our faith before God'. And the second is that they 'attest our confession before men' (IV.14.13). Not only does God bind us more closely to himself in the sacraments, but through them he binds us more closely to each other. By the sacraments we are 'welded together' in the church (IV.14.19). In his *Treatise on the Lord's Supper* Calvin writes: 'For as the bread, which is there sanctified for the common use of us all, is made of many grains so mixed together that one cannot be discerned from the other, so ought we to be united among ourselves in one indissoluble friendship' (*Calvin: Theological Treatises*, 151).

Knowing God and ourselves

'First the Lord teaches and instructs us by his word; then he confirms it by the sacraments; finally he illumines our minds with the light of his Holy Spirit and opens our hearts for word and sacraments to enter' (IV.14.8). Thank God for these three great blessings.

24. Baptism—
'Symbol of Adoption'

'When [baptized infants] have grown up, they are greatly spurred to an earnest zeal for worshiping God, by whom they were received as children through a solemn *symbol of adoption* before they were old enough to recognize him as Father' (IV.16.9).

Preaching on Ephesians 5:25-27, Calvin gave a brief statement of the main point of baptism and the Lord's supper. 'To apply the sacraments to a right use, even that which God permits and ordains, our Lord Jesus Christ must be our guide. In baptism we see the water, but thereby we must be lifted up higher to the blood of the Son of God, assuring ourselves that it is not the water that makes us clean, but that is only a pledge of the washing that was obtained for us when our Lord Jesus was crucified for us. In the supper we have bread and wine. Now to keep ourselves to that which is set before our eyes would be a withdrawing of ourselves from Jesus Christ. Our faith therefore must be lifted up and directed to him in whom all the parts of our salvation are wrapped up.'

Read: *Institutes* IV.15-16. [*1541* ch.11, pp.579-621.]

Scripture Text: 'We were buried therefore with [Christ Jesus] by baptism into death, in order that, just as Christ was raised from the dead by the glory of the Father, we too might walk in newness of life' (Rom. 6:4).

Notable Quote: 'We are baptized in the name of the Father, as the author of our salvation; in the name of the Son, who has performed all that belonged to our redemption; and in the name of the Holy Spirit, by whom we are sanctified, to possess and enjoy the incomprehensible benefits that are purchased for us by our Lord Jesus Christ' (Sermon on Eph. 4:1-5).

Prayer (on occasion of the baptism of a child)

Lord God, everlasting and almighty Father, whom it has pleased to promise that you will be our God and the God of our children: we pray that you may be pleased to confirm this grace in this child before you, begotten of a father and mother whom you have called into your church.

And as this child is offered and consecrated to you by us, may you will to receive him [or her] under your holy protection, declaring yourself to be his God and Saviour, forgiving in him the original sin of which all the descendants of Adam are guilty; and then sanctifying him by your Spirit, so that when he comes to the age of understanding he may know and adore you as his only God, glorifying you in all his life, to obtain from you always the remission of his sins. And so that he may obtain these graces, may it please you to incorporate him into the communion of our Lord Jesus, to be a participant in all his blessings as a member of his body.

Hear us, merciful Father, that the baptism which we communicate to him according to your ordinance may produce in him its fruit and virtue, such as is declared to us by your gospel. Amen.

(John Calvin: Writings on Pastoral Piety, 155-56.)

A look behind and a look ahead

After an introductory chapter on the sacraments in general, Calvin moves on to three chapters on the two sacraments that 'the Lord willed to be ordinary in the church'—baptism and the Lord's supper (IV.14.19). Calvin is concerned to neither minimize the sacraments nor magnify them improperly. Some 'weaken the force of the sacraments', he says, and others 'attach to the sacraments some sort of secret powers with which one nowhere reads that God has endowed them' (IV.14.14). Calvin insists that nothing be given to the sacraments 'which should not be given, and … nothing taken away which belongs to them' (IV.14.17).

Meaning of baptism

Calvin begins with a definition and descriptions of baptism. 'Baptism is the sign of the initiation by which we are received into the society of the church, in order that, engrafted in Christ, we may be reckoned among God's children' (IV.15.1). Baptism is 'a token and proof of our cleansing'. It is like 'a sealed document' to confirm to us that all our sins are forgiven (IV.15.1). Baptism unites us with the church and gives us 'the knowledge and certainty' of our 'cleansing and salvation' (IV.15.2). We are forgiven through the ministry of the church, that is, by the preaching of the gospel that tells us that we have been cleansed of our sins by Christ's blood, and 'the sign and testimony of that washing' is baptism (IV.15.4).

Blessings of baptism

Baptism demonstrates 'our mortification in Christ, and new life in him' (IV.15.5-6). Calvin's baptism liturgy of 1542 speaks of the 'double grace and benefit from God in our baptism', which means that 'God wills to be a merciful Father to us, not imputing to us all our faults', and that 'God will assist us by his Holy Spirit so that we have the power to battle against the devil, sin, and the desires of the flesh, until we have victory in this, and live in the liberty of his kingdom' (Billings, *Union with Christ*, 109).

In baptism we are united to Christ himself and 'become sharers in all his blessings' (IV.15.6). Baptism is not only an imitation of Christ's death and resurrection, it is also a participation in it. 'Just as the twig draws substance and nourishment from the root to which it is grafted, so those who receive baptism with right faith truly feel the effective working of Christ's death in the mortification of their flesh, together with the working of his resurrection in the vivification of the Spirit' (IV.15.5). In his commentary on 1 Corinthians 10:1-5 Calvin uses the story of Israel's exodus to illustrate the blessings of baptism: 'In baptism our pharaoh is drowned, our old man is crucified, our members are mortified, we are buried with Christ, and removed from the captivity of the devil and the power of death.' Baptism not only unites us with Christ in blessing but also in suffering. In a comment on Matthew 20:22 Calvin writes, 'Let us remember that we were baptized under this condition and for this end—to fix the cross to our shoulders.'

Baptism has continuing importance and power in the Christian's life. 'It is given for the arousing, nourishing, and confirming of our faith' (IV.15.14). 'As often as we fall away, we ought to recall the memory of our baptism' (IV.15.3). The 'fictitious sacrament of penance', therefore, is not needed (IV.15.4).

Baptism is also a confession of our faith. It first shows us that God is ours and then it shows other people that we are God's. It is 'the mark by which we publicly profess that we wish to be reckoned God's people' (IV.15.13).

Administration of baptism

Only ordained ministers may baptize. Emergency baptism of dying children by lay people is not permitted, and not needed, since, in Calvin's view, salvation is not tied to baptism. He explains: 'God declares [in Gen. 17:7] that he adopts our babies as his own before they are born, when he promises that he will be our God and the God of our descendants after us' (IV.15.20).

Though baptism is important, it is not required for salvation. If for some good reason—not because of sloth, contempt, or negligence—we cannot receive the sacrament from the church, we may still obtain God's grace 'by faith from the word of the Lord'. In the case of an infant who dies unbaptized, the grace of God is not so bound to the sacrament 'but that we may obtain it by faith from the word of the Lord' (IV.15.22).

Baptism does not depend upon the merit of the one who administers it. In rejecting the error of the Donatists, Calvin agrees with Augustine that 'whosoever may baptize, Christ alone presides' (IV.15.8). Calvin illustrates: 'If a letter is sent, provided the handwriting and seal are sufficiently recognized, it makes no difference who or of what sort the carrier is.' Baptism in the name of the Father, Son, and Holy Spirit is 'not of man but of God, no matter who administers it' (IV.15.16).

Calvin was critical of the 'alien hodge-podge' and 'theatrical pomp' that had been added to 'Christ's institution' of baptism by the Roman Catholic Church (IV.15.19). He was concerned that 'external pomp does not corrupt the simple institution given by Christ' (Comm. Acts 8:38).

Mode of baptism

Calvin uses the imagery of immersion when he says that God cleanses us within 'as truly and surely as we see our body outwardly cleansed, submerged, and surrounded with water' (IV.15.14). The early church, he points out, used immersion (one or three times), pouring, and sprinkling. These details, Calvin believes, are of no importance, but 'ought to be optional to churches according to the diversity of countries' (IV.15.19).

> Baptized into your name most holy,
> O Father, Son, and Holy Ghost,
> I claim a place, though weak and lowly,
> Among your seed, your chosen host.
> Buried with Christ and dead to sin:
> Your Spirit e'er shall live within.
>
> Johann J. Rambach

Infant baptism

Calvin adds 'an appendix' to his treatment of baptism to deal with infant baptism. The appendix, chapter 16, is longer than chapter 15! Calvin notes that some will think his treatment of infant baptism too long, but adds that 'in such an important matter, we ought so to esteem purity of doctrine as well as the peace of the church' (IV.16.1).

Calvin states his purpose in IV.16 by the title 'Infant baptism best accords with Christ's institution and the nature of the sign.' He acknowledges that the argument of the Anabaptists against infant baptism was 'seemingly quite plausible' (IV.16.1) in their claim that God's word does not teach it. He is convinced, however, that infant baptism was not 'contrived by the mere rashness of men' but possesses God's 'sure authority' (IV.16.1) and the 'firm approbation of Scripture' (IV.16.8). He appeals especially to the unity of the covenant of grace. He uses the term 'covenant' or 'testament' fifty-three times in IV.16. Since the grace of the covenant was the same in the Old Testament as it is in the New Testament, Calvin argues that the sacraments must also have equal significance in both periods. The Anabaptists held that the Old Testament covenant was a material or carnal arrangement and that circumcision was a political and not a spiritual sign.

Calvin argues for 'the anagogic relationship' of circumcision and baptism, showing how 'these two signs differ from each other, and in what respects they are alike' (IV.16.3). The connection between circumcision and baptism beautifully affirms the continuity of the one divine covenant of grace. Colossians 2:11-12 explains that the 'spiritual promise' given to the patriarchs in circumcision is given to us in baptism (IV.16.3). There is difference in 'the outward ceremony' but continuity in meaning and purpose. Since baptism has taken the place of circumcision, Calvin concludes, it surely must be administered to the infants of believers, as circumcision was. Calvin notes that only the bodies of male babies were imprinted with the mark of circumcision 'which could be imprinted by nature, yet in such a way that the women might be through them, so to speak, companions and partners of circumcision' (IV.16.16). In the New Testament, of course, both male and female babies are baptized.

'But if the covenant still remains firm and steadfast, it applies no less today to the children of Christians than under the Old Testament it pertained to the infants of the Jews. Yet if they are participants in the thing signified, why shall they be debarred from the sign?' (IV.16.5) It is inconceivable to Calvin that Christ by his coming 'lessened or curtailed the grace of the Father' (IV.16.6). In fact, 'the Lord Jesus, wishing to give an example by which the world would understand that he came to enlarge rather than to limit the Father's mercy, tenderly embraces the infants offered to him' (IV.16.7). Calvin sees a spiritual equivalence in Christ's embracing infants and the baptism of infants. Christ's promise to them of the kingdom of heaven is tantamount to attesting 'that infants are contained within God's covenant'. 'If it is right for infants to be brought to Christ', Calvin concludes, 'why not also to be received into baptism, the symbol of our communion and fellowship with Christ?' (IV.16.7).

But Calvin believed that the earliest church fathers regarded the practice of infant baptism 'in the apostolic age as a certainty' (IV.16.8).

Having placed baptism in the context of the Old Testament covenant, which 'is no less in force today for Christians than it was of old for the Jewish people' (IV.16.6), Calvin goes on to make four assertions about the baptism of infants.

- Baptism confirms the promise that is given to believing parents. By it, parents 'see with their very eyes the covenant of the Lord engraved upon the bodies of their children' (IV.16.9).

- By baptism, infants receive the benefits of the nurture of the church and in time come to realize that God had made them his own even before they chose him (IV.16.9, 17).

The full force of the efficacy of baptism may be long delayed. In words that may represent his own testimony, Calvin writes: 'We indeed, being blind and unbelieving, for a long time did not grasp the promise that had been given us in baptism; yet that promise, since it was of God, ever remained fixed and firm and trustworthy' (IV.15.17).

- 'Infants are baptized into future repentance and faith, and even though these have not yet been formed in them, the seed of both lies hidden within them by the secret working of the Spirit' (IV.16.20).

But, as Calvin also writes, 'baptism is clearly unprofitable for many' (IV.17.22).

- When baptized children grow up, 'they are spurred to an earnest zeal for worshiping God, by whom they are received as children through a solemn symbol of adoption, before they were old enough to recognize him as Father' (IV.16.9).

Calvin says that in the case of adults, baptism should follow faith and repentance, but he argues that the baptism of infants ought to be viewed differently. In Abraham's case circumcision followed faith, but in Isaac's case it preceded 'all understanding'. When adults are 'received into the fellowship of the covenant' they should 'learn its conditions beforehand', but infants, 'by hereditary right, according to the form of the promise', are already included in the covenant from their conception (IV.16.24).

Calvin sees the benefit of infant baptism as past, present, and future. Before they are baptized, children of believers belong to God. 'God declares that he adopts our babies as his own before they are born, when he promises that he will be our God and the God of our descendants after us' (IV.15.20). 'The children of believers are baptized, not in order that they who were previously strangers to the church may then for the first time become children of God, but rather that, because by the blessing of the promise, they already belonged to the body of Christ, they are received into the church with this solemn sign' (IV.15.22). There is the expectation that the promise sealed in the sacrament will in the future lead to the child's faith. But what happens in the present? Calvin prefers to leave it 'in suspense' (IV.16.19). He does not invoke infant regeneration or the possibility of infant faith to support his case. Calvin simply states that children 'receive some benefit from their baptism: by being engrafted into the body of the church, they are commended more to the care of the other members' (IV.16.9). And parents receive much benefit. 'For how sweet it is to godly minds to be assured, not only by word, but by sight, that they obtain so much favour with the heavenly Father that their offspring are within his care' (IV.6.32).

> Our children, Lord, in faith and pray'r,
> We now devote to thee;
> Let them thy cov'nant mercies share,
> And thy salvation see.
> Thomas Haweis

Knowing God and ourselves

'Baptism should be a token and proof of our cleansing; or (the better to explain what I mean) it is like a sealed document to confirm to us that all our sins are so abolished, remitted, and effaced that they can never come to his sight, be recalled, or charged against us' (IV.15.1). When Luther was tempted by Satan to doubt his salvation because of his sins, he answered, 'I have been baptized.' So did Calvin. 'As often as we fall away, we ought to recall the memory of our baptism and fortify our own mind with it, that we may always be sure and confident of the forgiveness of sins' (IV.15.2).

25. The Lord's Supper—
'The Wonderful Exchange'

'This is *the wonderful exchange* which, out of his measureless benevolence, [Christ] has made with us; that, becoming Son of man with us, he has made us sons of God with him; that, by his descent to earth, he has prepared an ascent to heaven for us; that, by taking on our mortality, he has conferred his immortality upon us; that, accepting our weakness, he has strengthened us by his power; that, receiving our poverty unto himself, he has transferred his wealth to us; that, taking the weight of our iniquity upon himself, he has clothed us with his righteousness' (IV.17.2).

'The holy banquet is simply the liturgical enactment of the theme of grace and gratitude that lies at the heart of Calvin's entire theology' (Gerrish, *Grace and Gratitude*, 20).

Read: *Institutes* IV.17-19. [*1541* ch. 12, pp.623-667; ch.13, pp.669-706.]

Scripture Text: 'I am the living bread that came down from heaven. If anyone eats of this bread, he will live forever. And the bread that I will give for the life of the world is my flesh' (John 6:51).

Notable Quote: 'Let us remember that this sacred feast is medicine for the sick, solace for sinners, alms to the poor ... Therefore this is the worthiness—the best and only kind we can bring to God—to offer our vileness and ... our unworthiness to him so that his mercy may make us worthy of him; to despair in ourselves so that we may be comforted in him; to abase ourselves so that we may be lifted up by him; to accuse ourselves so that we may be justified by him' (IV.17.42).

Prayer

All speech far transcending and beyond all thought, wonderful exchanging—poverty for wealth: to our hopeless weakness, give your mighty power; through this body's eating, grant our souls new health.

Son of God now with us, make us sons of God: coming from the Father, raise us now to him. Dying with us human, give us Godlike life; knit our members to you, fasten limb to limb.

Word of God now calling us to purity, of this supper make us worthy to partake; flood us with thanksgiving for your sacrifice, once for all time offered humbly for our sake.

Author of all justice, turn our unjust ways; healer of all sickness, cure our dread disease. In this meal declaring your death till you come, make all men our brothers, living in your peace. Amen.

(*Piety of John Calvin*, 171-72.)

A look behind and a look ahead

In chapters 15 and 16 of Book IV Calvin has treated the sacrament of baptism, 'the sign of the initiation by which we are received into the fellowship of the church, so that, engrafted into Christ, we may be counted among God's children' (IV.15.1). In chapter 17 he comes to the sacrament of the Lord's supper, 'wherein Christ attests himself to be the life-giving bread, upon which our souls feed unto true and blessed immortality' (IV.17.1). 'Baptism is the sign and seal of our justification before God in Christ … the Lord's supper is the sign and seal of our sanctification in Christ through the work of the Holy Spirit' (Partee, *The Theology of John Calvin*, 273).

Calvin wrote 69 pages (in the McNeill-Battles edition of the *Institutes*) trying to understand and explain what happens in the Lord's supper. He wrote nineteen more pages about what the Lord's supper is not, and then added another chapter of twenty pages. That comes to almost ninety pages, more than Calvin gave to any other topic in the 1559 *Institutes*. Calvin also produced a number of separate books on the Lord's supper.

Although Calvin became increasingly burdened with refuting Catholic, Zwinglian, and Lutheran views, his writings on the Lord's Supper are not primarily polemical but pastoral. 'The flesh of Christ is like a rich and inexhaustible fountain that pours into us the life springing forth from the Godhead into itself. Now who does not see that communion of Christ's flesh and blood is necessary for all who aspire to heavenly life?' (IV.17.9).

What the Lord's Supper brings to us

Note John Calvin's title for IV.17—'The Sacred Supper of Christ, and What It Brings to Us.'

God has 'through the hand of his only-begotten Son, given to his church … a spiritual banquet, wherein Christ attests himself to be the life-giving bread, upon which our souls feed unto true and blessed immortality' (IV.17.1). Simply stated, the Lord's supper brings Christ to us—as if he were 'set before our eyes and touched by our hands' (IV.17.3). The signs of the bread and wine 'represent for us the invisible food that we receive from the flesh and blood of Christ ... the only food of our soul' (IV.17.1). 'By bidding us take, [Christ] indicates that it is ours; by bidding us eat, that it is made one substance with us' (IV.17.3). The supper is 'a help whereby we may be engrafted into Christ's body, or engrafted, may grow more and more together with him, until he perfectly joins us with him in the heavenly life' (IV.17.33). 'So then when we receive a small piece of bread, we know that Jesus Christ is the food of our souls, when we drink a drop of wine, it is to testify to us that his blood is our spiritual drink to comfort us and make us rejoice; in short, we have in him complete perfection of life' (*John Calvin: Writings on Pastoral Piety*, 122).

The Lord's supper is occasional (Calvin wished it to be more frequent), but 'the broader banquet' which it represents is ongoing (Boulton, *Life in God*, 186). The Lord's supper reminds us that Christ 'was made the bread of life, which we continually eat ... It assures us that all that Christ did or suffered was done to quicken us; and again, that this quickening is eternal, we being ceaselessly nourished, sustained, and preserved throughout life by it' (IV.17.5). The Lord's supper, then, does not bring about 'a communion with Christ, or a reception of his body, that is not available anywhere else, but rather ... it graphically represents and presents to believers a communion they enjoy, or can enjoy, all the time' (Gerrish, *Grace And Gratitude*, 133).

The Lord's supper supports, clarifies, and strengthens our union with Christ. It seals and confirms 'that promise by which he testifies that his flesh is food indeed and his blood is drink indeed, which feed us unto eternal life' (IV.17.4). By it we 'have a witness of our growth into one body with Christ, such that whatever is his may be called ours' (IV.17.2). The Lord's supper also enables us 'to confess openly before men that for us the whole assurance of life and salvation rests upon the Lord's death, that we may glorify him by our confession, and by our example exhort others to give glory to him' (IV.17.37). By strengthening our union with Christ, it deepens our union with his other body, the church, because 'we cannot love Christ without loving him in the brethren'. Augustine, Calvin notes, frequently calls this sacrament 'the bond of love' (IV.17.38). Our compassion and generosity, which come from our union with Christ, and are nurtured by our deep fellowship with each other, should not end at the church door but go out into the world to seek those in need. Calvin wanted almsgiving—a collection for the poor—to follow the celebration of the Lord's Supper, most likely at the door as the congregation departed. That way, sharing in the body and blood of Christ manifested itself not only in mutual love in the church, but also in love for the hungry, the stranger, and the naked (Comm. Matt. 25:31-46).

> Bread of the world in mercy broken,
> Wine of the soul in mercy shed,
> By whom the words of life were spoken,
> And in whose death our sins are dead.
>
> Look on the heart by sorrow broken,
> Look on the tears by sinners shed,
> And be thy feast to us the token
> That by thy grace our souls are fed.
>
> Reginald Heber

A real but spiritual presence

John Calvin taught a 'real but spiritual presence' of the living Christ in the sacramental action rather than in the elements as such, writes Jaroslav Pelikan (*The Melody of Theology*, 81). Calvin believed that his view of the Lord's supper was the same as that of the early church. He was convinced that Augustine was 'wholly and incontrovertibly' on his side (IV.17.28).

In the Lord's supper Christ is really and truly present, but not in a physical sense. How can it be that Christ's body remains in heaven, and we feed upon his flesh and drink his blood in the Lord's supper?

Following Mary's example in Luke 1:34, who asked, 'How will this be, since I am a virgin?' Calvin believes that it is permissible for us 'in a difficult matter to inquire how it can take place' (IV.17.25).

The Swiss Protestants led by Zwingli believed that the Lord's supper was a memorial by which we remember that the body of Christ was broken and his blood shed for us on the cross. These Christians, said Calvin, define the eating of Christ's flesh and the drinking of his blood as 'nothing but to believe in Christ'. He adds that 'it is not the seeing but the eating of bread that suffices to feed the body, so the soul must truly and deeply become partaker of Christ that it may be quickened to spiritual life by his power' (IV.17.5). 'The supper is a gift; it does not merely remind us of a gift' (IV.17.6). B. A. Gerrish writes that for Calvin, 'the sacred banquet prepared by the father's goodness is the actual giving, not merely the remembering, of a gift of grace, and precisely as such it demands and evokes the answering gratitude of God's children' (*Grace and Gratitude*, 156).

The Catholics taught that at the sacrament the bread and wine were changed into the body and blood of Christ. This 'fictitious transubstantiation', Calvin argues, lacks 'the support of antiquity' and disregards the fact that 'Christ's body is limited by the general characteristics common to all human bodies, and is contained in heaven' (IV.17.12). Furthermore, the Catholic view violates the definition of a sacrament by denying the reality of the outward symbols, bread and wine, that lead us from visible things to invisible spiritual realities (IV.17.14).

The Lutherans insisted that 'in, with, and under' the bread and wine are the physical body and blood of Christ, so that there is a literal eating of Christ's flesh and drinking of his blood, as we eat the bread and drink the wine. Lutherans, Calvin believed, erred in thinking that only by Christ's descending physically could we really partake of his flesh and blood. 'They do not understand the manner of descent by which he lifts us up to himself', said Calvin (IV.17.16).

The Swiss and German Protestants failed to unite into one church because Luther and Zwingli could not agree about the nature of the presence of the Lord in the Supper. Philip Melanchthon's son-in-law, Christoph Pezel, reported that after the impasse at Marburg, Luther picked up a little book written by Calvin on the Lord's supper and praised it highly, saying: 'I might have entrusted the whole affair of this controversy to [Calvin] from the beginning. If my opponents had done the like, we should soon have been reconciled' (McNeill, *The History and Character of Calvinism*, 153). If this story is accurate, Luther may have agreed more with Calvin (as Melanchthon did) than most Lutherans. Later Lutherans bitterly attacked Calvin for the Consensus Tigurinus, in which he and Zwingli's successor, Heinrich Bullinger, hammered out an agreement on the Lord's supper. Despite their consensus there remained some difference between Calvin and Bullinger. Bullinger believed that God truly offers what the sacraments symbolize: outwardly we eat the bread, and inwardly at the same time we also feed upon Christ. Calvin held the Lord's supper is a symbol that represents and exhibits the body and blood of Christ to us, and at the same time an instrument through which God distributes the body and blood of Christ to us.

Calvin understood Christ's words 'This is my body' as a metonymy in which the name of the visible sign is also given to the thing signified, as in 1 Corinthians 10:4 (cf. Exod. 17:6), where we read that 'the rock from which water flowed in the desert was Christ'. When Christ gave the sign of his body, he did not hesitate to call it his body. In one sense Christ is not present in the elements of the Lord's supper; he has risen and is at the right hand of the Father (Mark 16:6). In another sense he is in the bread and wine of the Lord's supper, for 'the presence of his majesty has not departed' (Heb. 1:3; IV.17.26). Christ is truly present in the sacrament, but not physically, just as he is truly but not physically present in the preaching of the word. 'It is certain that if we come to church we shall not only hear a mortal man speaking but we shall feel (even by his secret power) that God is speaking to our souls, that he is the teacher. He so touches us that the human voice enters into us and so profits us that we are refreshed and nourished by it … If our Lord gives us this blessing of his gospel being preached to us, we have a sure and infallible mark that he is near us and procures our salvation, and that he calls us to him as if he had his mouth open and we saw him there in person' (Sermon on 2 Tim. 1:2). The same is true in the Lord's supper. 'For though he has taken his flesh away from us, and in the body ascended into heaven … He feeds his people with his own body' (IV.17.18).

How does it happen that in the Lord's supper we really receive the body and blood of Christ? Calvin answers this in several ways. In his commentary on 1 Corinthians 11:24, he writes that the risen Christ 'sends down the efficacy of his flesh to be present in us'. He sends down not his flesh which remains in heaven but 'the efficacy of his flesh'. 'Christ descends to us both by the outward symbol and by his Spirit, that he may quicken our souls by the substance of his flesh and of his blood' (IV.17.24). In a sermon on Ephesians 3:14-19, Calvin says that 'it is true that [Christ] really comes down to us by his word, and really by the power of his Holy Spirit, but that is in order that we should mount up on high to him'.

Roman Catholic theologians, Calvin claims, 'enclose Christ in bread'. Calvin answers that the manner of eating is 'spiritual because the secret power of the Spirit is the bond of our union with Christ' (IV.17.33). Calvin stresses the role of the Holy Spirit in the Lord's supper, as did the Eastern Orthodox Church. It seems 'unbelievable that Christ's flesh separated from us by such great distance, penetrates to us, so that it becomes our food' until we remember 'the secret power of the Holy Spirit', he writes (IV.17.10). If the Holy Spirit is absent, the sacraments achieve no more than the sun shining on blind eyes or a voice sounding in deaf ears (IV.14.9, 12).

In his treatment of the Lord's supper, Calvin repeats an important doctrine that he set forth in Book II. 'Therefore since the whole Christ is everywhere, our Mediator is ever present with his own people, and in the supper reveals himself in a special way, yet in such a way that the whole Christ is present, but not in his wholeness. For ... in his flesh he is contained in heaven until he appears in judgment.' In the Lord's supper 'the whole Christ is everywhere, yet everything which is in him, is not everywhere' (IV.17.30). Paul Helm explains, 'Christ in his divine nature [is] everywhere present, in his human nature localized in heaven, but the whole Christ [is] present by the efficacy of the Spirit's action in the worthy receiving of the Lord's supper ... In an "ineffable" way Christ is wholly present at a place even when he is not physically present at that place' (*Calvin at the Centre*, 301-302).

In a sermon on Matthew 28:1-10 Calvin said:

> Even though our Lord Jesus Christ is in heaven and does not show himself to be seen by the eye, still with his word he gives us the bread and wine that we receive here as a living image, in which we contemplate ... that the Son of God truly lives in us, in a fashion incomprehensible to our senses. We do not at all need to drag him from heaven to have this union which is spoken of here. It is an inestimable privilege that he gives us, when he makes us know his incomprehensible power and the wonderful virtue of his Holy Spirit, who makes things that are separated by a great distance nevertheless to be united.

Calvin sums it up this way: 'For it is enough for us that, from the substance of his flesh Christ breathes life into our souls—indeed, pours forth his very life into us—even though Christ's flesh itself does not enter into us' (IV.17.32). Calvin's opponents charged that he attributed 'no more to the power of God than the order of nature allows and common sense dictates' (IV.17.24). This is far from accurate. After many pages about the Lord's supper, Calvin writes, 'Therefore, nothing remains but to break forth in wonder at this mystery, which plainly neither the mind is able to conceive nor the tongue to express' (IV.17.7). 'Now, if anyone should ask me how this takes place, I shall not be ashamed to confess that it is a secret too lofty for either my mind to comprehend or my words to declare. And, to speak more plainly, I rather experience than understand it' (IV.17.32).

How we are to celebrate the Lord's supper

1. We are to celebrate the Lord's Supper in faith

Calvin writes that we take away from the Lord's supper no more than we 'gather with the vessel of faith ... Just as rain falling upon a hard rock flows off because no entrance opens into the stone, the wicked by their hardness so repel God's grace that it does not reach them' (IV.17.33). He quotes Augustine, who said that 'the rest of the disciples ate the bread which was the Lord, but Judas ate the bread of the Lord' and 'in the elect alone do the sacraments effect what they symbolize' (IV.17.34).

2. We are to celebrate the Lord's supper with humble self-examination

Calvin takes seriously the admonition of Paul that before partaking of the Lord's supper one must examine himself. Calvin writes, 'When Paul urges us to a holy and pure partaking of [the Lord's supper], he does not require that we examine one another, or every one the whole church, but that each individual prove himself' (IV.1.15). Calvin stresses, however, that 'if it is a question of our seeking worthiness by ourselves, we are undone' (IV.17.40-41). 'Let us remember that this sacred feast is medicine for the sick, solace for sinners, alms to the poor ... It is a sacrament ordained not for the perfect, but for the weak and feeble, to awaken, arouse, stimulate, and exercise the feeling of faith and love, indeed to correct the defect of both' (IV.17.42). Preaching in Geneva for a Sunday service with the Lord's supper, Calvin told the people: 'Know ... that this sacrament is a medicine for poor sick souls, and that the only worthiness our Lord requires of us is to know ourselves sufficiently to deplore our sins and to find all our pleasure, joy, and satisfaction in him alone' (*John Calvin: Writings on Pastoral Piety*, 133).

'John Duncan, when distributing the elements, saw a woman in a seat near the front of the church pass the cup untasted while the tears coursed down her cheeks. He left his place at the table, stepped down into the aisle, and, taking the cup from the elder, gave it himself to the weeping woman, with the words, "Tak' it woman: it's for sinners"' (G. F. Barbour, *The Life of Alex. Whyte*, 310).

Baptism is 'an entrance' into the church (and so is appropriate for infants) whereas the Lord's supper is for 'those who are capable of discerning the body and blood of the Lord, of examining their own conscience, of proclaiming the Lord's death, and of considering its power' (IV.16.30).

3. We are to celebrate the Lord's supper frequently

Calvin held that the Lord's supper should be 'set before the church very often, and at least once a week' (IV.17.43). Communion received yearly was regarded as sufficient in the medieval Catholic Church. Calvin believed that weekly observance of the Lord's supper was the practice of the apostolic church and was practised in the church for centuries. The frequency of communion in Geneva was restricted by the civil magistracy—against Calvin's continued protests—and a quarterly celebration was the most that could be achieved.

The Catholic mass

As we have already noted, Calvin devotes an entire chapter to the 'Papal Mass, A Sacrilege by which Christ's Supper Was Not Only Profaned but Annihilated' (IV.18). Calvin's vehement tone here is undoubtedly affected by the fact that 'the enemies of truth today do battle with so much rage, fury, and cruelty' (IV.18.18). He sets forth at least five reasons why he rejects the Catholic teaching.

- 'The mass is a sacrifice and offering to obtain forgiveness of sins' (IV.18.1).

- The mass is dishonouring to Christ, who is 'the sole and eternal priest' (IV.18.2).

- The letter to the Hebrews teaches that 'no further offering remains', and 'Christ also signified this by his last words … when he said, "It is finished"' (IV.18.3).

- The mass by its frequent sacrifices of Christ 'wipes out the true and unique death of Christ and drives it from the memory of men' (IV.18.5).

- The mass 'robs us of the benefit' that comes to us from Christ's death when it causes people to see 'new redemption in the mass' (IV.18.6).

God has 'given us a table at which to feast, not an altar upon which to offer a victim; he has not consecrated priests to offer sacrifice, but ministers to distribute the sacred banquet' (IV.18.12). The word 'sacrifice' in Scripture means 'a sacrifice of praise and reverence' and 'a sacrifice of propitiation or of expiation' (IV.18.13). The Lord's supper, Calvin argues, is the first, not the second; it is a 'thank offering' in which 'we do nothing but offer a sacrifice of praise' (IV.18.17). Augustine taught that 'the Hebrews in the animal victims which they offered to God celebrated a prophecy of the future victim which Christ offered; the Christians, by the most holy offering and partaking of the body of Christ, celebrate the remembrance of a sacrifice already made' (IV.18.10). The Lord's supper is God's gift to us, not a sacrifice offered by the church to God. In his commentary on Luke 22:17-20, Calvin wrote that Jesus 'bids the disciples to take: he himself, therefore, is the only one who offers'.

In summary, Calvin writes: 'The supper itself is a gift of God, which ought to have been received with thanksgiving. The sacrifice of the mass is represented as paying a price to God, which he should receive by way of satisfaction. There is as much difference between this sacrifice and the sacrament of the supper as there is between giving and receiving' (IV.18.7). B. A. Gerrish writes, 'The cross of Christ is thrown down as soon as an altar is raised up ... The Lord has given us a table at which to feast, not an altar on which to offer a victim; and he has not consecrated priests to offer sacrifice but ministers (servants) to distribute the holy banquet' (*Grace and Gratitude*, 148, 151).

In IV.18.7 there is a striking shift from divine gift to corporate act. The Lord's supper stands in a twofold opposition to the Roman mass—it precludes the language of work and sacrifice and it cannot tolerate any impairment of the sense of community. Calvin argues that private masses—'wherever there is no participation in the Lord's supper among believers', even though many people may be present—violate Christ's instructions for the disciples to take the cup 'and divide it among yourselves' (IV.18.8). Calvin rejects the Catholic practice of withdrawing the cup from lay people, pointing out that Matthew 26:27 states that 'the edict of the eternal God is that all should drink' (IV.17.47).

Arguing that the Catholic practice of displaying the consecrated elements to be worshipped was idolatry, Calvin asks, 'For what is idolatry if not this: to worship the gifts in the place of the Giver himself?'

(IV.17.36). He notes that the Council of Nicaea forbade 'us to fix our humble attention upon the symbols set before us' (IV.17.36). 'The only lawful adoration is that which does not rest in the sign, but is directed to Christ seated in heaven' (IV.17.37).

Knowing God and ourselves

Pray this thanksgiving prayer that was used at the end of the Lord's day service with the Lord's supper in Geneva:

> Heavenly Father, we offer you eternal praise and thanks that you have granted so great a benefit to us poor sinners, having drawn us into the communion of your Son, Jesus Christ our Lord, whom you delivered to death for us, and whom you give us as the meat and drink of life eternal. Now grant us this other benefit: that you will never allow us to forget these things, but having them imprinted on our hearts may we grow and increase daily in our faith, which is at work in every good deed. Thus may we order and pursue all our life to the exaltation of your glory and the edification of our neighbours; through the same Lord Jesus Christ, your Son, who in the unity of the Holy Spirit lives and reigns with you, O God, forever. Amen.
>
> (*John Calvin: Writings on Pastoral Piety*, 134).

26. Civil Government— 'Another Help'

'But if it is God's will that we go as pilgrims upon the earth while we aspire to the true fatherland, and if the pilgrimage requires *such helps* [as civil government], those who take these from man deprive him of his very humanity' (IV.20.2).

'The final chapter, "Civil Government", is one of the most impressive parts of the work. Like the Prefatory Address to Francis I at the outset, this chapter illustrates the vital contact of Calvin's thought with the world of political action ... The chapter abounds in quotations from the Bible, which here as elsewhere is his primary guide ... Calvin's closing sections are charged with power, and reflection on them will help to make possible an appreciation of the impact of his teaching on world history. But at the end he banishes any suggestion of reliance upon political action or advantage. Though we are menaced by the wrath of kings, we whom Christ has redeemed at priceless cost must obey God and endure all things rather than compromise piety or become slaves to the depraved desires of men' (McNeill, 1:lxv-lxviii).

The purpose of Calvin's theology 'is to glorify God, to save human souls, to transform human life and society' (Leith, *Pilgrimage of a Presbyterian*, 181).

Read: *Institutes* IV.20. [*1541* ch.16, pp.755-784.]

Scripture Text: 'Let every person be subject to the governing authorities. For there is no authority except from God, and those that exist have been instituted by God' (Rom. 13:1).

Notable Quote: Alluding to a proverb from Seneca's *On Clemency* (on which he as young scholar wrote a notable commentary), John Calvin agrees: 'It is indeed bad to live under a prince with whom nothing is permitted; but much worse under one by whom everything is allowed' (IV.20.10).

Prayer

We pray, O heavenly Father, for all princes and lords, your servants, to whom you have entrusted the administration of your justice … May it please you to impart to them your Spirit, who alone is good and truly sovereign, and daily increase in them the same, that with true faith they may acknowledge Jesus Christ, your Son, our Lord, to be the King of kings and Lord of lords, as you have given him all power in heaven and earth. May they seek to serve him and to exalt his kingdom in their government, ruling their subjects, who are the work of your hands and the sheep of your pasture, in accordance with your good pleasure. So all of us both here and throughout the earth, being kept in perfect peace, may serve you in all holiness and virtue, and, being delivered from the fear of our enemies, may give praise to you all the days of our life. Amen.

(John Calvin: Writings on Pastoral Piety, 127.)

A look behind and a look ahead

Calvin ends the *Institutes* not with heaven but with a discussion of civil government. We look forward to heaven, but in the meantime we live on earth. Calvin connects the same two themes in Book III, chapters 9 and 10—'Meditation on the Future Life' and 'Uses of This Present Life.' In the first nineteen chapters of Book IV, Calvin has taken us into the church. In this concluding chapter, we follow Calvin 'out of the sanctuary into the world' (McKee, *John Calvin: Writings on Pastoral Piety*, 31). And in that world, we find another help that God has ordained for us in our earthly lives, human government.

> Though far from accepting Calvin's theology, Jean-Jacques Rousseau paid tribute to the reformer who had helped shape Geneva's public life two centuries earlier: 'Those who only consider Calvin as a theologian do not understand the extent of his genius. The drawing up of our wise edicts, in which he played a large part, does him as much honour as his *Institutes* … As long as love of the homeland and liberty is not extinguished among us, the memory of that great man will never cease to be blessed' (Jean-Jacques Rousseau, *On the Social Contract*).

Calvin gives compelling reasons why he includes a chapter on civil government in a book on the Christian religion. 'Now since we have established above that man is under a twofold government [in III.19.15], and since we have elsewhere discussed at sufficient length the kind that resides in the soul or inner man and pertains to eternal life, this is the place to say something about the other kind, which pertains only to the establishment of civil justice and outward morality' (IV.20.1). 'The Calvinist piety', John T. McNeill writes, 'embraces all the day-by-day concerns of life, in family and neighbourhood, education and culture, business and politics' (*Political Duty*, vii).

Twofold government

Christians live under a twofold government, John Calvin writes. One aspect is 'spiritual, whereby the conscience is instructed in piety and in reverencing God; the second is political, whereby man is educated for the duties of humanity and citizenship that must be maintained among men' (III.19.15).

Robert Godfrey explains that Calvin's discussion of the twofold government is developed in the context of his thought about the two kingdoms:

> The language of two kingdoms (church and state) clearly did not mean for Calvin that one kingdom belonged to Christ and the other did not. It did not mean that one kingdom was for Christian living and the other was not. It did not mean that one kingdom glorified God and the other did not. Christ for Calvin was truly and fully king in both kingdoms, but ruled the two kingdoms differently (*Evangelium* 7 [2009]: 6-9).

Civil government is a positive good, not a 'polluted thing with which Christians will have nothing to do'. It is one way by which God initiates 'in us upon earth certain beginnings of the heavenly kingdom, and in this mortal and fleeting life affords a certain forecast of an immortal and incorruptible blessedness' (IV.20.2).

God ordained church and state as parallel institutions with distinct and separate responsibilities for ordering human life and society. The church 'pertains to eternal life'. Civil government 'pertains only to the establishment of civil justice and outward morality' (IV.20.1). But civil government is as necessary for humanity as 'bread, water, sun and air' and sees to it that people 'breathe, eat, drink, and are kept warm' (IV.20.3). God's presence is evident in the 'order of justice' when judges, senators, soldiers, captains, workers, and teachers all aid one another and so promote the well-being of all people (Comm. Isa. 3:4). Calvin argues that active participation in government is part of the Christian duty of love since such activity protects order and the rights and security of one's neighbour (IV.20.17). Calvin's vision of society included equal justice before the law, especially for the weak, and special provisions for the sick and poor. Fred Graham concludes that 'it was, for Calvin, the treatment of the weak in society that really determined the value of a political regime' (*Constructive Revolutionary: John Calvin and his Socio-economic Impact*, 62).

Each government has its own sphere of operation and should assist the other, but neither should interfere with the rights of the other. Calvin refused to secularize the state, or to politicize the church. 'Their function ought to be so joined that each serves to help, not hinder, the other' (IV.11.3). Calvin's view differed greatly from many in the medieval church who sought to bring the state under the control of the church, and some in the sixteenth century, even in Geneva, who wanted to bring the church under the control of the state. Calvin wrote, 'The church does not assume what is proper to the magistrate, nor can the magistrate execute what is carried out by the church' (IV.11.3). The church does not pass laws that govern the civil life of the people, and the state cannot dictate laws 'concerning religion and the worship of God' (IV.20.3). In his insistence that the church maintain full control of its own teaching and discipline, 'Calvin drove in a wedge between the church and state, the ultimate effect of which was to make him the father of the principle of a free church in a free state' (Warfield, *Selected Shorter Writings* 1:405). By his words and actions, he created 'something new in the Protestant world, and something in which lay the promise and potency of all the freedom which has come to the Reformed churches since' (Warfield, *Calvin and Calvinism*, 19).

Civil government provides that 'a public manifestation of religion may exist among Christians, and that humanity be maintained among men' (IV.20.3). It 'protects the outward worship of God' and 'defends piety and the church' (IV.20.2). Calvin does not require the state to execute the church's decrees, but insists that the state must support and encourage the church. The church, for its part, cooperates with the state in encouraging the people to live as good citizens.

Calvin, along with all Catholics and most Protestants of the sixteenth century, supported the ancient Justinian Code that prescribed the death penalty for serious heresies. By proclaiming anti-trinitarian views, Servetus committed an offence against the civil code of the empire accepted as legally binding on Geneva, rendering himself guilty and subject to criminal punishment. He was burned as a heretic on October 27, 1553—sadly, with Calvin's approval.

> 'In 1909, on the same spot where the Spanish heretic [Michael Servetus] was burned, the most moving expiatory memorial in human history was unveiled. The unveiling took place during the celebration of the four hundredth anniversary of Calvin's birth. Rendered into English the inscription on that memorial reads thus: "We, the respectful and grateful sons of Calvin, our great reformer, but condemning an error which was due to the age in which he lived, and being firmly devoted to liberty of conscience, according to the true principles of the Reformation and of the gospel, have erected this expiatory monument"' (McKay, *The Presbyterian Way of Life*, 14).

Magistrates

It is surprising to find Calvin describing magistrates as God's 'vicegerents', 'vicars of God', and 'deputies of God' (IV.20.4, 6). 'Civil authority is a calling', Calvin writes, 'not only holy and lawful before God, but also the most sacred and by far the most honourable of all callings in the whole life of mortal men' (IV.20.4). Magistrates have a 'holy ministry' to preserve the safety of humanity (IV.20.14). 'They are ordained protectors and vindicators of public innocence, modesty, decency, and tranquility' (IV.20.9). Magistrates are to remember that they are in a sense subject to the people they govern. In a sermon, Calvin stated that since God has set magistrates over us, 'it is certain that they are to that extent subject to those whom they ought to serve in ruling over them' (Sermon on Eph. 5:18-21).

The exercise of force is legitimate for magistrates, but Calvin warns that they must avoid both 'excessive severity' and 'cruellest gentleness'.

O God, your judgments give the King,
   his son your righteousness;
with right he shall your people judge,
   your poor with uprightness.
And then the mountains shall bring forth
   to all the people peace;
the hills because of righteousness
   their blessing shall increase.

Psalm 72,
Reformed Presbyterian Book of Psalms.

Furthermore, civil government has the right to wage war 'to preserve the tranquillity of their dominion, to restrain the seditious stirrings of restless men, to help those forcibly oppressed, to punish evil deeds' (IV.20.11). Wars are permissible only when there is 'extreme necessity'. They should not be governed by 'anger' or 'hatred' and must avoid 'implacable severity' (IV.20.12).

Governments have a right to tax people for legitimate causes, but rulers must remember that taxation is 'almost the very blood of the people ... to impose them upon the common folk without cause is tyrannical extortion' (IV.20.13).

Discussing different types of government, Calvin prefers 'aristocracy, or aristocracy tempered by democracy', an example of which he saw in the government God ordained for the Israelites (IV.20.8). John T. McNeill explains that Calvin was speaking of 'an aristocracy of excellence', not of lineage, checked by the democracy of popular election. The best men should be chosen by popular vote from a restricted list of names selected by their experienced predecessors in office (*On God and Political Duty*). Given human frailty and sinfulness, Calvin held that there is safety in numbers, 'so that they may help one another, teach and admonish one another' (IV.20.8). Douglas Kelly writes, 'Governmental principles for consent of the governed, and separation and balance of powers are all logical consequences of a most serious and Calvinian view of the biblical doctrine of the fall of man' (*The Emergence of Liberty in the Modern World*, 17).

> Some modern Chinese thinkers have come to the conclusion that what Chinese culture requires from 'the Christian spirit' is … the teaching of original sin. Yuan Zhimin, a philosopher active in China's Democracy Movement, has argued that the Christian emphasis on sin provides 'the ultimate philosophical base for the establishment of social covenants, checks and balances of power, and the rule of law … Denial of man's sin and limitations is the spiritual root of tyranny; our awareness [of these], the beginning of democracy' (Samuel Ling, ed., *Soul Searching, God and Democracy*, 57).

Civil law

Laws are the 'stoutest sinews of the commonwealth', writes Calvin (IV.20.14). They need not recreate 'the political system of Moses', but must 'be in conformity to that perpetual rule of love' (IV.20.14-15). They may 'vary in form but have the same purpose' or the 'same goal of equity' (IV.20.15-16). 'Equity' meant 'a fairness in human relations that balances strict justice with charitable moderation' (Horton, *Calvin on the Christian Life*). Though rejecting theonomy, Calvin was disposed to look for guidance for the Christian state in the Old Testament's instructions on social, economic, and legal matters.

Many have the mistaken idea that Geneva was a theocracy, governed by Old Testament laws, enforced by Calvin. Calvin exercised enormous influence in Geneva, it is true, 'but his authority was primarily moral, persuasive, and ecclesiastical, that is to say, ministerial' (Clark, *A Theological Guide to Calvin's Institutes*, 99). He was granted citizenship only in 1559, eighteen years after his return from Strasbourg and five years before his death. 'Calvin's name is so closely linked with Geneva that it is often forgotten that he was a resident alien, a hired hand, a Frenchman in a foreign land', writes Elsie McKee (*John Calvin: Writings on Pastoral Piety*, 11).

Christians may use law courts to settle disputes but must avoid hatred and revenge (IV.20.17). A lawsuit, however just, can never be rightly prosecuted by anyone unless he treats his adversary with the same love and good will as if the business under controversy were already 'amicably settled and composed'. But 'an example of an upright litigant is rare', Calvin admits (IV.20.18).

Some have found Calvin's views supportive of capitalism, with his allowance of reasonable interest charges in limited situations and his encouragement of thrift and diligence in work. Others see in Calvin's teaching 'the spirit of socialism, by its insistence upon communal responsibility and its demand that the general good should take precedence of all private interests' (Hunter, *The Teaching of Calvin*, 2). Ronald S. Wallace writes that Calvin's 'first concern in Geneva was ... to create at the heart of the city a community of the faithful in Christ whose ways of actual forbearance, love, and forgiveness would provide a pattern for the rest of civil society' (*Calvin, Geneva, and the Reformation*, 117).

The people

Scripture commands obedience to rulers, even wicked rulers, 'as far as possible' (IV.20.24). Calvin urges patience and prayer when Christians find themselves under wicked rulers, as the French Protestants did. Unjust rulers are raised up by God to punish our sins and promote our trust in God. We are 'to implore the Lord's help' (IV.20.9). Calvin notes that Paul calls rulers 'higher powers, not the supreme [power]' (Comm. Rom. 13:1).

Calvin discouraged rebellion. 'Private citizens ... may not deliberately intrude in public affairs' (IV.20.23). Calvin, however, believed that rulers were subject to criticism and correction from the Scriptures. In his letter to Francis I, written in 1535 for the first edition of the *Institutes* and appearing in all subsequent editions, 'the young scholar ventured ... boldly to admonish the proud and absolute monarch of a great nation' (McNeill, *On God and Political Duty*, ix).

Calvin adds some hope of relief from persecuting rulers by pointing to divine intervention in history. Sometimes 'open avengers' are raised up, 'armed from heaven' to punish wicked rulers (IV.20.30). God directs the affairs of history, including the overthrow of governments. This is a warning to rulers—'Let the princes hear and be afraid' (IV.20.31). There is also, Calvin writes, some hope from 'lesser magistrates' who have the duty to protect the people. When the higher magistrates, including the king, become abusive and tyrannical, these lesser magistrates have the obligation to organize and lead resistance. If they do not, they are guilty of wicked treachery, 'because they dishonestly betray the freedom of the people, of which they know that they have been appointed protectors by God's ordinance' (IV.20.31). McNeill comments, 'This emphatic and suggestive passage … was not less but more influential in that it came as a concession at the end of a discussion that is anxiously conservative' (*On God and Political Duty*, xix).

Persecution of French Protestants increased under Henry II, and in England and Scotland under Mary Tudor and Mary of Guise, and Calvin's counsel about obeying political authorities was severely tested. Calvin expressed himself more strongly. In a sermon on 1 Samuel 8, preached in the early 1560s, Calvin said that 'since kings and princes are bound by covenant to the people, to administer the law in truest equality, sincerity, and integrity; if they break faith and usurp tyrannical power by which they allow themselves everything they want: is it not possible for the people to consider together taking measures in order to remedy the evil?'

Calvin ended his commentary on Daniel, published in 1561, with a warning to unjust rulers:

> For earthly princes lay aside all their power when they rise up against God, and are unworthy of being reckoned in the number of mankind. We ought rather utterly to defy them whenever they are so restive and wish to spoil God of his rights, and, as it were, to seize upon his throne and draw him down from heaven.

Assessment

While Calvin's treatment of civil government includes many helpful ideas, it cannot be applied in every point directly to modern life. Calvin lived in the Christian city of Geneva. During his time, however, Protestants in France and other places were a threatened, persecuted minority.

Calvin's thoughts on resistance to wicked government no doubt will be of interest to Christians in the world today who find themselves in similar situations of oppression and persecution.

Calvin's ideas about civil government have had significant influence in modern political thought. David Steinmetz writes, 'We stand in different circumstances [today] ... We can, however, learn from ... Calvin ... that a tolerably just political order enhances human life and that Christians have legitimate reason to be grateful for it' (*Calvin in Context*, 208). Douglas Kelly writes that Calvin, in his views of the state's allowing and supporting one church only, was 'backward-looking', but in 'his doctrine of the limitations of all civil authority, and the people's right to resist it', he was 'forward-looking' (*The Emergence of Liberty in the Modern World*, 27).

Knowing God and ourselves

Calvin begins the last chapter of the *Institutes* by declaring that 'a zeal for piety may be more vigorous in us to testify our gratitude' to God for giving us civil government as a help in our earthly pilgrimage (IV.20.1). He closes the last chapter, as he begins the first chapter, with a call for piety, love for and obedience to God whatever the cost. He reminds us again of one of his central themes, our redemption by Christ and union with him. And he closes with great all-embracing words: GOD BE PRAISED. 'To grasp the *Institutes* as a whole is to know that these notes sound through these lines and doxology with which this remarkable treatise, in each of its editions, is brought to a close' (Reist, *A Reading of Calvin's Institutes*, 119).

> But since this edict has been proclaimed by the heavenly herald, Peter—'We must obey God rather than men' (Acts 5:29)—let us comfort ourselves with the thought that we are rendering that obedience which the Lord requires when we suffer rather than turn aside from piety. And that our courage may not grow faint, Paul pricks us with another goad: That we have been redeemed by Christ at so great a price as our redemption cost him, so that we should not enslave ourselves to the wicked desires of men—much less be subject to their impiety.

Conclusion

In his biography of John Calvin, *The Man God Mastered*, Jean Cadier writes:

> I am thinking of the man who said to me a short time ago as he came out of a lecture, 'I have just been converted through reading the *Institutes*.' And when I asked him to tell me what exactly had been the message which had effected this transformation in his life, he replied: 'I have learnt from reading Calvin that all the worries about health and about the uncertain future which had hitherto dominated my life were without much importance and that the only things that counted were obedience to the will of God and a care for his glory.'

Prayer of Thanksgiving

Heavenly Father, we offer you eternal praise and thanks that you have granted so great a benefit to us poor sinners, having drawn us into the communion of your Son, Jesus Christ our Lord, whom you delivered to death for us, and whom you give us as the meat and drink of eternal life.

Now grant us this other benefit: that you will never allow us to forget these things, but having them imprinted on our hearts may we grow and increase daily in our faith, which is at work in every good deed.

Thus may we order and pursue all our life to the exaltation and your glory and the edification of our neighbours; through the same Jesus Christ, your Son, who in the unity of the Holy Spirit lives and reigns with you, O God, forever. Amen.

Words of 'Thanksgiving',
offered at the close of Sunday worship in Calvin's Geneva,
(*John Calvin: Writings on Pastoral Piety*, 134).

❖

Bibliography:
list of books referred to in the text

A Theological Guide to Calvin's Institutes (2008)

Barth, Karl, *The Theology of John Calvin* (1995)

Battles, Ford Lewis
_____ An *Analysis of the Institutes of the Christian Religion of John Calvin* (1972)
_____ *The Piety of John Calvin* (1978)

Billings, J. Todd, *Union with Christ* (2011)

Boulton, Matthew Myer, *Life in God: John Calvin, Practical Formation, and the Future of Protestant Theology* (2011)

Calvin, John. The sources of quotations from the *Institutes*, commentaries, theological treatises, sermons, and letters are given in the text, and are taken from available English translations. Prayers of Calvin are taken from *Devotions and Prayers of John Calvin*; *John Calvin: Writings on Pastoral Piety*, edited by Elsie Anne McKee; and *Lifting Up Our Hearts: 150 Selected Prayers from John Calvin*, edited by Dustin W. Benge.

Canlis, Julie, *Calvin's Ladder: A Spiritual Theology of Ascent and Ascension* (2010)

Charry, Ellen, *By the Renewing of Your Minds: The Pastoral Function of Christian Doctrine* (1997)

Davies, Horton, *The Vigilant God: Providence in the Thought of Augustine, Aquinas, Calvin and Barth* (1992)

Douglass, Jane Dempsey, *Women, Freedom, and Calvin* (1985)

Dowey, Edward A, *The Knowledge of God in Calvin's Theology* (1994)

Dyrness, William, *Reformed Theology and Visual Culture: the Protestant Imagination from Calvin to Edwards* (2004)

Edmondson, Stephen, *Calvin's Christology* (2004)

Engel, Mary Potter, *John Calvin's Perspectival Anthropology* (1988)

Fuhrmann, Paul T., *God-Centered Religion: an Essay Inspired by Some French and Swiss Protestant Writers* (1942)

George, Timothy, *Theology of the Reformers* (1988)

Gerrish, B. A., *Grace and Gratitude: The Eucharistic Theology of John Calvin* (1993)

Gordon, Bruce, *Calvin* (2009)

Graham, W. Fred, *The Constructive Revolutionary: John Calvin and his Socio-economic Impact* (1971)

Helm, Paul, *Calvin at the Centre* (2010)

Horton, Michael, *Calvin on the Christian Life: Glorifying and Enjoying God Forever* (2014)

Hunter, Adam Mitchell, *The Teaching of Calvin: a Modern Interpretation* (1950)

Jones, Serene, *Calvin and the Rhetoric of Piety* (1995)

Keller, Timothy, *Prayer: Experiencing Awe and Intimacy with God* (2014)

Lane, Anthony N. S., *A Reader's Guide to Calvin's Institutes* (2009)

Leith, John
_____*John Calvin's Doctrine of the Christian Life* (1989)
_____ *Pilgrimage of a Presbyterian: Collected Shorter Writings* (2001)

Mackay, John, *The Presbyterian Way of Life* (1960)

McCormack, Bruce L., *For Us and Our Salvation: Incarnation and Atonement in the Reformed Tradition* (1993)

McGrath, Alister E.
_____ *A Life of John Calvin* (1990)
_____ *Christian Theology* (1994)

McKee, Elsie Anne
_____ *Institutes of the Christian Religion: 1541 French Edition* (2009)
_____ *John Calvin on the Diaconate and Liturgical Almsgiving* (1984)
_____ *John Calvin: Writings on Pastoral Piety* (2001)

McNeill, John T.
_____ *On God and Political Duty* (1950)
_____ *The History and Character of Calvinism* (1954)

Mouw, Richard J., 'Calvin's Legacy for Public Theology', *Political Theology* (2009)

Nichols, James Hastings, *Primer for Protestants* (1947)

Oberman, Heiko A.
_____ 'Initia Calvini: The Matrix of Calvin's Theology' in *Calvinus Sacrae Scripturae Professor: Calvin as Confessor of Holy Scripture* (1994)
_____ 'John Calvin: The Mystery of His Impact' in *Calvin Studies VI* (1992)
_____ 'Pursuit of Happiness: Calvin Between Humanism and Reformation' in *Humanity and Divinity in Renaissance and Reformation* (1993)
_____ *The Dawn of the Reformation: Essays in Late Medieval and Early Reformation Thought* (1986)

Ozment, Steven, *The Age of Reform 1250-1550: An Intellectual and Religious History of Late Medieval and Reformation Europe* (1980)

Parker, T. H. L.

_____ *Calvin: An Introduction to His Thought* (1995)

_____ *Calvin's Old Testament Commentaries* (1993)

Partee, Charles, *The Theology of John Calvin* (2008)

Protestant Scholasticism: Essays in Reassessment, edited by Carl R. Trueman and R. S. Clark (1999)

Reed, R. C., *The Gospel as Taught by Calvin* (n.d.)

Robinson, Marilynne

_____ *Gilead* (2004)

_____ *Lila* (2014)

_____ Preface to *John Calvin: Steward of God's Covenant* (2006)

_____ *The Death of Adam: Essays on Modern Thought* (1998)

Schreiner, Susan, *The Theatre of His Glory* (1991)

Selderhuis, Herman

_____ *Calvin's Theology of the Psalms* (2007)

_____ *John Calvin: A Pilgrim's Life* (2009)

Stroup, George W., *Calvin* (2009)

The Cambridge Companion to John Calvin (2004)

Thompson, Bard, *Liturgies of the Western Church* (1961)

Torrance, Thomas F.

_____ *Scottish Theology* (1996)

_____ *Theological Science* (1969)

Wallace, Ronald S.

_____ *Calvin, Geneva, and the Reformation* (1988)

_____ *Calvin's Doctrine of the Christian Life* (1959)

Warfield, B. B.

_____ *Calvin and Augustine* (1974)

_____ *Calvin and Calvinism* (1931)

_____ *Selected Shorter Writings of Benjamin B. Warfield* (1970-73)

Wendel, François, *Calvin: the Origin and Development of his Religious Thought* (1963)

White, Robert
_____ *Institutes of the Christian Religion: A New Translation of the 1541 Institutes* (2014)
_____ *John Calvin: Sermons on the Beatitudes* (2006)

❧

Also published by the Trust

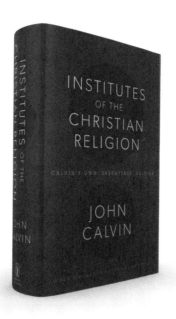

Institutes of the Christian Religion
John Calvin

Translated from the French Edition of 1541
by Robert White
920pp., clothbound
ISBN 978 1 84871 463 2

Also available as an eBook from banneroftruth.org

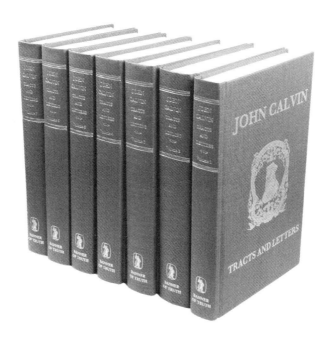

John Calvin: Tracts and Letters

Seven-volume set, clothbound
ISBN 978 0 85151 987 6

This seven-volume set, containing three volumes of Calvin's tracts and
four volumes of his letters, will delight all who have come to relish the
writings of the sixteenth-century reformer of Geneva.

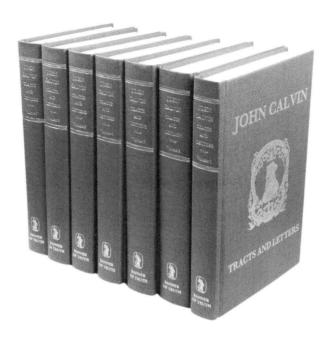

John Calvin: Tracts and Letters

Seven-volume set, clothbound
ISBN 978 0 85151 987 6

This seven-volume set, containing three volumes of Calvin's tracts and
four volumes of his letters, will delight all who have come to relish the
writings of the sixteenth-century reformer of Geneva.

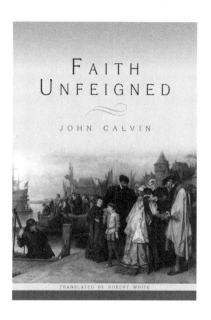

Faith Unfeigned
Four Sermons concerning Matters Most Useful for the Present Time with a Brief Exposition of Psalm 87
John Calvin

208pp., clothbound
ISBN 978 1 84871 086 3

Time has not diminished the importance of the issues which Calvin raises. His four sermons in this book are, in a sense, as contemporary now as when first preached in 1549. The pressure to conform to non- or sub-Christian religions and cultures is something no Christian can escape. The need for an open and sincere profession of faith in the Lord Jesus Christ is as vital as ever. To ponder the preacher's words is to be reminded of the cost of discipleship, and of the need for a much larger vision of God's saving grace and of the goal to which the Christian believer is being led.

The Banner of Truth Trust originated in 1957 in London. The founders believed that much of the best literature of historic Christianity had been allowed to fall into oblivion and that, under God, its recovery could well lead not only to a strengthening of the church, but to true revival.

Inter-denominational in vision, this publishing work is now international, and our lists include a number of contemporary authors as well as classics from the past. The translation of these books into many languages is encouraged.

A monthly magazine, *The Banner of Truth,* is also published. More information about this and all our publications can be found on our website or supplied by either of the offices below.

THE BANNER OF TRUTH TRUST

3 Murrayfield Road   PO Box 621, Carlisle
Edinburgh, EH12 6EL   Pennsylvania 17013,
UK   USA

www.banneroftruth.org